'The Vision of Mac Conglinne'
and other plays

PADRAIC FALLON was born in Athenry, Co. Galway in 1905. He moved to Dublin while he was in his teens, and his first poems were published there by 'Æ' (George Russell). He married in 1930, and had six sons, of whom four survive. His middle years were spent in Wexford, and it was there that he wrote a series of radio plays. He moved back to Dublin in 1963, and then to Cornwall in 1967, before returning to Ireland. His last years were spent in Kinsale, Co. Cork. Padraic Fallon died in 1974. His *Collected Poems* were published by Dolmen Press a few months before his death. In 1990 Carcanet published a new *Collected Poems*, adding previously unpublished work.

IAN FALLON is the second of Padraic Fallon's six sons. He was born in 1943 and educated at St Peter's College, Wexford and Trinity College, Dublin. He was art critic of the *Irish Times* from 1963 to 1998 and its literary from 1977 to 1988. He is the author of six books, including *An Age of* (1998), a study of Irish culture from 1930 to 1960.

Also by Padraic Fallon from Carcanet

'A Look in the Mirror' and other poems

PADRAIC FALLON

'The Vision of Mac Conglinne' and other plays

CARCANET

First published in Great Britain in 2005 by
Carcanet Press Limited
Alliance House
Cross Street
Manchester M2 7AQ

A CIP catalogue record for this book is available from the British Library
ISBN 1 85754 663 6

The publisher acknowledges financial assistance from Arts Council England

Typeset by XL Publishing Services, Tiverton
Printed and bound in England by SRP Ltd, Exeter

Contents

Introduction

Various poets and dramatists – and even more so, certain poet-dramatists – owe a great deal to sound radio, though less to the relatively diffuse, hybrid, quasi-journalistic medium of television. (Radio has also been kind to composers and to musicians generally, though television is obviously much more effective in dealing with the visual arts.) Since poetry – stating the ultra-obvious – is primarily meant to be heard, a medium whose sole resource is sound brings verse back to its very origins when it was chanted or declaimed. And 'poetic' drama – realistic drama is obviously something very different – often flourishes best when there is a minimum of props and visual distractions to come between it and the audience.

Padraic Fallon's radio dramas occupy a very special niche in the genre. They are not 'scripts' in the ordinary sense, though when he came to write them he had gained considerable experience and expertise in radio scriptwriting. They are works of literature whose original medium was sound radio, just as the stage was the medium for countless other creative writers. He wrote with a remarkably sure sense of how his work would register in performance, but his aim was also to produce works of art which could be read by sophisticated people with a critical sense. This fact was recognised by various critics and fellow-writers, both in his lifetime and since. As one of them remarked:

> There is the danger, because of the sporadic and ephemeral nature of the medium, that radio drama as an art form could disappear and that [Padraic] Fallon's contribution be forgotten. Despite the notorious disinclination of Irish critics to say much in praise of any writer who has not received the acclaim of London or New York, and despite Fallon's own distrust of modishness in current literary criticism, it is hard to accept that his name will not be better known. He did not in his lifetime seek easily won acclaim... He used a modern art form, radio, to transmit his vision. About lesser artists the legends grow and the book-trade prospers. Yet, if radio drama in this country ever justified itself as a distinctive and creative form, it did so by Padraic Fallon.'[1]

So wrote an eminent historian and scholar of the Irish theatre, the late Micheal O hAodha, who while head of drama in Radio Eireann was instrumental in having Fallon's plays performed (he even produced some of them personally). Perhaps O hAodha overstresses the poet-playwright's degree of isolation, though he had become an unfashionable figure in the last decade of his life and even something of a recluse. There was in fact a high degree of critical and public interest in him during the 1940s and 1950s, and he himself was genuinely surprised and flattered by the positive reaction of (often quite unliterary) radio listeners to what he himself had considered rather difficult and esoteric works. (Other listeners, however, found them incomprehensible.)

Neither was this interest confined to Ireland, as O hAodha's tone might suggest. Several of the plays were performed on the now-vanished BBC Third Programme, a number were translated into German and broadcast from Radio Hamburg (Nordwestdeutscher Rundfunk), and at least one was performed in Dutch. Much more recently, several have been translated into Hungarian and broadcast from Budapest. All this is proof that Fallon is no narrowly national writer whose idiom is circumscribed by circumstance, and who does not export without an effort of cultural adjustment. In fact his roots and allegiances were ramified and multiform; they included French Symbolism, the Irish Literary Revival (especially Yeats), Neo-Platonism, the English Metaphysical poets, and the Elizabethan dramatists. Add to that a deep, lifelong engagement with myth, both classical and Celtic.

Though the golden age of radio drama is long past, and plays of such length and complexity as his are shunned by most modern broadcasting stations, various literary historians have treated them respectfully.[2] This is mainly on account of their literary merits, rather than their effectiveness as radio entertainment, since performances have become rare and the people who listened to them originally form a rapidly shrinking tribe. So too do the actors and actresses who performed them, and who included some of the finest talents of their day, on the stage as well as on sound radio. None of Fallon's plays was printed in his lifetime, though a section of *Diarmuid and Grainne*, his first major work, did appear in the *Dublin Magazine* shortly after its first performance on Radio Eireann. Various lyrics from them, too, appeared independently in print.

Starting with *Diarmuid and Grainne* in 1950 and ending with *Riverside* in 1964, no less than fourteen of Padraic Fallon's radio plays were performed on the air. The early plays made something of a critical sensation – that is not too strong a word – though the very last ones received relatively little attention and by then he was becoming a Man Out of Season. By the early 1960s an entirely new taste in poetry had taken over, based largely on Anglo-American literary models, while the sudden rocketing to fame of Beckett's plays in the 1950s gave an entirely new twist and direction to Irish drama in general. (It will not be forgotten that *Embers* and *All that Fall* were written for radio.)

However, these works should not be viewed merely in the context of sound radio; they were part of a general rebirth of verse drama which began shortly after the Second World War. The heady success of Christopher Fry's works (*The Lady's Not for Burning*, *Venus Observed*, *The Dark is Light Enough*, and so on) nowadays seems of little more than period interest, but their verbal colour and fluent, accessible Neo-Romanticism obviously

'The Vision of Mac Conglinne' and other plays

answered some urgent contemporary need or mood. Discriminating audiences in Britain were weary both of 'socially significant' drama and of West End meretriciousness, just as in Ireland they were growing increasingly tired of peasant realism and imported farces. Apart from the Beckett works already mentioned, Dylan Thomas created a small classic in *Under Milk Wood*, Louis MacNeice wrote prolifically and well for radio, while W.H. Auden's translation of Cocteau's *Les Chevaliers du Table Ronde* made a positive impression when it was performed on the BBC Third Programme. And in Ireland, the poet Austin Clarke wrote several plays for radio which still keep their special niche and their own following.

Padraic Fallon's works, however, differ from those of most others in that he often utilised blank verse, prose dialogue and lyric verse together in the one work. The lyrics – generally declaimed at moments of dramatic stress or exaltation – are always dramatically relevant but can also stand on their own feet as verse; in fact, a large number were included in the *Collected Poems* I edited for Carcanet Press in 1990. They could be equated very roughly with operatic arias, while much of the verse dialogue correspondingly can be regarded as the equivalent of recitative. (It is noteworthy that Chinese classical plays use interspersed lyrics in much the same way, though they are sung rather than declaimed.) Fallon also made frequent use of the device of a narrator – part explicator and 'link man', part commentator on the action like a one-man chorus, and partly an intrusion of the poet's own voice (he sometimes speaks in lyric form). In his own words:

> My verse plays are not a mere extension of my poetry but an integral part of it. Indeed my lyrics can be taken as the high points of, or as correlative to, the continuous drama that goes on in the psyche where worlds are meeting and where history is always of the present. The long poem is a form I haven't any great liking for, so I invent my own equivalent which is drama suitable for broadcast on sound radio. In that I can relate the prose-verse vision of the poet to an inner unity.

Today, in lieu of actual performances, a good deal might be done through the medium of the audiobook, which has come as such a boon to poetry-lovers in particular. Padraic Fallon, however, did not live to see its rise to popularity, though various recordings of his plays have been preserved in the Radio-Telefis archives. Leading Irish composers – Gerard Victory, Brian Boydell, etc. – supplied the incidental music to them, and the BBC production of *Diarmuid and Grainne* had a score by Matyas Seiber, then highly regarded in the English musical world.

This work was first broadcast by Radio Eireann on 19 April 1953 and was the second of Fallon's major works to be heard, *Diarmuid and Grainne* being the first.[3] It had been written in the summer of 1951 – typed out at the poet's County Wexford home in less than a fortnight, in a veritable fever of inspiration. The part of Ligach was played by Una Collins, who had previously created the role of Grainne, and whose lovely voice was silenced for ever when she was still in her thirties. This performance was re-broadcast shortly after the poet's death in 1974, as an *in memoriam* tribute, and it was his favourite of all his plays (which, incidentally, include some stage ones).

The original medieval tale, *Aisling Meic Coinglinne*, is a medley of prose and verse, at times bitingly satirical towards the clergy in general and clerical gluttony in particular; it has even been surmised that its author was a disillusioned monk. In the twentieth century it became familiar to thousands of Irish schoolchildren (including myself) in a prose version by Father Peader O Laoghaire, who predictably removed most of its raciness and all of its anticlericalism and entitled the bowdlerised result *An Craos-Dheamhan (The Hunger Demon)*.

Some remnants of this anti-clerical stance persist in Fallon's version, since Muinchenn has a good many traits in common with the type of authoritarian, invulnerably self-satisfied Irish bishop who flourished as late as 1960. However, the setting is mythic rather than medieval and the real theme is the rivalry between two kings, Cathal of Munster and Fergal of Ulster, for possession of Queen Ligach. They symbolise South and North, Summer and Winter, respectively, while Ligach may be taken as a type of the Great Goddess, as well as the inspirational White Goddess beloved by Robert Graves, whose favours may bring death or madness. In character Cathal is Bacchic, impulsive, choleric, warlike; by contrast Fergal is cold, calculating, legalistic, a civilian and not a soldier. Ligach plays one against the other and her chosen instrument is Mac Coinglinne himself, a bard, goliard and healer who is also gifted with powers of prophecy and second sight.

The scene in which he is flogged at the pillar obviously relates to the ancient ritual sacrifice of the King-God at Midsummer Eve (see Frazer's *The Golden Bough*); the manner in which his body is set adrift in a coracle recalls the death of Orpheus, his singing head relates to the legend of Brian, while his rebirth from the sea links him with the Taliessin myth and also with the Finding of Moses. The Yewtree which challenges him at Ibar's Island is a traditional symbol both of death and resurrection. And Mac Conglinne's eventual triumph over the Hunger Demon is also the conquest of winter and dearth, and the renewal of warmth and life. He is also, it seems, the prophet of a New Order. (Incidentally, some of his arguments in favour of women have an oddly topical ring, at a time when numerous feminists have attempted to resurrect the ancient matriarchal culture.)

However, the play has many levels and the mythic is only one of them; the unending battle of the sexes is central, and it is fought with all the weapons men and women can command. The beatings and humiliation Mac Conglinne endures from both king and clergy suggest some allegory of the poet-prophet at war with the established order and the ruling orthodoxy. However, there is a near-Rabelaisian exaltation of eating and drinking, and the plot is interspersed with moments of almost slapstick farce, grotesque humour and scurrilous mockery. The dramatic content of *Mac Conglinne* can stand very firmly on its own feet, without benefit of mythic or philosophic props.[4] But binding it all together is the powerful, almost primeval power of Fallon's own quasi-pantheistic vision. The frequent exuberance and rich verbal orchestration may be, at first, an obstacle to latter-day taste – but taste, after all, is largely a matter of fashion.

The Poplar

This play was first broadcast on 6 December 1953, only a matter of months after *The Vision of Mac Conglinne*. Compared with its predecessor it is a relatively short work, lasting under an hour in performance. It is beautifully shaped and deceptively simple, almost folklike. Like certain other of Fallon's works, it began life as a short story which was published in the *Dublin Magazine*.

The theme has some basis in fact, and the character of Jerome was based on an uncle of the poet by marriage, Peter Nolan. (Those familiar with Fallon's poetry will know him as 'the old Land Leaguer' mentioned in the poem 'Three Houses'.) But while Jerome's membership of the Land League in Parnellite times is also founded on reality, his real-life prototype was guiltless of murder or even violence. His daughter Ellen is also based on a real-life person and is even given her name.

The time is about 1923, in the infancy of the Irish Free State. Jerome, the central character, belongs to a dwindling older generation who had once marched under banners proclaiming 'The Land for the People', at a time when Parnell and Michael Davitt had largely succeeded in channelling the old agrarian violence into organised public agitation. By contrast, his son James is typical of the new Ireland recovering from a decade of civil war or upheaval; unlike their forebears, he and his sisters now have property, or at least expectations in life, relative political stability, and above all a new, emerging social order which has more or less broken the back of the old Ascendancy class. Their main ambition is to lead decent and law-abiding lives, free from unrest or violence. In some ways they represent the kind of lace-curtain, *petit bourgeois* respectability which was largely to dominate Irish life for several decades.

Though Jerome is shown as a model husband and father, for him justice is not necessarily the law of the land but something men may be forced to take into their own hands if necessary. He is intrinsically a good man, a 'decent' man, yet he has committed murder – judicial murder in a sense, the last-ditch justice of the underdog, but still murder. As a believing Christian he can know no peace; and while deeply aware of his guilt he knows too that he will never truly repent, even though that means his eternal damnation. By gunning down his bullying landlord, he was in effect retaliating against a system which kept him and his kind in social and economic subjection, not to mention frequent insult and humiliation. And now, in any case, changing values have made him redundant, like the poplar with which his own life-force seems intimately linked.

The landlord-tenant relationship in late nineteenth-century Ireland was a complex business and we know there were plenty of good, conscientious, hardworking landowners as well as the usual quota of absentees and exploiters – just as there were many shiftless, chronically ungrateful tenants who at times could grow violent and vindictive. Nevertheless, evictions of whole families – sometimes of entire small rural communities – were common and the Great Famine had already shown up the inherent hope-lessness and inequity of the old agrarian system. The repressive policies of Arthur Balfour in the 1880s merely exacerbated existing tensions. Even after the Wyndham Land Act of 1903, rural grievances lived on and ancestral land hunger was a potent force behind the growing nationalist revival.

However, *The Poplar* is only incidentally social history. Its real theme is the dialogue between a man and his soul, haunted by an insoluble moral conflict and the imminence of death, and intermittently tortured by the gulf of misunderstanding between him and the younger generation. The poplar tree, which is so mysteriously connected to him and his own manhood, becomes his confidante and also his 'weather gauge' (something indispensable to a farmer). This dreamlike, nocturnal element is set against the daily trivia of rural life and gossip, and the bickering of Jerome's adult children and their small local ambitions. Such a contrast between dream and reality, poetry and everyday, mundane prose, is typical of Fallon's work as a whole.

The Hags of Clough

Fallon made three versions of this work, of which the third and undoubtedly the best is printed here. The first two (which survive in manuscript) are much shorter and are in prose dialogue with the usual interspersed lyrics, but the final version he recast in blank verse. In comparison with the quasi-mythological setting of *Mac Conglinne* or the early-modern one of *The Poplar*, it is placed in the eighteenth century, though with few or no histor-ical landmarks to pin it down in time more precisely. Unlike the first version, which was first broadcast on 30 June 1957, it was never performed and the poet almost certainly wrote it under a purely literary compulsion.

The Irish nobility and landowners of the time – particularly in the remote West – were still semi-feudal lords ruling over their counties, or baronies, or estates with almost plenary powers. One of the most famous of them, 'Humanity Dick' Martin,[5] when asked if the King's Writ ran in his country, replied: 'Egad it does, as fast as it can, when my good fellows are after it!' However, the character of the Earl of Leitrim is not based on any historical prototype, though the title did exist.

The Scholar, the leading character, is in some respects a blood-brother of Mac Conglinne – rhymer, healer, wanderer, blessed and cursed with second sight. He is also, it seems, a 'spoiled priest', given to spouting Latin in his cups. The Jockey, his twin, plays a kind of *Doppelgänger* role, and in a sense the brothers form a duality of light against darkness, or spirituality and intellect (however fallen or squandered) against animal carnality and man's darker instincts. The theme of two brothers in love with the same woman is of course common in folklore the world over. The Hags themselves are Furies of the folk imagination, akin to both the Erinys of Greek myth and the Witches in *Macbeth*. It is a curious feature that after their early appearance in the play they remain in the background as unseen, though not unheard, agents of temptation and retribution. Mephistophilis has a good deal in common with his prototype in *Faust* but is more urbane and less malevolent.

In many ways this is the most intellectually complex and 'metaphysical' of all Fallon's plays, which may explain why it never become popular in spite of its broad social span, its colour and violence and love scenes and moments of Bacchic abandon. Perhaps Leitrim's incestuous passion for his daughter was too much for audiences in the 1950s, just as the Scholar's moral dilemma – akin to certain characters in the plays of Kleist or Calderón – was on too esoteric a plane. He knows only too well that his destiny allows him to heal but not to profit by it, to love but not to possess, to warn but not be heeded like Cassandra. Perhaps he can also be viewed as a type of the artist, gifted with superior insight but doomed either to stand outside events or to intervene in them disastrously – an impassioned spectator rather than a participant, a Man Without a Shadow. Yet the play ends ambiguously rather than catastrophically, as though 'it was all a dream'.

Horses and the thunder of hooves dominate the play, particularly the great Stallion by which Leitrim wards off suitors from his daughter. The scene in which the Lady, finally purged of her neurotic terror, takes the tamed animal in hand is an apparent reference to the legend of the Virgin who tames the Unicorn, symbol of male lust and violence. Both here and in Leitrim's more cathartic cure, subliminal, potentially destructive passions and phobias are transfigured by the light of self-knowledge into natural and healthy expressions of the life force. By contrast, the centaur-like Jockey savagely rejects the Scholar's attempts to reason with him and meets his death at the hands of the terrible Hags who had egged him on.

In the original Radio Eireann production the Lady was played by Una Collins and that of the Scholar by one of the finest and most versatile of all radio actors, Thomas Studley (still living), who had taken the title role in the *Vision of Mac Conglinne*.

Brian Fallon, 2005

Notes

1 Quoted from *Written on the Wind: Personal Memories of Irish Radio 1926–76*, ed. Louis McRedmond (Dublin, 1976).

2 There is an almost eulogistic chapter on them in Robert Hogan's influential *After the Irish Renaissance* (Minneapolis, 1967, and London, 1968). A. Norman Jeffares is brief but respectful in his *Anglo-Irish Literature* (Dublin, 1982). Other Irish literary or theatre historians, such as Seamus Deane and Christopher FitzSimon, are similarly respectful.

3 He had written many scripts for Radio Eireann in the preceding decade including a dramatic adaptation of Gérard de Nerval's *Les Filles de Feu*. However, he never regarded these as part of his creative work and did not even bother to preserve them.

4 When Seamus Kelly, then *Irish Times* drama critic, reviewed the work for his newspaper, he wrote: 'The two and a half hours of its playing time seemed no more than twenty minutes, with no wavering of interest from first to last' (*Irish Times*, 4 May 1953).

5 Ancestor of the writer Violet Martin, who wrote under the pseudonym 'Martin Ross' in her partnership with her first cousin, Edith Somerville.

The Vision of Mac Conglinne

A Play in Two Parts

Dramatis Personae

Storyteller
Waiting woman
Queen Ligach, stepdaughter of the King of Ailech
King Fergal, son of the King of Ailech
Chief Doorkeeper to Fergal
Captain of Fergal's guard
Mac Conglinne, a young poet
Officers and soldiers of Fergal
Ulster voice
Fisherman
Woman
Three cranes
Yewtree
Muinchenn, Abbot of Cork
Monks
Cahal, King of Cashel
Herald of King Cahal
Demon
Master
Raven
The God
Aidan, a monk of Cork
Cork voices
King Pichan

Part One

STORYTELLER My story tonight is a story of Ireland, of two kings and a treacherous, beautiful woman.

(*Strings*)

> O woman. She is everywhere.
> An element.
> Behind each quarrel, at the back of every sermon;
> At the bottom of every bad debt.
>
> And yet I hail her.
> How can I help it? She
> Who divides herself around me like a calendar,
> Who is my twelve climates of feeling,
> Who musters me
> So many shapes, I live like the sun,
> A god within my year.

The woman is Ligach, the stepdaughter of Maolduin in the north, King of Ailech. The kings are Fergal, son of Maolduin, and Cahal Mac Finguine, King of Cashel in the south, two mighty men who can wax and wane, as equal as the north is to the south, as equal as the two parts of a foot rule, as one half of the year is to the other. And the woman stands with one foot upon each, and when she is a while with one she feels a desire for the company of the other; and the one from whom she is absent is nothing but a great hunger for her, a hunger that travels around him like a famine on circuit.

(*Strings*)

> O never will I love a woman.
> Give me a cat to nurse or a dog to pat;
> Give me a stone to kneel on. I
> Will be no woman's alphabet.

Look at her now. Her sun-room in Ailech is big and bright. In the green of the garden her fifty maidens are merry. They are wheeling and laughing. A golden ball goes from one to the other. But the game cannot end, for the lovely queen-pin is absent, the Queen does not play any more, she broods in the frozen sunlight of her window.

(*A soft trumpet*)

WAITING WOMAN Queen. O my Queen.
LIGACH I hear you.

WAITING WOMAN It is the King again. Fergal demands an audience.
LIGACH I have pleaded sleep.
WAITING WOMAN He carries a cure for sleepiness.
LIGACH I have pleaded weariness.
WAITING WOMAN He answers that he will cure that, too.
LIGACH I have pleaded melancholy.
WAITING WOMAN A sorrow shared is a sorrow halved, he says.
LIGACH I have pleaded coldness.
WAITING WOMAN He answers that his presence is warmth itself.

(*Sudden trumpet*)

He is here now.
FERGAL Ligach.
LIGACH This is the Queen's room, O King.
FERGAL Ligach, wherever the Queen is, that is the Queen's room.
LIGACH You have no rights of entry into my room.
FERGAL Wherever you are, there my heart is. May I not enter my own
heart, since my heart is your sun-room?
LIGACH I am tired of the words of love.
FERGAL That is not true.
LIGACH Weary of the litany.

(*Strings*)

Words stand around me
Like old and obsolete soldiers pensioned to sentry-go:
They bow me this way, that way,
Obsequiously on the paths I know.

They are afflicted by a palsy,
Their points are blunted, they are old for my age;
What can they in their rusted armour tell
To one so young, whose needs are a new language?

I repeat: I am tired of the words of love.
FERGAL And I repeat, you lie to me. You are not tired of the speech but of
the speaker: not so much tired of love as of the lover. Ho, there. You,
the doormen.

(*Ringing of gong*)

Bring in those men.

(*Echo of steps, etc.*)

CHIEF DOORKEEPER Softly now, Bigfoot. Fat buttocks, you, walk easy.
Soles must be silent here. O heavy heel, a strop on your backside for

this... their Majesties, the men. (*Whispers*) Laggards, to the earth
you! Rub your nostrils in it, make proper obeisance.

FERGAL You know these men, my Queen.

LIGACH They are mine.

FERGAL You have not seen them for some time?

LIGACH Not for some time.

FERGAL You did not miss them?

LIGACH I did not miss them.

FERGAL Did you send them on a mission?

LIGACH Have you questioned them?

FERGAL Have I questioned them? I have done more than question them. I
have scourged them.

LIGACH And they did not answer you? Why then do you expect an answer
from their mistress?

FERGAL I demand it. I do not expect it.

LIGACH I keep my rights to be silent. And my men have my rights to be
silent. In whipping them you exceeded your rights of kingship.

FERGAL Sometimes the man must overleap the king. You refuse to speak?

LIGACH I will speak as a queen.

FERGAL It is an aspect of you I would willingly leave to my people, to the
gapers at the door, to the loungers at the crossroads, to the lads at the
corner.

(*Strings*)

> As a queen you shine
> Like a stone after rain; and every man's prayer
> Though you have nothing for any man
> Gives you the face that he would sculpture.
>
> The long and lingering white thighs,
> I see them, and the birds below,
> Four delicate shanks. What an offering to the eyes.
> Each man uncovers you in that stone.
>
> Each man makes you with a look.
> But none dares break the stone, your queenly covering,
> Lest you vault naked, arched, arrowy and cold,
> Into the world, each breast a thunderbolt.

Be a queen to the people, wife, but to me you must be a woman. You
refuse to tell me to whom you sent those messengers?

LIGACH I think you know already.

FERGAL I have followed a little chain of reasoning. Shall I wag it for you?
Call me that border captain.

(*Gong, etc.*)

CAPTAIN My Lord, I am here.

FERGAL Your duties are?

CAPTAIN One week in two I keep the watchman's ford in Slieve Fuat. I
question, I pass, I detain, I admit, I turn back.

FERGAL You detained these men. Why?

CAPTAIN At my Lord's order. And following that order I had them
searched. I list my findings. Item, an oak apple; item, a white cloak,
with six undercloaks to match; item, a brooch of gold for those
cloaks; item, a bag of seed wheat; item, a queen bee in a stone jar;
item, the half of a woman's shift, item, the half of a queen's head-
dress; item, a sword of war. That is my enumeration.

FERGAL You have done well. Shall I read the story, Queen? Shall I deci-
pher this cypher of apples and bees and cloaks?

LIGACH Could I stop my Lord?

FERGAL Certainly. No man can speak if a woman's mouth is on his mouth,
or find zest for speech if her breast is on his breast.

LIGACH I will leave you the faculty of speech.

FERGAL Ah. Then all that is left to me is to withdraw into my kingship. I
speak henceforth as the law speaks. I shall assemble the court. I shall
accuse you of holding commerce with my enemy and the enemy of
Ulster, Cahal of Munster, but the penalty I can already whisper in
your ear.

LIGACH Banishment?

FERGAL Certainly not. And have you inside a month within the crook of
his arm? Are you curious about your punishment?

LIGACH You will tell me as you will.

FERGAL I will tell you now, my love. Deposition. Deprivation of queenly
rights. Deprivation of the rights of a citizen. As a person of no rights
you shall be a slave, and as a slave I shall purchase you from the
commonwealth and enrol you among my body-servants.

LIGACH You will not dare.

FERGAL Then, my Queen, you will not close your doors against me and
refuse me audience.

STORYTELLER I end this scene thoughtfully with the clamour of gongs.

(*Gongs and music*)

I open this next scene on a sight that gives pleasure to my soul. It is
the throne-room of Ailech. The King is carved in colours on high,
sea-greens and the acid blues predominate. Below him the assembled
court is a multicolour like bedded flowers. Those are the lawmen,
the laymen, the white clerics, the holymen, the wisemen, the heroes,
the schools, and immediately under the great Kingseat, where his

The Vision of Mac Conglinne

two tanists support the sacred heel of the King, is the assembled college of the poets. On a lower throne of ivory and blue sits the Queen. She is faintly smiling. Her eyes have caught up the stare of the poets and you can see every carolling boy of them laying down his metres like carpets before her, so that she may pass down in a stately progress through the ages, and every bald and bawdy ancient of them arranging her in his eyes like an image in a bed. I dare not look on her any longer. Her glance is a crepitation up my backbone. I could leap nine cubits for her. I will do the chariot trick for her. I will do the dangerous sword trick. I will do the wild feat of the spear and balance my bulk upon the point –

(*Gongs*)

Hush. It is the King speaking.

(Fergal's *voice comes forward from the background*)

FERGAL The oak apple is a greeting from royalty to royalty and has the double meaning that the days of love will come again. You agree?

MANY SOFT VOICES We agree, Lord.

FERGAL The white cloak, the six sub-cloaks, the golden brooch, all symbols of kingship. Why do they go from north to south, from Fergal's country to Cahal's country from the Queen? It is evident that she offers him kingship over her.

SOFT VOICES It is evident, Lord.

FERGAL The bag of seed. My reading is: I offer my lands to your sowing.

VOICES, SOFTLY That is our reading.

FERGAL The queen bee reads: I am ready to leave the hive.

VOICES We agree with that reading.

FERGAL The half of a queen's shift, the half of a queen's crown. I have left a king's bed. I seek the other half of my crown in the bed of another king.

VOICES That is our reading.

FERGAL You will agree, then, that the Queen has been making overtures to Cahal of Munster, my hereditary enemy.

SOFT VOICES We agree, Lord.

FERGAL Then, it remains only to name the punishment. You agree?

SOFT VOICES We agree.

YOUNG POET I do not agree, my Lord.

FERGAL You are a young poet. Have you orders of merit which give you a right to be heard?

YOUNG POET My Lord, at this moment I am endowed with grace and dowered with the loveliness of all the world, for I sit within sight of the Queen's face. This gives my small years a right to be heard greatly.

FERGAL I give you permission to speak. Your name?

YOUNG POET Anier the son of Conglinne, my Lord, a master of the alpha-
bets, of no country but the sea, one who has been rolled from one
seatop to another and got drunk with gravity in all the great homes
of this world.

FERGAL Say your say.

MAC CONGLINNE The Queen is saying it for me, Lord. Very silently, but
her soft thunder is all around her and the earth is speaking for her.
The different trees are singing in one still voice that this queen is not
of the kind that accepts a judgement she does not give. She is law
and lawgiving. She is that which she is.

FERGAL She is the Queen of Ulster, Mac Conglinne, and my queen. As
such she is not the law but amenable to the law.

MAC CONGLINNE King, she is a woman and her throne is her own will.

FERGAL Not so, Poet.

MAC CONGLINNE By my hand, I assert it, for she is the business of the
poets and our vision of life. In the wayward will of women we
live and love and die. She bears us and buries us. She is our year
of life.

(*Strings*)

On her changing levels
She demands of me more than one body;
So I invent myself
Everyday anew till there is enough of me.

I am my father and my son.
I am a town. I am a country. I establish her.
But she is flown, she is gone,
When the time comes for me to inhabit her.

She is my labour and my law. She lures me,
Loves me, lives with me, loathes me, leaves me, that is her way;
Yet when I take at last the grave she offers me
What a large legacy I leave in clay,
I who have lived like a god the lifelong day.

(*End of music*)

King, it is the business of a woman to bear man, rear man, and love
man. But it is also the business of the woman in the woman to tempt
him beyond himself so that he spends himself in extending the ways
of life and the breadth of life. She is the spark in his inertia, the little
white ewe of the New Year that tempts the drowsy ram till his horns
run gold and his stamping wakens the whole of the heavens. It is

even her business to deceive him, so that his anger and horror and hate make him welcome his inevitable end and the peace that the grave offers.

FERGAL I think you invert wisdom, Mac Conglinne. Do the Ulster poets agree with you?

SOFT VOICES We do not.

MAC CONGLINNE I am not disconcerted. Do I agree with myself among the confluence of my selves? I lay down this lady as a law, and I challenge the poets of Ulster to contradict me if I assert that they have behaved at this trial as the King's bondman, and that they have left empty the seat under the willow, the tree of the Goddess, where the poet is both votary and king.

SOFT VOICES This stranger is insulting, King.

FERGAL I agree. Yourselves can name his punishment.

SOFT VOICES Banishment from Ulster.

FERGAL I have good rodmen. If I suggested whipping?

SOFT VOICES His art exempts him.

FERGAL Let it be banishment, in that case.

MAC CONGLINNE I take it as an honour to be banned from Ulster. But I crave a boon before I leave.

FERGAL Is there good reason for this?

MAC CONGLINNE Is there a greater reason than justice?

FERGAL There is no greater reason than justice.

MAC CONGLINNE I demand that this assembly listen to the Queen, if the Queen should wish to speak.

FERGAL She has our permission. The Queen may speak.

MAC CONGLINNE King, you use a churl's speech when the occasion asks for bended knees.

FERGAL Now, by my royalty, Mac Conglinne, you have offended a king.

MAC CONGLINNE By your lack of it, O Royalty, you offend a queen and the order of poets to which I belong.

FERGAL I am entitled to have you whipped for lack of reverence.

MAC CONGLINNE I am entitled to lampoon you for lack of true majesty.

(*Gong, then clamour. Gong again*)

FERGAL Mac Conglinne, your peers can name the number of strokes you shall have.

MAC CONGLINNE King, I have no peers in this assembly. I will allow the assembled poets, however, to name the number of stanzas in which I may satirise you, pulverise you, blister you and flay you.

FERGAL Will the assembled poets allow me to name the number of this man's strokes?

SOFT VOICES You have our permission, O King.

FERGAL How many stanzas will you use to lampoon the King, Mac
     Conglinne?
MAC CONGLINNE I will number them by the strokes, O King.
FERGAL I do not think you will live that long. I order you five strokes for
     every consonant and ten for every vowel in the alphabet.
MAC CONGLINNE Calculate that, O King, in one number.
FERGAL Thirteen at five is three score and a quarter, five at ten is two
     score and a half. I add these and get five score and three-quarters of a
     score. Does the total satisfy you?
MAC CONGLINNE I asked that I might display to the court your ignorance
     of learning. Wise men shall know from now on that I am being
     punished by an ignorant churl of a provincial nobody of a king, who
     is so backward that the true alphabet has not yet reached him
     through his learned men. I shall have great pleasure in composing
     five score and three-quarters of a score of stanzas on the King's
     ignorance and churlishness, on his lack of majesty and variety –
FERGAL Variety?
MAC CONGLINNE That he cannot be thirteen men in one and keep his
     queen interested.

   (*Laughing strings as the* Queen *laughs*)

     I have amused the Queen?
LIGACH You have pleased me, Mac Conglinne.
MAC CONGLINNE It is my hard fate not to have been born a king. It is my
     hard fate.

   (*Strings*)

             I have many mirrors for a woman.
             O the delight of the long glass;
             And the little glass that nurses one blue eye;
             And the silver one that fills with a red mouth.
             I have two long shafts of light for the rich thigh.

             I hold a running glass like water
             When hair comes tumbling from the pin
             Of a May morning to stream down from the shoulder
             In waves of sunlight over the white skin.
             You will stand there like a swimmer.

             But for the secret night,
             There is plain gold in the room that will take a candle
             And make it seven; while I lean from the shadows
             With a peacock's feather in my hand,
             All eyes, all bright and foreign eyes.

The Vision of Mac Conglinne

FERGAL Now by all the gods, Mac Conglinne!

MAC CONGLINNE It is my regret, Queen, that I was not born a king.

LIGACH I could almost regret my royalty, Mac Conglinne.

FERGAL Take this poet away. Rope him to the pillar-stone on the green and give him the number of strokes he has been adjudged. After that, turn him loose in a wicker boat on the Foyle, that he may float out to the wastes of the sea where he belongs.

MAC CONGLINNE I bow to the Queen.

LIGACH You are pleasant company, Mac Conglinne. If I remember you tomorrow I shall be sorry for you.

MAC CONGLINNE That saying shall warm me, O Queen, when I sit before a big bonfire. I leave my farewells with you, as I shall leave the skin of my back on this pillar stone of the King's green.

(*Trampling sound, arms*)

ULSTER VOICE Come gently, Poet. Take his arm, there. No trouble, now. Move on, clapper-tongue, lively, bigmouth. We are only going to flay you alive.

(*Trampling dies out*)

FERGAL That is that. Now, where were we, gentlemen? Yes, the Queen was about to speak. Were you not, my love?

LIGACH I do not think so, my Lord.

FERGAL You will not defend yourself?

LIGACH It is not necessary. That poet has spoken for me the words I bade him speak.

FERGAL You know this poet, then?

LIGACH For some minutes only. His mind was open and I entered him. There is one thing, my Lord, I did not ask him to mention, for it is my wish always to play in my own drama and bring myself to a crisis.

FERGAL What thing is that?

LIGACH I would wish that captain who arrested my messengers to be brought before me.

FERGAL It is done. Bring in the captain of the ford.

(*Gong*)

CAPTAIN (*Ulster accent*) I am here, Lady.

LIGACH King, bid him eat the oak apple that he seized, the apple that he pawed, the apple that he stuffed in a common pocket among shreds of tobacco and bits of strings. It was a message from one throne to another. Now, it is soiled and it must to a garbage pail.

CAPTAIN I did but the King's will, Lady, and a soldier's duty. But I will eat the apple.

FERGAL Give him the apple.

CAPTAIN I have no taste for such greenery as is not boiled with old bacon, but I will eat it. By God, it is a heavy apple.

(*Sound like a lump of iron hitting the ground*)

My good big toe. Is the bloody thing made of bronze? Excuse the soldier's tongue, Lady.

LIGACH Eat it.

CAPTAIN I eat it.

(*Sound of a monstrous crunching*)

Is this quartz?

(*Bray of music*)

Is this limestone?

(*Bray of music*)

Is this the great rock of time?

(*Bray of music*)

These teeth noises – by God you must excuse me, Lords and Lady. Such mouth music I never made nor heard before.

(*Bray of music*)

This is the first subsoil of all the world.

(*Bray of music*)

And here I come to the core. I have eaten the earth, Lady.

LIGACH You have also eaten something that is less pleasant. You have eaten poison, good captain. Now you must die. But don't hurry yourself. It does not cause me much inconvenience.

CAPTAIN I have not deserved this.

LIGACH Why not? The good soldier is promoted and his trade is to die.

(*Sound of falling body. Crash of music*)

VOICES He is dead. He is dead.

FERGAL He is dead. And Cahal of Munster would have died likewise.

LIGACH I have given you a proof by demonstration.

FERGAL We record that. It is not a pleasant way of giving evidence.

LIGACH I have also taken a revenge for the whipping of my seven messengers.

FERGAL I would prefer law and not revenge.

LIGACH I would point out, too, that it is now time for you to ask pardon of me before the court for this public humiliation of a queen.

FERGAL I must do that.

LIGACH Further, you will agree before sureties to certain demands I will make on you as to our future relations. This must be your reparation.

FERGAL Name your demands.

LIGACH Insurance of my privacy. Freedom from the demands of a husband unless I will it otherwise –

FERGAL WHAT?

LIGACH Rights of my personal freedom to travel and entertainment. Indulgence of my fancies.

FERGAL By my oath, no.

LIGACH Equal rights of sovereignty. Separate establishments in the same establishment.

FERGAL Am I a king or a cuckold?

LIGACH I demand these as my rights, for they were a queen's rights of old. I shall put it to the assembled court, now, as is my prerogative.

FERGAL By my soul, you won't. You will get back to your carpet and play kitten. You will toss the ball among the girls and make eyes at the guards. You will regard your reflection in your polished nails and bore yourself to death; but what man has won from woman, what rights he has beaten from her throughout the ages, you will not obtain from Fergal of Ulster, by leading him into a little trap. Bow to the court and run now to the women's quarters.

(*Raucous music. Then tripping music as if women were running*)

STORYTELLER Phew. I end this scene with my handkerchief. For things are very hot here.

(*Music. There are hints of the sounds of a man being scourged*)

I open this scene with a scourging. The poor poet is strapped against the tall pillar-stone on the King's green and the soldiers are gathered round him.

(*The* soldiers *all speak in Ulster accents*)

CAPTAIN Lieutenant, begin the alphabet.

LIEUTENANT Beth, luis, beth, luis, nion – Sergeant, begin the alphabet.

SERGEANT Certainly, sir. Beth, luis, nion, beth, luis, nion –

CAPTAIN Corporal.

CORPORAL Present, Sir.

SERGEANT Begin the bleeding alphabet.

CORPORAL Sorry, Sir, I only knows my pees and cues.

CAPTAIN Lieutenant, the alphabet I said.

LIEUTENANT Yes sir. Sergeant, the alphabet.

SERGEANT Yes, sir. (*Whispers*) You son of a stunned pimp, how did you get your stripes? Have you been to school to any master except the paymaster?

CORPORAL The alphabet it is, Sir. (*Whispers*) Any of you lousers who've lain and lazed your life away at school remember your bleeding letters?

SOLDIER Beth, luis, nion, fearn, sáille, etc.

SERGEANT Enough. Stand by the captain and call out the trees. Corporal, call the tally. All ready, Sir. We begin with consonant beth, the good birch tree, and very apt if I may say so, Sir.

CAPTAIN Is the scholar ready?

MAC CONGLINNE I am ready.

(*Strings*)

> I am learning my letters
> The painful way.
> Not by attention, not by the rote of my fingers,
> But by rough strokes from the hand of a tree.

> Scholars, come to me.
> The consonants are mine, the vowels bleed on my side.
> Put up your slates, schoolmasters, all the world
> May cypher the alphabet on my backside.

> The lovely grove of trees
> The learned planted will leave scars on me.
> But my seat will be a seat of learning
> When I reach the last black vowel, the tall and hissing Yewtree.

SOLDIERS Flog him! Flog him!

(*A hissing music, raucous laughter. Short interlude of this music becoming raucous and jerky, ending in a violence. Sudden silence*)

SOLDIER And wham. By God, I buried that black vowel in his bum.

CAPTAIN Well struck. And how is our scholar now?

MAC CONGLINNE Bumptious.

LIEUTENANT By God, he speaks.

MAC CONGLINNE (*roaring*) Speaks? I can bawl, I can bellow like a bull, I can bell like the brute-throated bigmouth of the pack. O you men of Ulster, you have struck blows today that will resound in many hedge-schools. While you beat me, I lost myself in many stanzas, a stanza for every blow, and they shall be rods upon your backs till the Day of Doom.

(*Resonance of strings*)

> In Ulster a sour and sacred king
> Had a bad wife. But he was worse.
> And worse than he were the bonded people.
> Here on all of them is the poet's curse.

CAPTAIN Shut him up, shut him up. Bawl, shout, cry.

MAC CONGLINNE I can outbawl you. My god is the God of Eloquence.

> That King was never a king in bed
> For the Queen she was never there
> But walking the walls with a pain in her head –

CAPTAIN Wrap this shirt round his mouth.

MAC CONGLINNE Or tempting a guardsman by the pillar.

(*In music, the sounds of a struggle*)

CORPORAL Cripes, that man has strength.

SERGEANT He is quiet enough now. The half of his teeth are down in his jersey.

CAPTAIN Lieutenant, have a chariot prepared. He must to the river now, and immediately. We have listened to a blasphemy that might cost us our heads.

LIEUTENANT Sergeant.

SERGEANT Sir.

LIEUTENANT A chariot at once. Detail two men to follow me to the kitchens. We will ration up and leave for the Foyle river at once.

SERGEANT Two of youse, at the double. After me. Quick march.

CAPTAIN I need a drink. Call to the mess before you leave.

LIEUTENANT Am I going?

CAPTAIN Do you think I am? The nastiest jobs fall to the lowest in rank. Quite properly.

LIEUTENANT Is the poet to be left alone?

CAPTAIN What can he do? Steal the pillar stone?

LIEUTENANT The scholar has fainted.

CAPTAIN It may be a trick. They are full of tricks, these scholars. A minor poet stole my wife for a week one time on the pretence of teaching her something. He sent her back because she knew more than he bargained for. Well, he seems safe enough. We can be off.

(*Music. Quiet, dreamy*)

MAC CONGLINNE There is someone in the middle of my pain.

LIGACH It is I, Mac Conglinne.

MAC CONGLINNE The bad Queen.

LIGACH Not so, Mac Conglinne. A queen needs to be royal, not good. You will agree with me on that.

The Vision of Mac Conglinne　　　　　　　　　　　　　15

MAC CONGLINNE More thoroughly if I had not been beaten for it. You
must want something from me, if you break the tabus to look upon a
naked and beaten man.

LIGACH I speak from inside you.

MAC CONGLINNE No use, in that case, to ask you to touch me and let my
head full upon your breast.

LIGACH You are there now. My child, my boy, my man.

MAC CONGLINNE I think you are my Lady of the Willow Tree.

LIGACH I am your lady and still I am not your lady. I am a queen, Mac
Conglinne. My favours are a commonwealth.

MAC CONGLINNE I sigh on that account, but I must agree with you.

LIGACH Your pains have gone.

MAC CONGLINNE Why yes, and that is a wonder. I think that my red
alphabet has healed.

LIGACH Pain is but a thought. I have given you another one.

MAC CONGLINNE That is right. I can think, now, of nothing but you.

LIGACH You are my favourite among the poets.

MAC CONGLINNE I thank you. And now I know, indeed, that you have
come to ask me for something.

LIGACH You sing of women. It is always one woman who is no woman but
all women. You sing of me.

MAC CONGLINNE I sing of you.

LIGACH So, you must serve me.

MAC CONGLINNE So, I must serve you. You will bring me beatings and
contumely, you will bring me hunger and thirst. You will leave me
wifeless and houseless, but I will serve you. Have you not ordained
me under the willow tree?

LIGACH You have my thanks, you have my love, you have my art. You
shall be taken from here to the banks of the Bann. They will put you
in a wicker boat. When they do, you must ask for clothing. A woman
standing by will take off her cloak and offer it to you. It will be
folded and you must not open it. You will travel far but you must
not open it. Where you shall land, in that place you must call for the
King, and you will fast on him till he comes. The king will be Cahal
of Munster. You will give him the folded cloak. But in the
midwinter to come, you must be in Cork. You must be in Cork. I
kiss you now – from the outside. You are my beloved.

MAC CONGLINNE Queen, I tremble. This is my initiation. Forgive me if I
tremble.

(*Rumbling music of a chariot. Sound of voices. Steps*)

LIEUTENANT Is there any life in that hulk, Sergeant?

SERGEANT Corporal, does that corpse kick?

The Vision of Mac Conglinne

CORPORAL Soldiers, listen to that stiff's ticker.

SOLDIER There is a faint pulse. In some hole and corner of him there is a spark of life. What will I do with the captain's shirt? A breath tighter and it would have noosed him.

CORPORAL Softly, fool. Give me that shirt.

SOLDIER This poet is alive, nobles.

SERGEANT So much the worse for him.

SOLDIER He is talking about the Queen.

LIEUTENANT Lord, must the shirt go back upon his mouth? Boot him one in the belly. Put out that little spark.

(*Sudden strings*)

MAC CONGLINNE A marvel has happened to the scholar,
      His books light up.
      The birds and beasts he has inked in manycolour
      On the white margin speak to his fingertop.

      They are praising a queen.
      The Bull, the Lion, the serpent on the branch
      Of the tall and tinted tree,
      And the griffoned eagle are singing, praise to the queen of all
                                      lands.

LIEUTENANT Hoist up the carcase and let us be shortening the road.

STORYTELLER I end this scene with the grunt of straining men.

(*Interval of music*)

    I open this scene in darkness and torches.

ULSTER VOICE King or no king, I'll no' give my coracle without payment on the nail.

LIEUTENANT Knock him on the head, Sergeant.

ULSTER VOICE Ye'll not do that, Mister. Hola, my sons, neighbours! Ye see, sogers, we're clannish hereabouts and we keep a guard on the village. We put our trust in the King all right, and we drink the goodman's health of a feasting day, but we keep an eye on him all the same.

LIEUTENANT What do you want for the coracle?

ULSTER VOICE Well, a coracle is an expensive piece of manufacturing these times. Have ye tokens or kind?

LIEUTENANT What do you think? Do you expect me to carry a bull or a bloody ram about with me on the King's business?

ULSTER VOICE Moderate your language, Mister. We're all Kirk here. You will give me ten tokens for the coracle.

LIEUTENANT I will. Ten bleats from my Daddy's goat. I'll give you two tokens.

ULSTER VOICE Do ye want a good coracle, or no?

LIEUTENANT No. The very worst will do.

ULSTER VOICE (*ominously*) The very worst. Lads, he said the very worst.

VOICES He said the very worst.

ULSTER VOICE Light all the torches to Bran's causeway. Spread the nets
along the path. Touch the bonfire, and bring the beer down to the
river's brink.

LIEUTENANT Fisherman, if you are considering a quarrel, I would advise
you to the contrary. I will give you ten tokens –

ULSTER VOICE Noble, we will give you a coracle without charge. We did
not understand the king on whose business you move, the king who
owns all coracles but sacrifices one to his mother, the great White
One, when it is the time and number. We are ignorant people and we
beg your pardon.

(*A wild music in the distance*)

They are ready below. Let us go down, now, with your holy burden.

LIEUTENANT Sergeant, you hear what I hear.

SERGEANT Sir, there was one word struck pleasantly on my two ears. The
word was beer. I remember, now, that these people hold an autumn
festival that is different from ours.

LIEUTENANT Carry the poet down.

CORPORAL You stiffs, shoulder the dead one here. Right. Ready. Beat,
beat, beat –

(*Distant drums take up the corporal's rhythm. Through it the* Storyteller
speaks)

STORYTELLER Fires have been lit on a small green above the River Bann
where there is a hut or two, a pillar stone, and a tiny jetty of alder
wood. The seapeople are making something of a ceremony in their
reception of the poet's body. Three women take it from the soldiers,
the only women on the green. They wash him and tend to his hair,
they rub his cheeks with a limewash, a coracle is taken from the
causeway, it is lined with ivy leaves, and the poet is placed in it. We
seem to have struck on some old relic of Dionysian days –
(*Suddenly a bitter wailing, then quiet*)

FISHERMAN Nobles, he is to be divided now. The head we set adrift on the
river that it may prophesy to us. The rest we keep.

LIEUTENANT Not so, fisherman. The King's order is that the unmaimed
body be set adrift.

FISHERMAN The King is ignorant.

LIEUTENANT The King is a king. Lift up that coracle, now, upon your
shoulders, men.

The Vision of Mac Conglinne

FISHERMAN It is an imperfect sacrifice.

LIEUTENANT It is warranted by the king of this land.

FISHERMAN That is a good point. I will make it clear to my brothers. Wait for me. We will move in procession.

SERGEANT (*drunk*) What's the bloody row about? And where are the women? Time we saw a good round dance.

LIEUTENANT You're drunk.

SERGEANT Of course I'm drunk. That's why I'm a soldier, so I can get drunk oftener than the land-tillers and the turfcutters and the foresters who can manage it only at Christmas. 'TENTION. You there, who have you permission to lift that body? Not the ivy ale. Wait for orders! Lieutenant.

LIEUTENANT The body may be removed, Sergeant.

SOLDIER Corporal, there is a little life in this body still.

CORPORAL Lift it. Ready, lads. Steady.

(*A wailing music begins. The drums keep rhythm*)

CORPORAL A beat, a beat, a beat. Halt. To the ground, now. And now, gently, into the water. Easy now, the bloody ozier in this basket is rotten. There. Why look, look. The water has revived him.

(*An awe of music*)

SOLDIER I said he was not dead. He's sitting up.

(*Crash of cymbals*)

MAC CONGLINNE I am cold. I was told to ask for a cloak.

SERGEANT Won't you have a jacket of water soon enough? You're a troublesome bloody man.

MAC CONGLINNE I will not leave without a cloak. I will leave a curse on the black police of Ulster if I am not provided with a cloak. Am I to go to Hell naked and indecent? Is there a tall woman near me?

WOMAN I am a woman, and I will provide a cloak.

SERGEANT My God, woman, it would be better if you gave that cloak to a man who could use it.

VOICES O what a cloak. O what a cloak.

(*Strings*)

> The whiteness of seven ram lambs.
> A gold seam from Wicklow.
> But the woman folds it in seven folds and leaves it
> In the coracle with a poet.

SERGEANT Push the bastard off before he breaks my heart.

(*Strings*)

My curse on poets.
They are more wayward than women. They gad
From word to word. They have many gods.
They are quite mad.

They undermine kings.
They upset queens. You will find them in a bed
Sacred to a priest or in the straw of a harlot.
They have no stability. They are quite mad.

Say goodbye to Ireland, bigmouth. And say your prayers. What the
hell is wrong with those people behind us, Corporal?

CORPORAL They are expecting the poet to sing a prophecy, Sergeant. It is
an old custom that the head should sing. And look at him! Has he
lighted a torch in the boat that he should blaze so brightly?

VOICES Vo. Vo.

(*Soft music. Trumpets inset giving hints of the Last Post*)

MAC CONGLINNE I go on a journey
　　　　　　To which there is no ending.
　　　　　　I move without mourning
　　　　　　Into the beautiful heart of a woman.
　　　　　　I am now a story.

　　　　　　I will not be lost;
　　　　　　For the footprints of tall ones go before me
　　　　　　From god to god. I will recover my ghost.
　　　　　　I will recover a country.
　　　　　　In the green of Cork I will be a story.

(*His voice is growing distant as he ends. Music*)

VOICES Vo. Evoe.

SERGEANT The devil's cure to him. There goes a lovely cloak. Corporal,
hail me that woman that bestowed the cloak. She may have something else of note.

CORPORAL I thought of that myself, but she's disappeared.

SERGEANT Nothing left us, so, but the ivy ale.

STORYTELLER I end this scene with a wish for the ivy ale. For one would
need to be drunk, indeed, to follow the poor poet in his coracle of
ozier. The night plucks him to the seaboard. He disappears out of
ken. Yet there are mariners' stories coming into this port and that
port of a golden head that floats and sings upon the wastes of the
waters in the Irish Sea. But you know what sailors stories are. You
can divide them by a woman into half and then by another woman
into half again. But one delicate morning in October, when the skies

were watercolours of hazy blues and early sunrays, on the Bar of Wexford where a few mild monks of Ibar's community were knotting a torn herring-net, a salt-white coracle of ozier wattles moved towards them on the tide from around the Raven Point. It was the wonderful golden head of the poet they noticed first. Then, as slowly he whorled past them, they saw he was green ivy to the chin, that his face was moulded like a mask of molten gold, and that he lived. Past them he went on the stream, with three curious young seals hang-dogging him, and around the muddy swirl of the holy island where the tall yewtrees quivered slightly and whispered to the three cranes that stood on sentry-go by Ibar's painted house. The coracle brought him to the wooden landing and the cranes hissed. The three cranes hissed and the first of them stepped forward.

(*Music. Croak*)

FIRST CRANE Do not enter.
SECOND CRANE Pass on your way.
THIRD CRANE Goodbye.

(*Strings*)

MAC CONGLINNE Good birds, you slight me. You threaten me.
You speak short to Mac Conglinne
Who knows you, who has picked your brain
For the pattern of your living.
FIRST CRANE Do not enter.
SECOND CRANE Pass on your way.
THIRD CRANE Goodbye.

(*Strings*)

MAC CONGLINNE You fish from one leg
And the fish you catch, you lay them in a wheel.
Do not be proud of your knowledge.
I know all the delicate steps of your dance-reel.
FIRST CRANE Do not enter.
SECOND CRANE Pass on your way.
THIRD CRANE Goodbye.

(*Strings*)

MAC CONGLINNE I know what you spell
By wheel and dance. It is my command
You waken the voice of the Yewtree to welcome
Mac Conglinne to his own land.

(*Hissing music. An old, cold, measured voice from a height*)

YEWTREE This land is everybody's land and no man's land.

MAC CONGLINNE Yewtree, it is Ireland.

YEWTREE It is not Ireland, but little Ireland.

MAC CONGLINNE Yewtree, I think you know me.

YEWTREE I shall know everybody by the end of time. The knowledge is of small advantage to me. Have you something to give me?

MAC CONGLINNE Only a lesson in manners. Only to tell you that you are the part of a pattern, that there is life as well as death, and that the lady who supports your right side is about to get annoyed with your churlishness in receiving me. She will let you topple in a moment and you shall have a large accounting to make to your peers.

YEWTREE I see you have a right to come to land.

MAC CONGLINNE Yes, and also a right to leave.

YEWTREE You may land so.

FIRST CRANE You may enter.

SECOND CRANE Do not keep away.

THIRD CRANE Welcome.

(*Music*)

STORYTELLER The poet lands. And in a moment the island changes. The great Yew becomes formalised as a tall and painted sculpture. Two marvellous goats support it in the rampant way of heraldry, and one has a crescent moon on her horns, the other a wane. And from wooden houses all around a close-cropped green, quiet monks emerge to welcome the poet as if he were an ordinary pilgrim. And indeed he is, and very much too ordinary, for he is, of a sudden, mother naked, unwashed, and hungry. The ivy and the gold are gone and his salt-white face is peeling off skins of sun. He is drunk from the motion of the sea, he is a worn-out, shipwrecked, battered mariner, and the monks wash him and put milk drinks before him, but before he can touch the tableware he is asleep. He has not forgotten the folded cloak, however. It sleeps with him. It is a light in the dim dormitory. It is a crepitation of the sun. It is rushlight in glimmering candlesticks of gold, and the monks, amazed and wondering, have brought the ancient Abbot to view it. The Abbot, amazed and wondering, has sent messengers to the King, and the king is Cahal of Cashel whose royal household is a hundred and fifty miles away, and the runners are there before Mac Conglinne opens an eye. When he does the Abbot, folded in a musty old mantle, has gone asleep at the foot of his bed.

(*Chirpy morning music*)

MAC CONGLINNE Priest, does your brotherhood ever wash? I can count and distinguish seven different stinks upon your person.

ABBOT Eh?

MAC CONGLINNE Remove your seven odours from the bones of my ankles.

ABBOT You must speak louder, Son of the Cloak.

MAC CONGLINNE Do you mean to carry those to Heaven? If so, speak, that I may go the other way. (*Loudly*) Look, find some other place of rest.

ABBOT Plaice for breakfast? No, no, Son of the Cloak, it is not the season for plaice. Herring you shall have, goat's milk, cheese, bread panned and mixed from unblackened wheat, and stirabout, the lucky caul of spring oats.

MAC CONGLINNE Do I hear you mention food?

ABBOT Yes indeed, God is good.

MAC CONGLINNE Is there no person in this establishment with two good ears? Do I see a gong? Strike it.

ABBOT Indeed, breakfast will not be long now, and you may bite it. But you must be careful. Long fast has given you the narrow belly of a knitting-needle and the more fanciful of my brethren assert that the music you made coming up Hantoon was caused when you struck your ribs like heartstrings.

(*Strings*)

MAC CONGLINNE In the mad months
     The jackass stamps the hill till grass goes mad.
     The dog unloops itself
     From the doorstep, his face one wrinkled snarl.

     But the jackass has long ears
     And the dog will hear me if I call.
     I would wish this Abbot had long ears
     And I dog-madness so that I could howl.

A MONK Master of the Cloak, we apologise for our aged Abbot. He is deaf, but kind; he is old, but wise, he is failing, but the God is still within him. Speak to him with your fingertips.

MAC CONGLINNE I was impertinent, and I offer you my regrets, Brother. Can you tell me where I am, and the manner in which I came here?

MONK You do not know?

MAC CONGLINNE Would I ask otherwise?

MONK You fell into our quiet like a spark, Master of the Cloak.

(*Strings*)

     The brothers who haul the herring,
     The cotmen, the netmen, met you at sunrise there
     At the point of the Raven,
     You and the sun together.

Twinbrother of the sun,
O hazel one, ivy had twined you to the throat;
Your mouth was a song
Without sorrow or anguish or threat.

You arrived among the reeds
Of our holy and peaceful island without a sound,
And we found you worn and torn,
Wearied and many-scarred, dead like a man long drowned.

In your weedy coracle
Barnacle and shell had a long sea-lease;
But your cloak was new, your cloak was a miracle,
A golden tabernacle by your knees.

MAC CONGLINNE This is the cloak. By God, I remember something about this cloak. And still I remember nothing.

MONK You do not remember whence you came?

MAC CONGLINNE I do not. But there is something about that cloak that sticks in the thick of my gullet. How did Mac Conglinne arrive at a wonder like this? Look, look, this cloak is the worth of a kingdom.

MONK It is a heavenly cloak. We have not dared to touch it. Even as we washed you, your hands guarded it.

ABBOT Son of the Cloak, if you could get up now, we could break our fast together, and you could tell me your story if you have it in mind to tell me.

MONK And the cloak seemed to evade us, it avoided our fingers, it shifted, it changed its place. Our Abbot said a wonder of that kind did not fall to be dealt with by a single shrine-keeper, so he sent word of it to King Cahal of Cashel –

MAC CONGLINNE That is it. You have taken my tongue from my mouth and spoken for me. That cloak is the King's.

MONK The King's? You could not have stolen that cloak from the King.

MAC CONGLINNE Have I thief-signs on my forehead?

MONK You have not. You have the signs of the tall poet, you have the swagger of the Hazel-man.

MAC CONGLINNE I am Mac Conglinne. I do not know how that cloak was given to me, but I know I am under bonds to present it to Cahal of Cashel.

MONK It is a present worthy of him. It is a god's raiment. You will break your fast now.

MAC CONGLINNE I have lost the gift of hunger.

MONK You must eat to travel. And Cashel is a long way.

MAC CONGLINNE I will munch on the road. No. There is something else comes back to me. I am to stay where I land until the King comes.

MONK Your cloak expects a large and kingly condescension, it requires a mighty obeisance from the King, if he has to travel so far for it.

MAC CONGLINNE I remember that as a condition.

MONK I respect your memory.

MAC CONGLINNE I am also to fast until the King comes. And now, O Lord, because of this obligation on me, hunger is gnawing at my every gut.

ABBOT Will the Son of the Cloak breakfast with me now? I am old and morning hunger is not good for me. There is herring on the grill, butter that has talked with salt and raspberry, bread from a horsemill, white and brown, buttermilk, sweet milk with a lacing from a jar –

MAC CONGLINNE If you hear thunder, it is my gums falling one on the other. Bring this Abbot to a pot and boil him.

MONK I shall take him to his table.

MAC CONGLINNE Why does he stink this way?

MONK He bears the odours of his office, Mac Conglinne, the smells of mortality. This is the sign of the Yewtree, the tree of death. Sleep now, since you cannot eat.

MAC CONGLINNE How can I sleep with this demon in my belly?

MONK I will ask the Abbot to lay his hands on you. I could give you sleep but it is his privilege.

ABBOT What does he want to go to sleep for, and breakfast awaiting us? The young waste too much time in sleep. What? Fast till the King comes? But the King will not come here. Our oratory is not a place he wishes to patronise. Well, well. If he wishes for sleep, let it be so. Lift my right arm. Leave your eyes to my eyes, Son of the Cloak. You see into my eyes. You see the pool. You see the salmon. The pool sleeps, the salmon sleeps. The Son of the Cloak sleeps – now. You will sleep until the King comes. But if he never comes, Son of the Cloak? I cannot await breakfast until then.

STORYTELLER But the King does come. With round cursing and martial threats he takes the green route by Fethard and Rossbercon –

(*Martial music with a hint of fun*)

– takes a dipping, chariot and all, at the old bridge of Ross where the barrels hold up the bridge –

(*Squawk of music*)

– at Wexford where there is wattle and mound, a multitude of geese, and a couple of boys bobbing for eels. All the menfolk, as usual, are out beyond the Bar fishing the famous herring that cannot be smoked, and all the women are in each others' houses playing some cardgame or other with fireirons. But the Custom House is very busy. There are ten carracks loading great barrels of yew and twenty Customs men in charge of them. Cahal halts in his tracks.

(*Blare of music*)

CAHAL What have those men in those barrels?

A MAN Wine of the country, Lord, a bishop's brew.

CAHAL Let it be a brew for a king. Tip me a barrel. Stave in the head, Crowfingers. Your king is thirsty.

(*Crashing wooden music*)

Good, good. I will hold it myself, I will tilt it.

(*Gulping music*)

By the gods, it is rich. Let the stream from which that liquid is drawn be called the King's River. Tilt me another.

MAN Lord, another will bring pimples, a red nose and the yellow trembling.

CAHAL That is for little bellies, good man. For Wexford bellies. Henceforth they shall be called yellowbellies. Where is this fellow Ibar's island? Yonder? Now, how may a chariot skim that waste of water?

MAN By the ferry, my Lord, a scant furlong to the north there.

CAHAL Away then, away. Is a king to be delayed by every man who offers him a barrel?

(*Hurry of music*)

STORYTELLER The hasty king is ferried over the wide Staney, and he rumbles over the ruts of Ardcavan where slow streams wind like heavy cattle through the reed country. He comes to the wooden causeway. It resounds.

(*Trumpets*)

A MONK My father, the Abbot.

ABBOT No need for the finger-spelling, my son. I know the King is here.

(*Strings*)

> I have heard wheels
> In Ross. The waters of the Barrow broke
> In a drift of steam. There are feathers on his heels.
> The tall tree croaked.

> The black bird has bright eyes.
> I am his speechman. I quote what he says to me.

The Vision of Mac Conglinne

I am at the end of his promises.
I look two ways over his country.

Bid the Son of the Cloak awaken. He has been a long time waiting for his breakfast. Tell them in the kitchens. Send him the smells of good food cooking, woodcock and snipe on the spit, and the great Arctic bird; have sauces in cup and soup in tureen, milk, buttermilk and mead, large bread and smallbread and sweetbread, bullmeat and pigmeat, the white chicken and the smoked haunch of the little bonave.

MONK This is a feast.

ABBOT It is a feast of smells, the delicate odours from the brazing charcoal. I do not think we shall eat this feast. But if not, we can eat of another.

MONK You are in a mood to prophesy.

ABBOT I have said my say for the moment. Do as I have bidden you. I will meet this king at my tree-seat.

(*Trumpets. Trumpets. Trumpets*)

HERALD The King. Spread the wool, unroll the rug, uncoil the round carpet.

(*Trumpets*)

The King.

ABBOT My Lord is welcome. May all trees smile on him. May all trees blossom through him. May he live in the fruit of all.

CAHAL After the welcome is accepted, after the compliments are returned, show me this blazing cloak that I have travelled leagues to see.

ABBOT You have been told the story?

CAHAL It is now the property of every sub-court in my portion of Ireland. And I think I shall have trouble with that Corkman, Muinchenn. He has laid claims to that cloak already. It is the cloak of his god, he asserts, the lad of the vine, the body who drinks ten tubs at a sitting and then warbles a stave or two. O glory be to God, I really must put law on the Pantheon. Can we not supply the market ourselves? We import more than we export and our theogany is lopsided. Do I wait much longer to see this cloak?

MONK The Son of the Cloak approaches, my Lord.

CAHAL I can see that. And I notice that the measure of light increases accordingly.

(*Faint trumpeting music in the background*)

I begin to think my journey was worthwhile. Who is the lad that carries it?

MONK He has a name, my Lord, but is nameless among nobles. You will not have heard of him.

(*Music comes forward. Final blast*)

CAHAL Bearer of the cloak, lay it softly on the carpet. Unfold it.

MAC CONGLINNE I will lay it down, King, but I will not unfold it. My errand ends when you accept this cloak from my hands.

CAHAL The cloak is then a present to me. By my hand, it is a royal gift. You will tell me who sent it?

MAC CONGLINNE My errand was determined for me, King, and limited to this act of handing you the cloak in person. I do not know who gave it to me, I do not know where I come from. Is the cloak itself no hint of the giver?

CAHAL I will open the cloak.

(*Music. A few short raps of excitement. A general gasp. A hurry-scurry of excitement and amazement*)

VOICES Oh. Oh. Now, by my hand.

CAHAL It is, indeed, a cloak.

(*Strings*)

> It is the living skin of a god.
> It stands, it flies, it lies down,
> It breathes, it grows, it spreads over the sod
> In greenery, in flower, it is softer than swansdown.
>
> It is speaking throughout a country
> And its words are gifts of the air: the tillage acres
> Welcome it, it clothes each tree,
> And talks in sap to the wide pastures.

Scholar, there is something hiding in it. What is it?

MAC CONGLINNE King, I do not know. My errand is ended, and I smell the marvellous smells of good food cooking. Without disrespect, my lord, my nose quivers, my gums drip, my teeth are ajar, my mouth grinds, my gullet is wide open and my belly is crying out for that food which is on spit and table.

MONK The scholar has fasted for a time no one knows, King.

CAHAL I am nosing that feast too. Let the scholar wait until this small packet can be opened.

MAC CONGLINNE O King, I am one leaping mad mass of appetite. If it is permitted I will dip with the scullion and horseboy, cook, server and tableboy, while you examine this package.

CAHAL Certainly not. You shall sit at my right hand. It is an honour I owe to the giver of this cloak. Why, what's here? Another cloak with its

The Vision of Mac Conglinne

seven subcloaks, fit for a king. And an oaken apple, greeting from
royalty with the double meaning that the days of love are not over; a
bag of seed, a woman offers me land for sowing; a queen bee in a
stone jar, a queen is ready to leave the hive for me; a queen's nightgown and the half of her crown – it is the half of the nightgown too.
Ha. And ha again. The meaning is too plain. It comes from a great
white bitch with whom I will have nothing more to do. Lead me to
the feasting chamber, good Abbot.

MONK We will pack the cloak, Lord.

CAHAL Aye. Give it to the bearers. It is kingly. It will cause admiration in
Cashel. So she has tired of her Northman.

(*Strings*)

> O Scholar.
> Bend to your book when a woman passes,
> Or your adventure
> Will exceed all your wildest guesses.
>
> If she is beautiful,
> Read your book. Histories
> Have no more terrible
> Story than the woman to whom you lift your eyes.
>
> If she be ugly,
> Still she is a woman. That is enough.
> Read your book, my boy,
> And stay with the simple stuff.

MAC CONGLINNE King, at this moment I would eat a woman if she were
broiled, boiled or on the fillet; if she were baked, brawned, browned,
underdone, overdone, or a mere juice in the black bottom of a
country skillet; and I would eat her family after and then begin with
her family tree. I tell you, King, I will eat your royalty if I am not
served at once. A greater hunger there never was since the word
uttered itself, than there is at this moment howling and yowling in
the snarling pit of my bowels.

CAHAL By the gods, that is a great hunger, Scholar. It is a notable hunger,
but I will see to it that it is royally satisfied. You will sit at my right
hand, and every second bit shall be your bit.

MAC CONGLINNE King, I will want all the bits at this table.

(*Music imitates the howl of a wolf*)

CAHAL By my hand, that is indeed the true howl of hunger. Monks, platter
the table there, lay on the big meats and the small meats, the gluti-
nous gravy, the luscious soup, bread in portion.

(*Music.* Mac Conglinne *howling*)

Gently now, Scholar. Here are the servers. Indeed, those smells give myself an appetite. Sit this scholar beside me. We will talk of women. I have great wisdom on that subject. I will teach the scholar.

MAC CONGLINNE King, you have an oak apple in your hand.

CAHAL That, Scholar, is a greeting from one royalty to another.

MAC CONGLINNE Give it to me. It whets my front tooth, it frets my back one. Give it to me, O King.

CAHAL By my hand, I cannot. It is tabu. I could eat it, but you would die.

MAC CONGLINNE I shall die but I will eat it.

CAHAL Then I must eat it myself to save you.

MAC CONGLINNE No. Leave it to me. You are eating it, you are munching it. You shall not rob me. I will follow it down your throttle. I go after it.

(*A prolonged howl of hunger*)

CAHAL Something has jumped from your mouth into mine, Scholar. By the gods, it could be your hunger that jumped from you to me. I am starving.

MAC CONGLINNE And I am no longer hungry. I think there was a demon in me and he is now in you.

CAHAL O wise demon. He knows that kings can provide what scholars cannot. Welcome, Demon. O when have I felt such a wonderful hunger? To the carving, monks, to the knife and the tall fork. No, never mind. The gods made fingers first. Toss me that great bird. That leg of mutton, now. That pot of broth. You are nibbling my piece of bread, Scholar. Back to your books.

I will clear this table and look for more. O lovely appetite. Away, all of you. Back. The King dines. That ham, oh mast and barley-fed beauty of the pigstye, my little bit of bacon. Snipe, woodcock, tastes for a small tooth. Have I cleared the table? Is there no more?

(*The foregoing has a background of music. Ends in a wolf-howl*)

Is there no more? Where are your pantries, Monks? Where are your storehouses, your kitchens and back-kitchens? Bring in the bacon, the stirabout, the birds, the fresh fish, the salt fish, the crayfish, the oysterfish. No, I will visit them in person. The King will make a royal progress through your foodstuffs. Lead on, lead on.

(*Hurried music as he visits place after place*)

Bones, marvellous bones.

(*Crunching music*)

Pottage of little oats.

The Vision of Mac Conglinne

(*Sucking music*)

A churn of cream.

(*Merry gobbling*)

Fleabites, fleabites. Where are the shoulders of mutton, the racks of young wether, the royal joints of the year-old-bull? Lead me to them, lead me.

(*A royal howl of hunger*)

STORYTELLER Only Mac Conglinne and the old Abbot are left at the table. That table is a curious sight. Every platter is bone bright with unused cleanliness, but there is not a pick of food on any of them. All signs of food have vanished into the King's mouth. What a royal digestion he must have!

MAC CONGLINNE It seems to me, Abbot, that I have started something.

ABBOT I would say that you have begun a season of dearth in the south, Scholar. I would say that many great houses shall feel the winter, and the smaller ones accordingly.

MAC CONGLINNE Can I have a drop of milk?

ABBOT Certainly, you are not guilty.

MAC CONGLINNE I said MILK. I will name it on my fingertips for you. M.I.L.K.

ABBOT Milk. I fear you will have to go to the goats for it.

MAC CONGLINNE I fear so too.

ABBOT They are in a pound beyond the causeway.

MAC CONGLINNE I will do without.

(*Music returning*)

Listen! The royal hunger is returning.

CAHAL (*booming*) Where is that scholar? I must thank him for my hunger. But bring wine, mead, bring buttermilk. We shall talk of women. I will tell him of that great bitch, Ligach, who wants me to love her once more. Scholar!

MAC CONGLINNE I am here, King.

CAHAL Never mind the women, Scholar, a good belly-hunger is much better than a queen. Its demands are less and can always be satisfied. I shall now proceed to tell you the tale of Ligach. You know why she left me? She wanted to have all my king's rights. She wanted to be king and queen at once. By the gods, I feel a nibble of hunger again. O lovely appetite. Is there any chicken in this house? Is there any roast beef or mutton broiled? Is there a salty hard piece of a pig? Is there anything at all?

(*Music*)

STORYTELLER I end this scene with a great hunger.

(*Music*)

End of Part One

Part Two

STORYTELLER I open this scene with a madness of feasting. Cahal is
delighted with his appetite at first. He displays it to ten chieftains on
his way home to Cashel. They are not so pleased as he is, for he eats
them out of house and home. He eats them to the scullery, to the
piggery, he lays bare the fowl-run and then climbs into the pigeon-
cote. He walks into the stubble-field and gnaws the sheaf in the
pointed stook. He picks the leaves from the trees as his chariot passes
beneath them, he catches at the tops of the grasses. His face is green
from grass-juice, greasy from fat bacon, grey with dust, and he is
anything but royal as the gates of his city open to him and he climbs
up the great Rock of Cashel.

HERALD Welcome to Cahal. Welcome to the son of the Bright One.

VOICES He is welcome to his own place.

(*Trumpets*)

CAHAL The welcome is accepted, the compliments are returned, we will
take the ceremony as completed. But where are the boiling pots, and
the bright braziers with their pleasant grills and delightful, whole-
some smells? Is there no food in Cashel, no green food, red food,
brown food, no beasts in pens, bulls on the hoof, birds in the run?
Have I no cooks, no potboys, no scullions? Have I no kingdom, no
revenues, no servitors? Does Cahal's household sleep when he goes
on a journey? Ring bells, gongs, bring whips and scourging staffs. I
am insulted, demeaned, I am hungry...

(*Wild music of hurrying servitors, tableware, clash of silver, murmur of
voices*)

STORYTELLER He eats Cashel down to the last pantry. He licks every plate.
He devours the substance of his nearer neighbours. He makes
excuses to visit his sub-kings and strips their households too. The
country groans under his vast appetite. The monasteries murmur,
for even in those days before Patrick there were monasteries and
religious settlements all over Ireland, some of them with the hue of
Christ on them covering an older image, as in Muinchenn's establishment at Cork where the traffic of the sea-people had touched the
Bible story somewhere and resolved it in their own way. Muinchenn
was a Briton, as we learn from the tale of the Tale of the Two
Swineherds, a righteous monk who would bow to nothing but his
own god. A clever man, too, and a headstrong, who put his own
establishment before all the other establishments of Ireland and was
ever a-tiptoe to glorify it. When he heard of the great cloak in the

King's possession, he set off for Cashel to lay claim to it. It was a curious procession, Muinchenn, alone, at the head of it, in a wine-painted chariot drawn by two milk-white asses whose bridles are the bright findrinny, whose trappings are of red leather. The monk himself has the formality of the wine-god. Behind him, his monks sing gentle hymns.

CAHAL I know what you are after, Briton, and you can whistle for it at full moon. The cloak is mine and I retain it.

MUINCHENN The cloak is the cloak of our god, King, and I must demand it of you.

CAHAL You are entitled to demand. I am entitled to refuse. Off with you, now, back to the hungry sides of the Lee river.

MUINCHENN I will fast you for that cloak, King.

CAHAL You will fast anyway, for I have no food to spare for you. And don't turn your donkeys into my stables. I have cattle fattening and I can spare you no hay, no wheaten straw, and no grain of any description. And nobody in this neighbourhood can spare them either. I have engaged them all to fatten stock and birds for me. I have a royal hunger for such things since the day I got that cloak.

MUINCHENN I notice you have not been to Cork lately.

CAHAL I knew you would notice that. I did not want to trouble you, for I guessed that you would trouble me about this cloak.

MUINCHENN Cork is the only place I have seen thriving since I set out upon my journey. The rest of the country has been harrowed by your hunger.

(*Strings*)

> Field and byre are swept clean,
> The rich dung of the beast is gone from the farmyard,
> The churns of yew are empty,
> There is no soft lowing from any barn.
>
> Cahal's hunger is great.
> It has the magnificence of a season of winter.
> There is a great void after his great heat.
> The king has emptied field and byre.
>
> But in Cork of the Lee,
> In the harbourage of my bells, the season is full of flavour.
> We sweat sweet oils, our girths are easy;
> We fill our cloaks with the warmth of good eating.

CAHAL It seems you invite me to Cork, Monk.

MUINCHENN That is not my intention, King. We are a free settlement who owe you no rights but a yearly tribute. But I think that in all Ireland, it is the only place at this moment where you could eat your fill of the ripe things of the world.

(*Strings*)

> The spits are laden and drip gravy;
> The cow misses her fat calf;
> The bell-wether is troubled about the tally;
> But the spit drips gravy, it roasts a lamb.
>
> The appled orchards, the quince, the pear,
> The plum is in the jar. We are fat and happy
> In Cork of the Lee this year.
> Cahal leaves us alone; so the spit drips gravy.

CAHAL What I want to come at is this: do you challenge me to a feast or a battle?

MUINCHENN Neither, King. But for that cloak, I would offer you seven days of rich feasts, seven nights of dancing, seven serving-maids for your night-guard, seven vats to be on hand for your drinking; and for your occasional picking, a large fat county of arable households.

(*A wolf-howl of hunger from* Cahal)

CAHAL My hunger has spoken for me. You are cheating me by temptation. You can have your blazing cloak and may it burn you to the bottom. When do I progress to this feasting?

MUINCHENN It will be ready when the sun falls to the lowest rung. That is the time of our feasting.

CAHAL Now, hurry that sun. I famish, I famish. You shall earn that cloak, monk, you shall pay for it. I will eat you out of house and home and out of the surrounds of Cork. I will eat you down to the very sandals of your season. Give me bonds for that cloak and that feasting. Hurry, hurry. (*Wolf howl of hunger*)

STORYTELLER Muinchenn returns to Cork. He is received with acclamation in the monkhouses and with wonder in the farmhouses. He has struck a mighty bargain. All agree with that. All the same, the sly farmers are already removing their stock into Kerry and to the summer booleys in the hills. And larders go underground. In West Cork, indeed, there is rioting when Muinchenn's tall fellows are seen upon the roads and some hardy spirits engage them from ambush as is the traditional way of the West Cork people. Muinchenn is hard put to it to keep his word. But in the end he is ready for Cahal. The stores groan, the piggeries squeak, the sheepfolds bleat, the byres and paddocks bellow, the butchers' shops are ringing with cold iron, there is a great scraping of pots and pans in a hundred kitchens. The charcoal-burners and the furzemen are up and down with their donkey-loads. Then, two days before his time, the King arrives.

(*Music in kind from above*)

He is hasty, avid, ravenous. His progress is a rhythm of wolf-howls. The country yields before him as to a wolf-pack. He is mad, snarling, vicious. He is a mighty hunger.

(*Trumpets. Trumpets. Trumpets*)

CAHAL The mighty dinner, Monk. It is ready, it is boiled, broiled, baked, braised, browned –

MUINCHENN There is nothing yet. It is not the time.

CAHAL Time. My belly has changed time. It has issued edicts that the day begins with my breakfast, that the sun must reach its zenith at the middle of my lunch, that it must decline into my dinner at afternoon, and go to sleep in my supper and be absent from the sky whiles I sleep. I offer you a new calendar, and it is your duty as my vassal to accept it.

MUINCHENN I do not accept it.

(*Strings*)

> I take my time
> From the steps of God. I find him
> In the divisions of the days in which he circles the womb.
> One year is his flow and his ebb. The year is his rhythm.

CAHAL I want my feasting. I will have it, I will bolt it. (*Wolf-howl*)

MUINCHENN It is a time of annual fasting, of preparation. We are down on the sun's ebb and we wear black. Can I break the heavenly order because the King is hungry?

(*Wolf-howl in music*)

CAHAL O the lying Abbot of Cork.

> His promises are plenty. He gives bonds for a feast.
> But I find myself in a hungry country.
> I am offered a black fast.
>
> He is a holy man.
> He moves by order: his rota is axled on a year;
> But for the King there is only a little can
> Of holy water. He blesses hunger
> And leads me to a table that is bare.

MUINCHENN King, that satire is not a fair saying on the ways of a priest. I follow the law, but you would have the children of this town of Cork

The Vision of Mac Conglinne

sing about me as if I had sinned in hospitality. I would ask you to withdraw it.

CAHAL I will not withdraw it.

MUINCHENN Then by example you will allow free tongue to every minor satirist, every catchpenny quarreller, every subversive talker inside the kingdom. That is an example that will round on you, for after the priest will come the king. One is no more sacred than the other.

CAHAL I will withdraw it if the board is laid.

MUINCHENN The board will not be laid until the proper time.

(*Wolf-howl of music*)

CAHAL I must have food. I must have filling.
  I must have swilling, I must have solids.
  Lids must be off for me and tables laid.
  The King's belly lays down that law.

MUINCHENN Small bread and whey-water
  Is all man's lot in Cork for two days more.
  No bright beef, no milk, no butter.
  We fast by the law's letter.

CAHAL I will go out into your country. I will beggar farmers, I will strip chiefs, I will have every house boiling pots for me within the hour. There will be no law in the country of Cork but the King's hunger.

MUINCHENN You will destroy festival, interfere with fertility, and enforce famine in the future. There is a demon in you.

(*Wolf-howl of music*)

I know, now, there is a demon in you and if he is not exorcised, you will eat up the country and your kingdom will be a kingdom of hunger. I will exorcise this demon.

(*Savage music*)

DEMON You will not exorcise me, Monk. I will break your bells.

(*Clash of bells*)

I will blast your holy water.

(*Water music*)

I will burn your books.

(*Whirl of flame-music*)

I have already done it. There is in Cork, now, not a bell nor a book nor a drop of holy water. Come on, King, and let us eat.

(*Flourish and crash of music*)

MUINCHENN God help us all.

(*Successive flourishes of music at a distance*)

FRIGHTENED MONK Father Abbot, the buttery is gone.
MUINCHENN God help us all.
ANOTHER MONK Father Abbot, a demon has entered the slaughterhouse.
MUINCHENN God help us all.
ANOTHER MONK Father Abbot, the kitchen is cleared. The King's mouth is
    a demon's mouth.
MUINCHENN God help us all.

(*The flourishes are going into the distance*)

MUINCHENN He is stripping this street, he is stripping that street,
        Every larder, every larder.
        There is no more grocery, no more sweet,
        The rich are lost, the poor are poorer.

        He will go into the country.
        His tongue will be in every house.
        From here to Doneraile he will be eating
        Till he comes to Pichan's dwelling beyond the mountain.

        There he will be stayed
        By a richness of victual, by such a hosting of food
        That even his appetite, enraged as it may be,
        Could not consume to the full moon.

        I will go there.
        I will wear this wonderful cloak I have.
        I will pluck this demon by the hair.
        I will bring him down to his grave.

    Come with me to the oratory, my sons. We shall pray and I shall
    array myself in this miracle of raiment. I will go to Pichan's house
    and I will lay this demon.

(*Flourish of music*)

STORYTELLER I end this scene with a paternoster. King and demon are
    ravaging the country towards Doneraile and rumours of the ravage
    travel before them from tongue to tongue. The rumours are the
    faster and they go farther. They range over Munster. They are over
    the Suir and the Nore. They are up the Barrow. They shiver along
    the Slaney. And from every little hill they leap to other hills. They
    reach Mac Conglinne at Elphin in Roscommon, where he has put

himself to school to a very old master. This teacher has divined the reign of Christ in his numbering, and Mac Conglinne is mastering the attributes of His divinity and altering his poetic psyche until it is in tune with his new beliefs. The news of Cahal's ravages disturbs him. His sudden problem makes him silent in the school, but silences are accepted there as a mental process.

(*Strings*)

>The poet is quiet.
>Leave him. His leisure works for him.
>Behind his still eye
>His silences are busy, they gather in a rhythm.
>
>He works without end,
>Dependent on everything, yet dependent on
>One thing only, the self that has no end,
>The self that he flies and follows, the self that is one.

At the hour of afternoon sleep, a raven perches on the top of the thatch where the poet has tossed his cloak. The master sees it first.

MASTER You have a visitor, Mac Conglinne. That bird wishes speech with you.

MAC CONGLINNE I suppose you know what the bird wants to say to me.

MASTER I can divine that. She says it is time you gathered up your cloak and went down to Cork to cure the King. Raven, am I not right?

(*Squawk of music*)

RAVEN You are right. But you might do me the honour of allowing me to deliver my own messages.

MAC CONGLINNE How am I to cure the King?

RAVEN Let your wise master answer that.

MASTER That is something I cannot answer.

RAVEN I trust your ignorance will make you humble.

MASTER Raven, I accept the rebuke.

RAVEN That is well. Gird yourself up, Mac Conglinne. Take staff and scrip. You can sell your books and buy bacon for the price you get. You will need food in Munster, where there is little enough since that demon in the King went on the rampage.

MAC CONGLINNE But how am I to cure the King?

RAVEN Won't the time tell you that, and your own special knowledge of the situation in which you find yourself? Didn't the demon go from you into the King? If you were the passage in, you must be the passage out.

MAC CONGLINNE I refuse to offer myself as a passage. That demon could stick in me.

RAVEN That demon thinks more of herself than to bother with a poverty-stricken little man who hums a song now and then and thinks he overtops the world. Begone now, and have no more talk out of you. It is time for you to remember that you made a promise to be in Cork the day the lynchpin falls out of the year. You have but the quarter of a day to get there, and it is a good journey enough.

MAC CONGLINNE I'd say it was a good journey. But I remember no promise and I do not know how to cure the King.

RAVEN You made the promise, and you will know how to cure the King. Are you not a poet?

MAC CONGLINNE I will take your word for it.

(*Strings*)

> Drink in fine houses and a rush chair
> Over the embers, people of quality
> In a ring around me, every face aware;
> That is to be a poet. But that is not a poet.

> For the hungry god in me
> Is wild when I waste myself on foolish faces.
> He would have me forever in the agony
> Of delivering him by wild guesses.

> I say my say once
> That others may say it after me.
> They have the credit, I have the pains,
> The god has the authority.

> I guess right, I guess wrong.
> But I know my wrongness, and the god knows it.
> I sacrifice myself in every song.
> Death on death is the hard way of the poet.

Master, will you give me a round of old bacon for my painted book, a piece of leather for two sandals?

MASTER I will give you that. And you may keep your book.

RAVEN He will need no book. He will invent a new one. Hurry now, and put your bits together.

MAC CONGLINNE I suppose you couldn't give me a lift on your back, Raven?

RAVEN I am of the order of ravens. If the gods wished you a carrier they would have sent you that litter-bird, the pigeon, the jade of the woods, whose courting keeps half the world awake when the sun would have them sleep. Go by Slieve Aughty and Limerick, thence to Fermoy, and if you are not there before they close the guesthouse, you might as well stay at home.

MAC CONGLINNE Goodbye Omen, farewell Squawk. I go to cut out sandals.

RAVEN Good luck to the road.

MAC CONGLINNE

(*Strings*)

> Now, poor shanks, you must be spindles
> And wind me a quick road to Cork.
> Bless you, big toe; and you, the tiny one,
> I trust you are up to heavy work.
>
> O ball of the foot, I am no lightweight;
> Ankle, up-gatherer, you hold all the reins
> Of this five-horse chariot of my foot,
> Keep the sweet instep arched upon its ways.
>
> And heel, O sacred and sunny heel, I know
> Something is happening to you as I take the road.
> A wing lifts my foot from heel to toe,
> And I above it tread tall air like a god.

MASTER (*going into distance*) Farewell, Mac Conglinne. Lucky the road.

(*A flying music with pleasant whirls*)

STORYTELLER Slieve Aughty and the waters of Loughrea.

(*Whirl of music*)

The stones of Ennis.

(*Whirl of music*)

The waters of the Shannon.

(*Whirl of music,*)

Cattle plains of Limerick.

(*Whirl*)

Blue mountains of Cork.

(*Whirl*)

The blue washing of the sea.
We will leave the poet to his running. We will go before him. For something has been happening in Cork. Something sad, sorrowful and dreadful. Muinchenn has returned from exorcising the demon.

The Vision of Mac Conglinne   41

He has returned safely and soundly, but he has returned without his cloak. He and his frightened community are gathered in the wooden oratory, Muinchenn huddled head-down in the great chair of the Abbot, his monks, ordained and lay, mouths to the floor upon the sacred cedar wood.

MUINCHENN It could not be because I was afraid of IT.

MONKS (*as in a litany*) You did not fear it, Father.

MUINCHENN Did I not face it hardily?

MONKS You faced it hardily, Father.

MUINCHENN I repeated the ordained words.

MONKS You repeated them.

MUINCHENN I did not fear to sprinkle the water.

MONKS You sprinkled the water.

MUINCHENN Then it was the bell. I lacked a bell.

MONKS It was the bell.

MUINCHENN Why did my sons not provide a bell?

MONKS The demon broke all the bells. O Father, what are we to do?

MUINCHENN We shall pray.

MONKS Let us pray.

MUINCHENN My sons, it has been a shame for me and it has abased me that a priest of my quality should have been subdued by a demon and robbed of the cloak that came to me out of the heart of the god. To you now, I confess that it was pride before a fall. But there was also a thing I had not taken into account, brothers. It was the position of the sun in the heavens. Our god is down upon his knees tonight. He is tired, grey, worn. His body is at the last. But in an hour or so there will be a resurrection from the sea. The young one will come that is still the old one. Earth will tremble and turn upon the axle. The name of the tree will change, and another mighty digit shall be added to our numbering. My sons, with the help of our young god, I will try again.

MONKS The people are on the seashore. They are ready for the young god with welcomes, with psalms, with shouting. The ozier basket is ready in the reeds.

MUINCHENN And the green is empty?

MONKS No one is there on the green.

MUINCHENN The guesthouse is ready?

MONKS The door is open. Hinges squeak. Fleas abound, coverings and beds are grey with dirt. Last night's wash is still in the footbath. The towels smell. The guesthouse is ready.

MUINCHENN Then we can begin. Who is the youngest brother this year?

AIDAN Aidan, Reverence. And I am ready, I stand at the door. I have a wisp of the barley-god in my hand and the two seeds of fire are

beside me in my brazier. And when I hear the cry in the guesthouse,
I will succour the marvellous child.

MUINCHENN We will begin, then. Where is my bellringer?

MONK Here, Worship.

MUINCHENN Ring my bell.

MONK Reverence, there is no bell.

MUINCHENN Make a bell, some bell, any bell, dumbell. What do I say? I
have not lost reverence, but my temper scatters. I lose my thread.
We will do without a bell. Let us play.

MONKS Oh. Oh.

MUINCHENN My sons, it seems that I slip into unnatural errors of speech. I
shall withdraw for a time. The choirmaster will lead you. I am lost
for the moment, I am cowed and cursed, and I know that my temper
is swelling. If I remain, Brothers, I feel that I will pull down the
house in order to assert myself. And that would be bad example and
unwarranted expense. I bow to you and I retire. You shall pray for me.

MONKS We shall pray for you.

(*Music*)

STORYTELLER Muinchenn retires to his dormitory. His defeat by the
demon trembles in him in a terrible temper. His teeth gnash.

(*Quirk of music*)

His hair comes out in fistfuls.

(*Quirk of music*)

His nails rip sheet and covering.

(*Quirk of music*)

And outside in the dark, footsore, with a droop in every bone in his
body, the student Mac Conglinne arrives in a town that is myste-
rious and deserted. It is a night of the three things, wind and snow
and rain about the door, so that the wind left not a wisp of thatch,
nor a speck of ashes that it did not sweep in one door and out
through the other. And that was the way he found the guesthouse.
The doors open and slapping, all winds and draughts loose in the
place, the beds tumbled, the fleas hopping and a mournful blackness
over all things.

(*Background music to go with above, culminating in a kind of creaking,
gusty, door-banging climax*)

MAC CONGLINNE I suppose if I blessed this house, there is no one who
would reply to me?

(A hiss of music)

Rain, I do not ask a reply from you. You have talked to me too much all this evening.

(Hiss of music)

Nor an answer from you, west wind.

(Soft whispering music)

And you, O snow, may whisper elsewhere.

From the three weathers, roof, I ask you to shelter me. Door, do your duty and shut up. By my soul, if this is the far-famed hospitality of the clerics, I will pick my living from profane houses. The washtub? It smells greasily. The towel? It stinks. The bed? Why, it is ready to go nightwalking all by itself. The flea is my guestmaster tonight.

(Strings)

> The flea is my guestmaster in Cork tonight.
> His arms are open to me.
> He welcomes me well; I know that
> He is glad of my company.
>
> He is red-mouthed as a woman
> And he lies as close to me.
> I would have chosen a different sort of lover.
> Yet I accept his hospitality.

No fire, no food, no master in the house. The taxpayers should learn of this, the farmers who salt pigs, the men who buy and sell, the tradesmen who ply this art and that art. By my soul, I will make a satire and I will publish it. They shall learn of this Cork cleric from Slieve Mish to Rathlin Island. My god is the god of eloquence. For once he shall do my bidding, and not I his.

THE GOD I will do that, Mac Conglinne. Speak now and you shall be heard a mile away.

MAC CONGLINNE Glory be to God, I never heard your voice before. It sounds very like my own.

THE GOD It is your own. What other voice can I use except your voice, seeing that you were endowed with me at your birth and I with you? Not that I care for your voice very much. I keep on thinking how much better I could do on my own.

MAC CONGLINNE I won't argue with you, for I am in a hurry to blast those monks of Cork. Are they at their prayers or in their sleep?

THE GOD Never mind that. Let us say our say and I promise we will make ructions.

MAC CONGLINNE Then, let us say our say.

(*Strings*)

> You have put me out, speaking to me out of the air like that. I can
> think of nothing.

THE GOD I shall say it for you.

(*A major music*)

MAC CONGLINNE (*after a moment*) That is a voice that will be heard. But
I'm damned if I understand a word you are saying.

(*Music continues. Stops on a jarring chord. A gentle knocking*)

AIDAN I am Aidan, the youngest brother. I come to welcome the occupant
with fire and food. I hurry and I tremble and I worship and fear, for
this is the first time, Lord, such a mighty voice has resounded in
Cork from such a frail if heavenly body. I will make the fire. Already
the milk is warmed and the woman follows me.

MAC CONGLINNE Well, you got results, queer fellow. But I can't say much
more about your performance.

(*Laugh of music*)

> But milk, old one. Can we thrive on that, we the viney lads who love
> the vat? You with the spark, O cowled one, I am not pleased with
> you. I do not love the service.

(*Strings*)

> A scum of water and a dirty towel
> Is my cleansing in Cork of the clerics;
> I, who have wished in the silver vowel of a spring,
> I am not pleased, O clerics, O Corkmen.
>
> A dark house is no welcome,
> For a house speaks from the hearth, the warm tongue
> Of fire is pleasant and the laden table.
> I did not find them here in Cork.

AIDAN My Lord...

MAC CONGLINNE I am no lord. I am a poet.

AIDAN Grace be around me. A poet in the house on this night, the god's
night? O my dear and sainted halo. There will be a riot in ritual, a
clangour in commentaries, and a storm in the holy water.

MAC CONGLINNE I see you've had a pleasant training in evasions. I see that
you can beat the usual retreat behind the clerical wall. But I will

accept no excuses. I am right, I am firm. I have been insulted by lack of welcome, by the meagreness of fire, by a weakness of cow's milk. And you, it seems, are insulted because I will not be a child and cry for its nanny. Let us, mutually, put the case into quatrains. The poets of Ireland will judge between us. Any little technical assistance I can give you, I will, since you do not appear much of a metre-man to me, and your head is tonsured on that spot where the sun should spreadeagle wildly in long hair.

AIDAN Do not make a satire on our establishment, O Poet. Our reverend Abbot is in a temper already. He has failed to dislodge the demon from the King and he has lost his cloak and something of his mind. You will be disciplined if you do.

MAC CONGLINNE

(*Strings*)

> I do not like big sticks.
> I carry the slender hazel wand,
> The long and lively tongue that never breaks,
> The elastic fellow that has no end.

> No end at all
> For he goes up to the nut and lives in it.
> He is the matter in a nutshell.
> A sweet voice and I deliver it.

> For I am the salmon in the pool.
> The hazel knows me. I am friend to a friend.
> Big sticks are the tools of the fool.
> I carry the tall and slender wand.

The little monk has gone.

STORYTELLER Indeed the little monk has gone. He is flying, rushing, he is tumbling over his habit and badly frightened. Bump, through one door; bash, through another; bish, through the third. And his reverend Abbot is glowering at him over a praying stool. He gathers his breath.

(*Music to go with above*)

AIDAN O Father Abbot.

MUINCHENN Brother, is excitement part of the ritual?

AIDAN O Father Abbot.

MUINCHENN You are frightened, afraid. Brother, this is a simple, a reverend and a yearly ritual. The child you have welcomed to the house need be no cause for fear. It is merely a symbol. It is human and ordinary. The woman will take it up. The woman will feed it, warm it. And the brothers will transform the house in a twinkling till it shines and glitters and welcomes.

AIDAN O Father Abbot, it is not a child that has come. It is a poet.

MUINCHENN Do I hear correctly? Does the demon still mock me? Am I out of my mind?

AIDAN It is a poet, Reverence.

MUINCHENN It is a poet.

(*Strings*)

> The house that has emptied itself,
> That is dead, that is a tomb
> Which must be refurbished by the One beyond wit
> Has given itself to a poet, to a coxcomb.
>
> He will speak loudly for a child,
> He will be heard outside the cradle, his bitter wit
> Is not the comment of the humble and the mild.
> God knows him. But he stands opposite.

The poet spoke to you, boy. What did he say?

AIDAN He is making a satire upon the monks of Cork, because he was not received and warmed as a guest.

MUINCHENN That is the poet's way. He shall not make that satire except he speak through scourges and rods. The brothers must out to him without delay. They will remove him to the green and knot him to the plllar-stone. They will scourge satire out of him until his flesh and skin break loose from his bones. But his bones must not be broken. And when that has been done, let him be dipped soundly in the River Lee, aye, without a stitch of clothing. And after that he may inhabit the guesthouse until morning, for it is now desecrated and the ritual of the year cannot be completed with regularity. His death must absolve us from that, death by crucifixion. To the guesthouse now, to the guesthouse.

(*Hurry of music ending with a recurrence of the phrases used in the first scourging at Grianán Ailech*)

STORYTELLER That is the poor poet learning his lessons over again.

(*Strings*)

> A bitter thing it is
> To be creature to a tongue, to a current of speech
> That will carry you out of yourself
> Beyond all reach.

What do you say, tongue?
Have you so much to give
That I should die so many deaths
That my tongue may live?

They have flayed him to an empty skin. He is bloodless and breath-less, but there's an undaunted devil in him somewhere. He is still mocking when they toss him over the long reeds into the sluggard River Lee.

(*Splash, splash of music*)

MONK Mud to mud.

(*Splash of music*)

MONK Mind to mind.

(*Ditto*)

MONK The stay of the river.

(*Ditto*)

MONK The blight of mankind.

(*Ditto*)

MONK Let him bide by his element for a while, the unstable man in the unstable water. Learn of mutability, Poet.

MAC CONGLINNE

(*Strings*)

I am among the reeds of the Lee and they talk to me
As my peers, for the reed is royal.
O tall sceptre, a starry man in Egypt
Lifted you in jewels. He knows you for an equal.

Flow on, lovely river. Do not mind me.
I have friends in this court, stately and tufted lords
Who have sway over a country, who find me
A mud-relation and understand my words.

MONKS Have you had enough of water, Poet?

MAC CONGLINNE I would like more land, Monk, if it weren't for the tithes you would grab from me.

MONK Push him under a little more.

(*Bubble of music*)

MONK I shall repeat my question about water, Poet.

The Vision of Mac Conglinne

(Bubble, bubble)

MONK The scholar has the speech of water, now. He talks in bubbles. Pull
him to the bank. I think he is senseless, or his tongue would still be
wagging.

ANOTHER MONK Up with him, Brothers. Now who will carry this oozy
mass of the River Lee? God spare us, the vesper hour has come and
gone. We have not sung, we have not prayed. The child has not
come from the water, as in every other year from time out of mind,
and we have spent our time in scourging a poet.

MONK Lift up this waterman. Holy father, what a weight! Certainly if this
man has divinity, it would weigh before the Lord.

MONK At least something comes to us from the water. There is a symbol
in that if one could read it. Ah, to be a wise man.

MONK Better to be holy.

MONK Better to be lucky, for to be lucky is to find the heaven that is at
the end of holiness. Up, sweet brother of the tongue, you have
neither luck nor grace, but certainly you smell to the highest of the
heavens.

(Music flourish)

STORYTELLER The unfortunate poet is lodged in the icy guesthouse for the
long night. He gathers his skin about him for warmth and sleeps in a
palpitation of the flea-world. He does sleep. He has learned the
secret of pain from somebody he cannot remember at the moment,
some She that he has met at some time or other, but there have been
so many Shes in his life that he cannot distinguish his teacher. But
she is warm inside him. She is a thought without a visual symbol and
in thinking her out he forgets that he ought to be in plaster and
under a vegetable drug. The monks wake him in the morning. They
come bearing gifts. The gifts are: sour faces, sour words, and sour
judgements. They array themselves before his pallet and stand
silently until the stately Abbot enters slowly. His every step is a
pondering, his every look is a rendering. When he stops the world
stops, and he envelops the earth in a vast silence.

(Appropriate music)

MUINCHENN He is awake?

MONKS He is awake, Father.

MUINCHENN Let him stand. Let him bow.

MONKS You must stand. You must bow.

MAC CONGLINNE

(Strings)

This Abbot, it seems,
Demands largely like a king.
Is he a tall tree among trees?
What is his family? Does he hail from some royal thing?

MUINCHENN I think largely, I believe profoundly,
I live wisely. In that I am a king.
God is my family tree
And tall enough to my thinking.

MAC CONGLINNE I do not think I shall stand for you. Instead, I would ask
you to make obeisance to me.

MONKS Make obeisance to him?

MAC CONGLINNE This Abbot is self-chosen.
His qualities are worldly, his cloak too large for him.
His signs are only the signs of a servant.
Give him a mattock. Set him to till.

MONKS Oh. Oh.

MUINCHENN I suppose I must sit in judgement for this insult. I shall do so
with justice and calm, as might be expected from me. I think generally and not particularly when I condemn him to be crucified after
the fashion of a malefactor.

MAC CONGLINNE There was a certain malefactor whom you may not have
heard of yet. He was condemned to crucifixion too, but his sin was
Divine Justice. I shall take it as an honour to suffer a death of that
kind, for I am tired of the injustice of this world where a man is
whipt clerically and half-drowned for no sin at all but for some mild
objection to a failure in hospitality, a hospitality which is due to him
and which is well paid for by the community.

MUINCHENN I tell the world there was no lack of hospitality on the part of
the monks of Cork. You come to us on a night that is one night of
the year for us, you take over a house that is prepared for another,
and you lampoon holy men whose only business it is to serve God
and deliver him credibly to a world that is lost to all the sins.

MAC CONGLINNE I would have begged pardon of the monks of Cork if I
had known of this thing, but it was not explained to me. I was taken
and flogged and half-drowned and not allowed to ask a question
or say a word. I have been evilly treated, for if I did evil it was
unwittingly.

MUINCHENN You have continued your evil. You have insulted an abbot.
And in me, all abbots and religious are offended. To condone that is
to cheapen offence. And so, I will not remit my judgement.

MAC CONGLINNE How can I expect justice? The face I look on is not a just
face.

The Vision of Mac Conglinne

> The heraldry of that white face
> Is that of the lawman who wins arguments.
> It is painted law but not justice.
> It is pride rampant. It lacks God-sense.

MONKS Oh. Oh.

MUINCHENN You see? You still follow the ways of pride. Will you die with some wild lampoon in your mouth?

MAC CONGLINNE You will die with some wild opinion of your own worth.

MONKS Oh. Oh.

MAC CONGLINNE I charge you, now, with the murder of a body, my body.

MONKS Oh. Oh.

MAC CONGLINNE I charge you, too, with the murder of a soul, your soul.

MONKS Oh. Oh.

MAC CONGLINNE You may take me to your death-tryst at your peril. I am ready as you will never be ready.

MONKS Oh. Oh.

MUINCHENN You may take him away. He has earned so many deaths, he is lucky he can die but the one time.

MAC CONGLINNE Cleric, there is something you have forgotten.

MUINCHENN I have overlooked nothing.

MAC CONGLINNE The law lays down the offence for which crucifixion is the legal punishment. How will you justify yourself to the King, when the poet-schools of Ireland bring my death before him?

MUINCHENN That need not trouble you. My conduct is impeccable. You have been judged guilty by a convocation of the clergy, over which I presided. The sentence is a matter for me. Away with him, now.

MAC CONGLINNE Not so fast, if you please. I have a right to ask a boon of you.

MUINCHENN If it is to liberate you, Scholar, you can shut your mouth.

MAC CONGLINNE It is only a minor boon, a thing that is insignificant and small, but I warn you in advance that I shall try to make more out of it.

MUINCHENN Name it.

MAC CONGLINNE I must have sureties first.

MUINCHENN You may trust in my mercy.

MAC CONGLINNE I will trust in my sureties, Monk, and in the bond of God I will put on them. That is not a right, but it is a custom.

MUINCHENN Name your sureties.

MAC CONGLINNE Ibar of Little Ireland, Cahal of Munster. And all of your brotherhood that are present here shall take a pledge that I may have this boon.

MUINCHENN My sons may do so.

MONKS We take the pledge of fulfilment.

MUINCHENN You can name your wish now.

MAC CONGLINNE Let my satchel be given to me. Let it be opened. It is my
wish now to eat those two wheaten cakes that are in it and the round
of old bacon. I believe in food for a journey, and by the signs of
things I would seem to be going on a long one. I would eat my meal
at the door, with a spark of the sun at my head, and the people of
Cork watching me. I demand to be taken there.

MUINCHENN You may be taken there.

(*Music*)

STORYTELLER Poor Mac Conglinne. He is taken to the door from which
the poor of Cork are fed every evening before the vesper bell, but
around which they gather early, playing pitch-and-toss and the
horseshoe game and the sly gamble of the shell-and-pea.

MAC CONGLINNE I need a knife.

MUINCHENN Let him have a knife.

MAC CONGLINNE It is the law that the man who eats must give tithes to
a man who is poorer than himself. I am cutting a just tenth of my
mite and I will give it to anyone who can be found to be poorer
than I am.

(*Clamour of beggars. Music*)

> The beggars of Cork, the rough-and-tumble men,
> The lazy women who never delouse,
> The one-legged men, the blind stick-tapper, children
> On arm-crook and shawl, they are after me with their claws.
>
> I save myself from the outstretched fingers
> With difficulty. I would feed these poor
> If I had plenty; but this poet has hungers
> Inside himself that knock at every door.

Before God, you rag-and-bone people, it can never be known if any
of you stands in greater need of these tithes than the man who has
them in his hand; and since possession is nine-tenths of the law, I
propose with God's consent to put them into my own belly. For
my journey yesterday was longer than any of yours. And my ill-
treatment in Cork was worse. I was received by curs and hounds,
and stripped and scourged and dipped in the waters of the Lee. And
in the presence of my Maker, O you evil monks of Cork, I say that it
will not be charged to me by the fiend when I reach the Judgement,
that I gave you these tithes, for you deserve them not.

MUINCHENN I did not bargain for this oration to the laity, Scholar.

MAC CONGLINNE You can overlook law but not custom, Monk. I put the case to your congregation.

MONKS The scholar is right, Father.

MUINCHENN Then take him to his well. But I will wait here within my house. I will lose no dignity on him.

MAC CONGLINNE That is a pity, for I have lessons for you still. Note that I have eaten enough for three days to come and that there is no time limit within which I must take the drink that goes with that meal. It is my intention accordingly, O Monk, to fast for another three days, and then for three days more to be drinking water and doing penance for my sins. I think, O you bad Abbot, that I have obtained nine days of respite from you in spite of yourself.

MUINCHENN I allow no trickery, Scholar.

MAC CONGLINNE The stretching of a custom is no trick.

MUINCHENN I shall ponder it. In the meantime, go to your drink. Get out of my presence, for neither your face nor your ways are a pleasure to me. Take him to this well and stick his head in it.

MAC CONGLINNE Not so, Monk. I go to a drinking and not a drowning, and I shall take my drink in my own way – (*Fading out*) There is a method in all things.

(*Music*)

STORYTELLER And what a drinking, and what a method of drinking! The poet reaches the well, guarded by the monks, but accompanied by half the population of the town of Cork. On the flag before it he halts, he loosens his cloak and the big brooch of his cloak with the long pin. He lays the cloak down upon the flag and lies down upon it like a strong man about to perform the feat of the stone-sledging. His head is to the well.

CORK VOICE What is he at at all, boy? Is it an acrobat the fellow is? What's he doing with the brooch?

MAC CONGLINNE My method of drinking, people of Cork, is to dip the pin of this brooch over my head into the water. Watch me. You see I gather water on the pin, and when I lift it it runs down the pinhead into one drop. I hold the pin over my mouth and the drop falls into it.

(*Laughter of the people of Cork in music*)

It is somewhat laborious, people. It will take a long time to satisfy my thirst, my legal and proper thirst, but you must admit that I have a right to stay alive while my thirst is unsatisfied.

(*Laughter in music*)

The Vision of Mac Conglinne   53

Am I not making a fool of that Abbot, that bad Abbot, Muinchenn,
O people of Cork?

MONK It was no part of our bargain, Scholar, that you should make the
people laugh at us.

MAC CONGLINNE It is a man's business to live while he may, Monk.

MONK He must die when his death is ordained, Scholar.

MAC CONGLINNE When God ordains it, Monk. But to give up life easily is
to commit the sin of suicide.

MONK Take this question to the Abbot, Brother. You must run, for we are
but objects of ridicule here before the people.

MAC CONGLINNE

(*Strings*)

> The monk has a quandary.
> He follows a trodden path. He does not lift his eyes.
> He is nervous of the glory
> I catch. He fears my sunrise.

> The monk is right.
> But so am I. He finds in abstinence
> And knee-bending all the glories I
> Startle each moment out of every sense.

MONK Brothers, we cannot stay here much longer. We are becoming a
mockery.

MONKS Does that matter? We shall stay here and be comfortable while the
scholar is uncomfortable.

MAC CONGLINNE Monks, I am always comfortable wherever I am. One of
the lessons the poet learns is to feel in different parts of himself, so
that he can unfold his own drama in one eye and regard it with the
other.

(*Strings*)

> In Cork by the Lee
> I am married to the earth. We lie so lightly
> That the earth may think me
> Thin and warm as early sunlight.

> We are happy together.
> We are two in one. We are so young
> That our drink is one bright drop of water,
> One small golden egg that falls through our marriage ring.

(*Heavy Abbot music approaching*)

MUINCHENN I will not have this, Scholar.

MAC CONGLINNE O the bad Abbot.

MUINCHENN I will not allow custom to be outstretched till it becomes
farce. You can stand up now. I allowed you to drink and the time to
drink. If you have not drunken what you need, it is your own fault.
Take him up, my sons.

MONKS A boon from you, Father Abbot.

MUINCHENN What boon do you want of me?

MONKS Time has gone astray on us today. We have not offered Mass nor
blessing and it is now past the noon. Let us have a respite for this
poet until these things have been done.

MUINCHENN Afterwards you shall do them. The day of his transgression
shall be the day of that man's punishment. You may rise up and take
him to the wood of the foxes. Let him cut his own tree, let him carry
it to the green, let him be crucified. I will not be mocked by a
mocker, I will not be demeaned. (*Fading*) I will not be dishonoured
in my community.

(*Heavy Abbot music recedes*)

STORYTELLER Poor Mac Conglinne is marched to the wood of the foxes.
An axe is thrust into his hands and an elder tree pointed out to him
on a ditch.

MAC CONGLINNE

(*Strings*)

> Elder tree, I fear
> You are unlucky for me. You will stretch
> My poor body on spokes of air
> Till nothing is beyond my reach.
>
> What will I be
> When bone on bone is racked around in a ring
> And I see the stars from the end of my heel,
> A sunwheel thundering?

STORYTELLER But the midwinter day is short. When he labours back with
his cross, the monks are tired and without food.

MONK This scholar is a great trouble to us.

MONK He is the points of seven pins pricking my skin. I could lay him
down and dance on him.

MONK What brought you to Cork, wonderman? Could you not have
holidayed somewhere else? B' l'ath Cliath is a great place for the
poetry and the drink. Or that fishtown by Ibar's island.

MONK Brothers, there is a void in me.

MONK There is a void in us all.

MONK I am never myself the day I do not spend the morning in my little chapel.

MONKS Nor I, nor I.

MONK Nor when I miss the morning's porridge.

MONK Little time today we had for praying. Let us, in convocation, pray the Abbot for a respite for this lost one until the morning.

MONKS That is a good thought.

MONK A good thought. We will halt here, now, and I will call Muinchenn. You may halt, Scholar. Scholar, you may halt. He does not hear me. Scholar, Scholar! Lord Abbot –

(*Heavy music of the Abbot*)

MUINCHENN Another respite.

MONKS This time it is for us, Father Abbot, for monks who have not said Mass, nor offered a prayer in the course of this day in our little chapel. We crave this benefit of clergy and we request it because it is our right.

MUINCHENN Rights, rights, boons, boons, respite, respite. Am I to hear nothing all day but those words? A demon loose in the country, a poet loose in Cork, and my monks fail me and do my bidding slowly.

MONK Not so, Father. We have failed in no thing. It is your own power and your own insight and oversight that have failed you and allowed that demon to overcome you and the poet to delay you.

MUINCHENN Which of you has spoken?

MONKS, ALL All of us have spoken, Father Abbot.

MUINCHENN I see. Many faggots make a bundle which cannot be broken. Let this poet have a respite till tomorrow morning. But let him be stripped, let him be bound to the stone, and let him have no food and no drink.

(*Receding Abbot music*)

STORYTELLER The unlucky poet is knotted once more to that tall stone. And the night comes down on him. He can hear the monks in the chapel, he can listen to the dogs barking on the horizon, he can feel the grass of the green thicken and crinkle with ice, and he can count more stars than comfort. But he falls asleep. He falls into the warm cloak of a thought. And the cloak is very like the cloak that he delivered to the King on Ibar's island. And there is somebody else inside the cloak. There is a tall and golden woman. There is a queen.

MAC CONGLINNE There is someone in the middle of my pain.

QUEEN It is I, Mac Conglinne.

MAC CONGLINNE The bad queen.

QUEEN Not so, Mac Conglinne. A queen needs to be royal, not good. You
have agreed with me on that before.

MAC CONGLINNE I did, and I don't know why. I carry a red alphabet for
you on my buttocks, the mud of the Lee in my gullet because of you,
and before me there is a great stretching of arms and legs that I am
not partial to. They call it a crucifixion.

QUEEN I know that.

MAC CONGLINNE I expect you do. And it is plain to me, now, that many
have been crucified because of you. Do you speak outside or inside
me?

QUEEN I speak from inside you.

MAC CONGLINNE No use, in that case, to ask you to touch me and let my
head fall upon your breast.

QUEEN You are there now, Mac Conglinne. My child, my boy, my lover.

MAC CONGLINNE You are my Lady of the Willow Tree.

QUEEN That is one aspect of me.

MAC CONGLINNE You are also a terrible nuisance to me.

QUEEN That is another aspect of me. But my business is to establish
myself. I need your help for that.

MAC CONGLINNE If you think to establish yourself with Cahal of Cashel,
you can put it out of your head. He calls you a great bitch. Your
name is farmyard muck to him and all that goes with it.

QUEEN I am aware of that. But it is not an expression I would wear to
dinner. The King is necessary to me.

MAC CONGLINNE Have you no pride, to follow him this way?

QUEEN I have proportion, I have business, I have being.

(*Strings*)

> I alternate,
> How can I help it? I
> Rise and fall with the spirit
> That moves me, that is me.
>
> Do not remark me.
> I am not remarkable. I am a country
> You know well.
> My demands are simple. My demands are me.
>
> I ask you to carry me.
> But I carry you too, though you grow taller and taller.
> And I the larger for you till the time
> Comes when you grow smaller.

You have this to do for me now, my poet. I am the great hunger in
Cahal of Cashel.

MAC CONGLINNE You are that great demon?

QUEEN It is one more aspect of me, the most terrible. It is my requiem side. And the day has now come when I leave it aside. In the morning you will go to the King.

MAC CONGLINNE If I go there, it will be on one side of a cross. Tomorrow I shall be a dead man.

QUEEN I will have talk with the Abbot Muinchenn.

MAC CONGLINNE That's all the good that will be. You do not know this Abbot.

QUEEN I do know him. He has his own dream of me. And he is steadfast to it.

MAC CONGLINNE

(*Strings*)

> Do you tempt every bed,
> You, O long hair, O white one, are you
> A different woman in every head,
> A woman of thousands? And who will wear you?
>
> Who will wear you when time ends,
> You, O long hair, O white one, every man
> Carrying you in his head to heaven,
> When time ends, will you be the only woman?

QUEEN I will be the only woman, Mac Conglinne.

MAC CONGLINNE I know you now, and I am lost. O Goddess, my heart is in my mouth for you and it will talk love. When you were a queen, you were the profane thought in my mind, and you were a hope there, too, that some day I might come on you when you were not queenly. I am lost, now.

QUEEN You are not lost. You will find me in every poem.

MAC CONGLINNE Is that enough?

QUEEN Nothing is ever enough. I am not enough in myself. But everything has enough to go on with so that it can will and desire and change, so that it is ever in the process of creation. Is not that enough?

MAC CONGLINNE Lady of the Willow Tree. But how will I know the way to release you from the kingly appetite?

QUEEN I leave that to you. Are you not a poet and master of arts? Are you not now in that visionary state in which things can happen? This Abbot, who is an ogre to you, has he not served you in that?

MAC CONGLINNE It was harsh service.

QUEEN His mission is to be hard. And I am afraid you will have some revenge on him tomorrow. You will be given his cloak.

MAC CONGLINNE I do not want his cloak.

QUEEN Tomorrow you will want it. It is the cloak of the delivery of a god, and in time you will become so proud of it that you will have to be removed from under it, for that is the way of things. You will become dry, arid, sterile and haughty, and you will misinterpret your god so much that he will find it necessary to remove you.

MAC CONGLINNE If I wear this cloak, I shall never be of that kind.

QUEEN It is in the nature of things for you to be of that kind.

MAC CONGLINNE I will leave the nature of things.

QUEEN Then you will cease to know me.

MAC CONGLINNE I will take you along with me.

QUEEN I am there before you. But what there is here of me remains till the fan is folded from before the face. I leave you now, I kiss you, I love you, and I will receive you when the world has ended for you.

(*Music of the Queen's going*)

STORYTELLER I end this scene with a sigh. To the poet his vision, to the storyteller his hard work and little profit, to the monk his abbot, to the abbot a matin bell that is cracked and newly made from a kitchen skillet.

(*Cracked skillet music. Sounds of rousing monks*)

MONK It is not a good omen, this cracked bell of the morning. *Pax tecum, pax tecum.*

MONK Fresh holywater has been blessed.

MONK My soul is cold. The Abbot must allow us Mass this morning.

(*Heavy music of the Abbot*)

MUINCHENN My sons.

MONKS Our father.

MUINCHENN After Matins, after Mass, it is usual for us to have some collation. This morning you must feast with me, for last night I had most unseemly dreams of good food and I awakened this morning with an appetite that climbs to the devilish level of the King's.

MONKS (*softly*) It is the demon, the demon of the King's.

MUINCHENN That is my dread, sons. It is as yet a baby hunger to the King's hunger, but big things begin small. Once the world was a tiny egg. You will fast with me this morning?

MONKS We will fast with you this morning.

MUINCHENN We will pray now.

MONKS We will pray now.

(*Heavy Abbot music recedes*)

STORYTELLER Prayers waken Mac Conglinne. He too feels a passion of
   hunger. He smacks his lips.

(*Quirk of music*)

   His gums are saliva.

(*Watery quirk of music*)

   But his teeth are warriors in white armour who clash with one
   another.

(*An iron music*)

   In the air above his head a hawk dives, no, it is that quarrelsome
   little bastard, the cock robin. But what a robin! Has he borrowed
   feathers from the eagle? He plunges at a little wren, the tiny gold-
   crest, and by God he's got him. And oh what a ripping of small
   plumes. The sky awakens. Chimneys are smoking. Dogs are sniffing.
   Cats are mewing at kitchen windows. Milk pails are clinking and
   there are the tiny chimes of good delph all along the streets. And oh,
   the smells. It is breakfast time in Cork. Mac Conglinne sniffs, sniffs,
   sniffs.

(*Quirks of music*)

   And now the stately Abbot Muinchenn begins a stately progress
   across the green.

(*Heavy Abbot music*)

MUINCHENN I smell good things.
MONKS The earth is gracious.
MUINCHENN It is the tables of the Corkmen I smell.

(*Quirky sniff of music*)

   O muttons, pray for me.
MONKS Oh. Oh. Oh.
MUINCHENN O Lard look down on me. My tongue sniffs. I cannot say a
   bird right.
MONKS The demon is in the Abbot.
MUINCHENN It is the feast in me. Again, again. My tongue tripes at every
   curd. I cannot speak to this scholar with this hunger in my mouth. I
   will return and read in my little cook. Oh. Oh.
MONKS Oh. Oh. Oh.
MAC CONGLINNE What a lot of 'Os' there are in Ireland this morning.
MUINCHENN I have no stomach for morning wit, please be gravy.

(*Quirk of music*)

MAC CONGLINNE O weighty Abbot

(*Strings*)

> O weighty Abbot, how could you be light
> From such a family tree
> As yours? I saw it in a dream last night.
> It was a vision that came to me.
>
> You are the son of honeybag and lard,
> Son of stirabout, son of butter,
> Son of a cow's cream, son of curd,
> Son of bacon-flitch, son of shoulder.
>
> Son of back, son of paunch,
> Son of leg, son of kidney,
> Son of pig's head, son of haunch,
> Shall I go on? Do you forbid me?

MUINCHENN You would not hurt me, Mac Conglinne, by finding my pedigree in food but for one thing; and that is that you should speak of it this morning when my tongue sloughs over.

MONK There is a demon of food talking through you.

MUINCHENN Not yet, not yet. It is a cream I had in sleep last night,

(*Quirk of music*)

MONKS Oh. Oh. Oh.

MAC CONGLINNE It is quite clear to me.

MUINCHENN Your sight will not help you much. You will die even if I am beflitched.

(*Quirk of music*)

MONKS Oh. Oh. Oh.

MAC CONGLINNE Old bacon, I can cure you.

MUINCHENN If you could, I would reward you.

MAC CONGLINNE In what way would you reward me?

MUINCHENN By allowing you to confess your sins and shriving you before death.

MAC CONGLINNE By my soul, there is a large sulk inside you. You will do much more for me, O Muinchenn. You will also take my body into consideration. You will release me from all bonds. You will let me have the ownership of that great cloak that I presented to the King on Ibar's island.

MUINCHENN It was you, then, who gave the King that cloak?

MAC CONGLINNE It was I.

MUINCHENN You are a power, then?

MONKS Oh. Oh. Oh.

MAC CONGLINNE (*imitating monks*) Oh. Oh. Oh. You owe me so much, I should hang out the usurer's sign. I will add to my offer. When I have cured you, I will cure the King.

MONKS (*softly*) A marvel amongst us, a marvel amongst us.

MAC CONGLINNE You are considering it?

MUINCHENN I am crunchidering it. That cloak, that cloak.

(*Strings*)

> It is raiment. A cloak of every stew.
> It was Muinchenn's. Now, a young rooster
> Because of an ignorance in Muinchenn's belly will go
> In God's guise and eat above me.

You may cure me, Scholar.

MAC CONGLINNE Sureties first, Monk. Name them.

MUINCHENN (*breathlessly to music*)

> Beef, mutton, lamb, a kid,
> Stewy smells that lift the lid.
> Tripe and sausage, wheat in milk –
> Stop me, I cannot help myself.
> Back rashers dripping smoke and fat,
> The brains of a pig, his little hat –
> O help me brothers – bacon boiled,
> Slices roasted, then half broiled.
> Brothers, brothers, I am lost
> In food, I'm soup-and-gravy tossed –

(*Blare of music. Sudden silence*)

MAC CONGLINNE You are cured.

MUINCHENN What did you do to me?

MAC CONGLINNE I allowed you to boil over. I have taken your hunger on myself.

MONKS Oh. Oh. Oh.

MUINCHENN You show no signs of my hunger.

MAC CONGLINNE It is because I am much larger than you are.

MUINCHENN I can see that, now.

MAC CONGLINNE That surprises me. I thought you had one little eye and that it was eternally turned upon yourself in adoration. Loose me, now. I have work to do.

MONKS It is a marvel. It is a marvel. Oh. Oh. Oh.

(*Music*)

STORYTELLER But Mac Conglinne is away to greater marvels, to the curing
of Cahal of Cashel and the salvation of South Ireland. He lifts his
five-folded, well-stropped cloak on to the slope of his shoulders, he
ties his shirt around the rounds of his fork, and in a twinkling his
heels are feathery with speed and he is striding over Raheen and
Bealnablath and coming to the Dun of Coba, the wide dwelling of
Pichan. The crossroads are peopled with quiet men in their Mass-
suits, men who say nothing but are waiting for something to happen.
So, unchallenged by any doorkeeper, Mac Conglinne bursts into
Pichan's enclosure where the soldiers are in chattering groups and
the women gossiping and the children running around, playing a
new game that they call King and Demon. The King is abroad
somewhere, somewhere unknown. And Pichan, his friend and
warrior-mate, awaits him in the great hall of the Dun, the wide
living-room where walls are lined with sleeping places, where
soldiers lounge, where they sharpen weapons on the big stone, where
they line the board at mealtimes, where they quarrel and take their
turns in boasting according to their orders.

　　Into the enclosure, turning cartwheels and doing wild juggleries,
comes this new and strange Mac Conglinne. He has been fasting, he
has been beaten till his mind has left his skin, he has been drowned
till all his life has gone inward, and now he is light, airy, and like a
shaft of the sun for power. Pichan watches him out of a tired dream.

(*A tired music*)

MAC CONGLINNE I do not amuse you, Pichan.
PICHAN You do your best, Scholar, but your best is of little use against the
King's worst.

(*Strings*)

　　　　He is all my friends in one.
　　　　I cannot deny him, he may have heart and all;
　　　　But what I give is given to a demon.
　　　　A demon is eating my heart, he is eating Cahal.

　　　　If there was help from God
　　　　I would meet it on my four bones and crawl with it
　　　　From heaven to Corcalee;
　　　　If my knees were to redden the earth, it is I would haul it here.

MAC CONGLINNE Help has come, O Pichan.
PICHAN I am not aware of it, Student. I only see a scholar before me who
　　demeans a high art by the trumperies of jugglers and twopenny
　　tumblers.

The Vision of Mac Conglinne　　　　　　　　　　　　　　　　　　63

MAC CONGLINNE Still I bring help, Pichan. What shall I receive from you if
    I keep the King from eating the whole day?
PICHAN A golden ring and a Welsh horse.
MAC CONGLINNE I see you put me in the penny place. My demands are
    larger.
PICHAN I can see that now. I will give you, too, a white steed from every
    house and fold from Carn to Cork.
MAC CONGLINNE That is my due. Sureties now, if you please.

> Kings and lords of the land,
> Poets and satirists must be pledged to me;
> Kings to enforce the dues, lords to spend
> On collectors, the poets to satirise for me,
> Satirists to travel, to spread the abuse
> Of the poets. In that way I get my dues.

PICHAN It is done. And you may begin now, for I hear the rush and the
    approach of my sick friend and King.

   (*Appropriate music*)

STORYTELLER It is the King indeed, and a changed King. The demon is
    showing through his face. He is lean as a tapeworm. And he seems to
    have wings on his shoulders, but that is only the cloak of Muinchenn
    that is awry and flying about in his great hurry. From the serving
    quarters there is a rush of servants, gillies and maidservants. They
    have placed him on the top king-seat of the board, they are loosening
    his boots, they have the utensils on the wash, but he pulls the hide
    table-covering on to his lap and starts to munch the barrowload of
    apples that have been piled on it in section and order. O what a
    munching.

   (*Appropriate munch music*)

   But there is another munching too, a tooth-on-edge kind that draws
   all eyes, even the King's.

   (*Appropriate tooth-and-edge music*)

   Now this is a strange sight. Mac Conglinne has taken the huge stone
   block on which the soldiers sharpen their points and edges, and is
   holding it with abnormal strength to his mouth. The King stops to
   watch.

   (*Tooth-on-edge music which recedes*)

CAHAL What makes you mad, Son of Learning?
MAC CONGLINNE I grieve to see a king eating alone.

CAHAL Small reason for grief in that. A king is always alone.

MAC CONGLINNE A king is a kingdom. He is his people's honour. If there were a foreigner here, he would be entitled to scoff at our bad manners if my beard did not wag mutually in movement with yours.

CAHAL That is a good point. I will give you an apple. This one is too large for you.

(*Crunch-crunch of music*)

This is large too.

(*Crunch-crunch*)

So is this.

(*Crunch*)

And this also.

(*Tooth-racking music begins again*)

MAC CONGLINNE I still eat my stone, O King.

CAHAL May you have good digestion. All those apples are too big for you.

MAC CONGLINNE And how that foreigner would laugh at us, at you.

CAHAL True. I will give you an apple. This one, no this, no. By God, you are a greedy man, Scholar. Is it necessary at all that I should give you an apple?

MAC CONGLINNE For your own honour and the honour of your kingdom.

CAHAL Here, before I change my mind. Catch, greedy one.

(*Whizz of an apple thrown*)

MAC CONGLINNE I catch, but it was ungraciously given. I have one, but better two things than one in learning. One is the path for another, King.

CAHAL Oh. Oh. Another. Am I made of apples?

MAC CONGLINNE You are a great tree of apples.

CAHAL Here, Scholar.

(*Another whizz of music*)

MAC CONGLINNE I have only two. And the number of the Trinity is one more.

CAHAL No.

MAC CONGLINNE King, you dishonour the Trinity.

CAHAL Do I do that? Here, then.

(*Another whizz*)

MAC CONGLINNE The number of the Gospels is four books. That is one more.

CAHAL I give you the four books of the Gospels. I cannot eat them.

MAC CONGLINNE Then, the floor of your hall falls under you.

CAHAL Here, here.

(*Another whizz*)

MAC CONGLINNE I have four. But there are five books of Moses.

CAHAL Why should you count them in apples? Count them in spears or
    buttons. Those I will give you.

MAC CONGLINNE The apple is blessed.

CAHAL Woe, woe.

(*Another whizz*)

MAC CONGLINNE I have five. But there is a number which consists of its
    own parts and divisions. Its half is three, its third is two, and its sixth
    is one. Give me that lovely number.

CAHAL You rob me, you reeve me, you unrobe me.

MAC CONGLINNE The sixth, King.

(*Whizz*)

I thank you. There were seven things prophesied of God on earth,
    however –

CAHAL Do you ask me for a seventh?

(*Wolfish howl*)

MAC CONGLINNE I do. And an eighth for your own royalty. And nine for
    the orders of heaven, and ten is the number of mankind. And the
    eleventh, King, is the perfect number of the Apostles after sin. And
    then, for the triumph of triumphs, Cahal, the number thirteen, the
    perfect number, Christ with his Apostles.

(*There is a whizz after each number above, but at thirteen there is a violence
of whizzes*)

CAHAL Take all, O devourer. Let me rise, let me reach for my anger. Let
    me rear and roar.

(*Snarl of trumpets*)

MAC CONGLINNE This is not kingly. If you curse me, you cut me off from
    Heaven. I remind you of the mercy you carry, for I stand in need of
    it. I have also something to say to you.

CAHAL I will calm myself. Be brief as my meal was brief.

MAC CONGLINNE I must ask a boon first. I ask it of your kingship.

CAHAL Are you entitled to that? Have you any degrees, Poet? Have you
    the signs of the houses on you?

MAC CONGLINNE Pichan will bear witness for me.

PICHAN I will bail him, Cashel.

CAHAL Ask, then.

MAC CONGLINNE Sureties, then, that my boon be granted.

CAHAL My princely word on it.

MAC CONGLINNE I will speak so. Because of you I came south to Cork. Because of you I transgressed in Cork. Because of you I was punished, and there is a curse on me still for my innocent transgression. It is in your power to release me from that curse, for you are an original brother.

CAHAL But if I release you, I must do a fast for it. Do you ask me to do that?

MAC CONGLINNE That is what I ask.

CAHAL By my faith, you will carry your curse along with you to the end of time.

MAC CONGLINNE King, your bond, your bails, your princely word.

CAHAL Student, ask me for a cow from every enclosure in Munster, ask me for an ounce from every householder, ask me for a cloak from every church, all to be levied by my steward, and yourself to stay feasting with me till the tax is heaped before you and the taxmen touching their caps.

MAC CONGLINNE It would not be lawful. Is it lawful that I should feast my body and give my soul to eternal perdition? I hold you to your bails and your bonds and your sureties.

(*Wolf howl from the* King)

CAHAL   This sprig of learning,
    With his satchel, with his wand, he walks
    The roads and the delicate bye-paths of all things
    Where the world is talking,
    And where no world talks.

    Learning is no load. He walks lightly
    And so deceptively, five things are graces in him,
    The solar month, the age of the moon, the sea-tide,
    The calendar of the perfect deity
    And the year in its rhythm.

    He slips through me. He enters
    From so many roads, he is before me here
    In the flash of my anger, and suddenly I see him
    With my country in his power.
    That is what learning has done for him. That is the way of
                                                            learning.

The Vision of Mac Conglinne   67

I will fast with you, Student, but I shall hate you.

(*Wolf music*)

STORYTELLER Cahal does fast, but if he sleeps, nobody else sleeps.

He dreams of fat pots.

(*Quirk of music*)

Poleaxed bullocks, skin-stripped by the cooks.

(*Ditto*)

Fires under black vats.

(*Ditto*)

The kitchen spits turning, brown smells on the hooks.

(*Ditto*)

The weighty belly of the table.

(*Ditto*)

The crunch and munch of everything.

(*Ditto*)

Food like a fable.

(*Ditto*)

ENOUGH FOR A KING.

(*Ditto*)

(*Wolfish music*)

CAHAL Where is that student?

MAC CONGLINNE I am here, nodding by the wall.

CAHAL Release me from my fast.

MAC CONGLINNE There will be no release, there will be no relieving.

CAHAL I will halve my dinner with you, I will give you three parts of my breakfast.

MAC CONGLINNE Sleep, King.

(*Strings*)

In little thatches
Where men who work the fields are tired out
Women sing sleepy snatches

To the cradle by the fire. They stir with one bare foot.

Let them sleep.
They have the right of labour. If a man
Turns over, there should be a warm meeting
On the pillow-side, for winter is on the land.

My words to greet kings are:
Justice; be gentle; start no great shows
That the man and the woman together
Sleep warm in the winter snows.

CAHAL I will take that scholar by the throat and throttle him. I will bottle him, baste him, roast him, toast him, I will thrust him into the wild den of my mouth. I will be the first cannibal king in Ireland.

(*Wolfish music*)

STORYTELLER But in the morning he is still fasting under bails and bonds and his stomach is still a mighty emptiness. The daylight hours are all to pass. The student calls on the clergy. He puts them in pulpits and they preach to the King. They get on well enough until one of them tells the story of the ravens who fed some prophet or other, and then there is a commotion in the royal pew. Wood flies, kneel-props whistle through the air. Towards evening, there is nobody in Pichan's house who is not tired, flat, flabby and flatulent with hunger, thirst, excitement and depression. At the supper-hour, the King is raving.

(*Wolf music*)

CAHAL That scholar, that scholar. Let him release me now, now, now.
MAC CONGLINNE King, I am here. I bring you another request.
CAHAL Bring me my supper.
MAC CONGLINNE I would prefer to bring you salvation from your appetite.
CAHAL Leave me my appetite. I shall dine on my salvation.
MAC CONGLINNE Those are demon's words.

(*Wolf music*)

DEMON They are demon's words, Mac Conglinne, for it is the demon who speaks to you now. You had better leave me alone, or I will come out to you as I did to Muinchenn of Cork. I took his cloak and I will take your skin, for you have very little else that is yours.
MAC CONGLINNE You will only come out to a good dinner, Demon. I know your nature. And when you come out I shall be ready for you.
DEMON I will be a blast in your mind.
MAC CONGLINNE My mind is withdrawn.

DEMON In your body a hunger.

MAC CONGLINNE I have a greater hunger.

DEMON Your soul shall not escape me.

MAC CONGLINNE It waits for a woman in Heaven.

(*Howling music*)

You hear, King?

CAHAL I hear nothing but my belly, Son of Learning. I ask you to release me this minute. Have the half of my house, the half of my authority, even the half of my dinner, but sit me down to a big table. Let me eat.

MAC CONGLINNE You have fasted for me, you have restrained your world-wide appetite for me, and you have given me that power over the demon in you. You have done that for me; now do it for yourself. Fast one night.

CAHAL I smell a mighty supper.

MAC CONGLINNE King.

CAHAL I do not hear you, Son of Learning.

MAC CONGLINNE It is not yet suppertime. Nothing is ready, nothing is prepared, we all fast and we will fast with you.

CAHAL Fasting is not food I like.

MAC CONGLINNE If you sleep you will not dream of fasting. Sleep till supper.

CAHAL No. You would trick me.

MAC CONGLINNE King, fast for me till supper as you have sworn to do.

CAHAL What else am I doing? But I ask you to release me.

MAC CONGLINNE Let me whisper in your ear.

CAHAL Approach me and I will bite your nose.

MAC CONGLINNE Still I shall say my say.

(*Strings*)

There is a secret in the King's hunger.
The hunger is not for food, otherwise
The King would be bird or boar,
The wing-beast or the foot-beast. It is otherwise.

There is a sweet mate somewhere.
She calls to the King.
This woman is the King's hunger;
She is his hungering.

CAHAL I think you are speaking of that great bitch Ligach, Scholar. I remember you now. You are that castaway who brought me the cloak I gave and took from that ass-eared Muinchenn. Have you a league

The Vision of Mac Conglinne

with Ligach? By my soul, if you have, you can take three jumps out of here on the toe of a royal boot.

MAC CONGLINNE King, I came to save you from her, to save you from that hunger for her that is in you.

CAHAL You lie, Scholar. The hunger I have is for food. For Ligach I have nothing but a wish to turn my tail on her and run.

MAC CONGLINNE King, take a scholar's oath. The desire for that woman is inside you. Fast one night for your own self and tomorrow I shall free you.

CAHAL You assert that?

MAC CONGLINNE Have my head otherwise.

(*Howl*)

DEMON Have his head now, Cahal of Cashel. Little curly Cahal, have his head now.

CAHAL By God, I recognise the turn of that phrase. Are you here within me, then, O you lovely dangerous bitch?

DEMON Do not believe the scholar. I am a table-worshipper. Bid them lay a table for us. Big, bright, groaning –

(*Howl*)

CAHAL I will fast tonight. I will purge this demon with prayer. I will fast till she bites her own nails, till she chews her fingers, till she starts viciously to make a dinner out of her own skin.

(*Wolf music*)

Fast with me, all of you that are in Pichan's house tonight. Pray for me, priests, bishops, any preaching will please me. Poets, pick your pearls for me; and you, Son of Learning, watch with me, watch with me. There is no fasting, no praying that I must shirk tonight to kick that woman out of her place in my belly.

(*Appropriate music*)

STORYTELLER So to the fast again. And if one night was bad, the second was a horror. Cahal was as loud as a den of animals. Where his tongue would pray, the demon substituted food words as in the case of the Abbot Muinchenn. He slept towards morning. And then Mac Conglinne rose up and went into the great kitchens where Pichan was lost in reverie before the cold fires.

PICHAN What to do now, Son of Learning?

MAC CONGLINNE This is cure day. I want, now, ash-billets for a large fire. I want four long, strong spits of hazelwood. I want four mighty pieces in slab of corned beef, red beef, wether mutton and a young ham. In addition, I must be supplied with twenty strong helpers of proven courage and with hammered cables of iron, and there must be dug into the floor and outside the house strong staples that will hold these chains.

PICHAN To do what, Son of Learning?

MAC CONGLINNE To do a terrible thing, master of the house, for which I must have your permission and your blessing. To take and bind the King, for that is necessary if he is to be cured.

PICHAN If it is necessary, it must be done. I shall get you what you require.

MAC CONGLINNE Softly as you may, O Pichan. We must be ready when he wakes up.

(*Music*)

STORYTELLER Mac Conglinne makes his fire, four ridges of it, four apertures, of four-cleft ashwood. And he put a name into the fire that is hidden to this day. And on each side of it he clamped one spit and its sizzling burden. And from one to the other he skipped so that no drop fell but what he gathered, and indeed, in his linen cap and his linen apron of the purest white, he was the master of the world's cooks. But when the King awakes, the King is astounded, for while the most marvellous smells await his nostrils, he cannot stir hand nor foot for all the chains and the mighty cables in which is he cobbled.

CAHAL Do they truss royalty in Pichan's house? Is this treason? Untie these things.

VOICES (*softly*) We have been ordered, King. We are advised it is necessary.

CAHAL O by the gods.

VOICES It is for your cure, King, and the care of your kingdom.

CAHAL O by the gods.

(*Wolf howl*)

I smell breakfast. Now let me free before I chew chains, rope, twine and tape, let me free to clear that table and I shall forgive you for this crime of handling me.

CORK VOICE O Lord, lads, are we wrong or right? Can he have law on us?

ANOTHER Pichan, away here for a minute.

PICHAN King, we regret this. But the scholar knows the thing to do.

CAHAL You, Pichan, I will forgive and exonerate, I will absolve for one mouthful of that smell.

(*Howl*)

MAC CONGLINNE Breakfast is ready, King. Come, now, and sit by this fire.

But you must eat in chains and cables. There is a reason for that
which will be shown to you.

CAHAL I will eat in buckets and iron collars, I will be Billy the Bowl. I will
eat standing, walking, rolling, flying, I will eat standing on my head
provided there is food brought to me. Scholar, you are a cook among
cooks. Come to Cashel with me, I sniff –

(*Quirk of music*)

Dish up, dish up. Wait, leave my hands free, boys, at least my hands.

MAC CONGLINNE You must have no freedom, King. That is a condition
you have accepted. Are the chains bedded in the ground without?

CORK VOICES (*softly*) They are indeed, Scholar.

MAC CONGLINNE Are they bedded within?

VOICES They are indeed, Scholar.

MAC CONGLINNE And he is tightfast to wall and floor.

VOICES He is indeed, Scholar.

CAHAL Begin, begin. I am a dearth among plenty. I am a starvation in
paradise, I am the sun that sees from afar the promised land of early
summer. Begin.

MAC CONGLINNE First, we shall talk.

CAHAL O God, this student. Will talk fill me? Can I crunch it, quaff it,
chew it? Can I gobble it?

MAC CONGLINNE I have a dream to tell you.

CAHAL Keep it for some woman in the night.

MAC CONGLINNE It is a dream about food, King. It is a prelude to a king's
meal, it is sauce, it is savour.

CAHAL I will give you ten beats of my pulse to tell me. After that, I will eat
or I will pull down this house upon us all.

(*Wolf howl*)

DEMON It is a trick, Cashel. Do not listen, little curly Cahal.

CAHAL I recognise the turn of that phrase. I will abate hunger, I will starve
it. I will listen to you, Scholar, for this bitch inside me bids otherwise.

MAC CONGLINNE I will begin, so.

(*Strings*)

> I walked in sleep last night
> Into this vision. I was hungry too.
> I saw a tall, well-filled house
> With great pantries of good food.

(*Lupine howl*)

A pond of new milk
In a plain that knows no cow's hoof.
A mighty pat of yellow butter
Thatched the roof.

(*Howl*)

The doorpost was white custard
Frozen till it stood,
The windows were white wine.
The doors were cheese, a lovely wood.

(*Howl, howl*)

The walls were smoked bacon.
There was that and more
In the naked cauldron
That bubbled on the fire.

Shall I tell you more, King?

(*Wolf howl*)

CAHAL Tell me more and I shall go mad.

MAC CONGLINNE I will give you the fable, then, in another way. It was in this country I met the wizard doctor who lives in the island of Eating. 'Limp is the look on your face,' says he. 'The shine of good food is not around you like a bright corselet. You are sick, you are ill, come with me.'

I went with him. We came to a lake of beer in which was a coracle of hard lard waiting for us, and we rowed over that lake to the wizard's dwelling. 'You have a desire of eating,' he says, ' that cannot be satisfied. And you are a burden to yourself and a plague to others, since it is your desire to be first at a feast, to grudge a share to others, to gobble, to push, to scrape, to shoulder away, to gather all plates and platters, mugs, jugs, and bowls before you. But I will cure you,' says he.

'What way will you cure me?' says I. 'For indeed, I would wish to be cured. I am built in a shameful way and I am in constant sorrow over my great and abnormal appetite.'

'I will cure you this way,' says he.

(*Strings*)

Go tonight to the well. Wash head and hand.
Then spread a calfskin by a fire of ash
Ripped octagonally, and call the noble woman
Of the fivefolded purple cloak. She is all men's wish.

The Vision of Mac Conglinne

Active, sensible, whitehanded, witty, merry
Is this woman. She is three tall graces in one.
The three nurses of dignity are about her.
Three joys are delicate colours in her skin.

With a tree-swaying sauntering walk she will come to the door
And wait like a stately avenue. Under her black brows
Are calm blue eyes that will receive you
Into her look as into a big house.

She will move around you with a woman's music,
The reed music of a riverside;
But her laugh is lively, her red mouth is such
It warms you with friendly humour that is fire and fireside.

O but you will go on a long journey
On her voice, man; you will go and come home
To a woman whose hair is down from her shoulders.
To a shining eye and a lifted comb.

CAHAL Are you describing Ligach to me, Poet? You are describing that
    great bitch as she was to me one time.
MAC CONGLINNE I am describing a process and a cure.
CAHAL You are filling me with an old desire and a wish that has gone from
    me.
MAC CONGLINNE I have not finished yet, King. Said the wizard doctor:
    'Let this maiden, who is without stain, give you three times nine
    morsels, each morsel the size of a heath-poult's egg. You will take
    these morsels into your mouth with a round swing, and while you
    are in the process of chewing them your eyes must move clockwise
    round your skull.' Now we shall proceed to give you your breakfast.
CAHAL Ah, that is talk to a purpose.
MAC CONGLINNE But first –
CAHAL Another 'but'. Are you a ram or a bullcalf, Scholar, that you butt
    me so much?
MAC CONGLINNE First, that cloak. You gave it to Muinchenn for a feast.
    Will you now bestow it on me for a mouthful?
CAHAL ROBBER!
MAC CONGLINNE It is a good, large-smelling mouthful of roasted beef. I
    put it to your nostrils. Smell.

(*Wolverine howl*)

CAHAL You may have my cloak.
MAC CONGLINNE I will take it off so.
CAHAL First, the mouthful.

MAC CONGLINNE The cloak first.

CAHAL I will submit.

MAC CONGLINNE I take the cloak, then. O mighty armful.

CAHAL That mouthful, now.

MAC CONGLINNE There is yet something else.

(*Despairing howl*)

It is not something for myself. It is for the kingdom and the natural order of things. A king must have a noble queen.

CAHAL I knew you were in league with that Ligach.

MAC CONGLINNE Is it Ligach that I talk of? I do not think so. I saw her once when I was in Grianán Ailech, but I remember her only as a distant, cold and difficult queen.

CAHAL She can be otherwise. O, she can be otherwise.

(*Strings*)

> She can call out of her hair
> So softly that one warm candle is her breath
> And all the shadowy air
> About each breast.
>
> I was her room. I know her
> For she filled me to curtain and window till my eyes
> Were my window-blinds at morning
> That stared inward on all beauties.
>
> Tell of her now, and I will break
> Countries apart to find
> That room inside me, and again, again
> Draw down each window blind.

MAC CONGLINNE A queen of that sort should have all the old prerogatives of a queen, otherwise she is a slave lifted to throne-level, she is a king's serf, his meaty bedfellow. You agree, King?

CAHAL I will agree to nothing but my breakfast, my mouthful of beef, my ham, my wether-mutton.

MAC CONGLINNE That is coming. The beef is bubbling, the mutton sizzling, the ham is humming. About this queen. She has rights that go back to the foundation of the world. She has queen's rights, privacy at will; freedom in travel and entertainment; indulgence of her fancies. A separate establishment.

(*Lupine howl*)

CAHAL I want my breakfast.

MAC CONGLINNE It is ready, it is ready. See it. O marvellous breakfast.

The Vision of Mac Conglinne

(Howl)

> King, for each of those old rights that have been stolen from the woman, for the return of them to the Queen that you must make, I will give your hunger one large mouthful.

CAHAL Robbery, larceny, treason. What is this crime you commit upon the King?

MAC CONGLINNE I put it to your nostrils. Smell.

(Howl)

CAHAL Whatever queen she is, she can have those rights.

MAC CONGLINNE There is yet something else.

(Prolonged howling)

CAHAL There is nothing else in the world but food.

MAC CONGLINNE Rights of equal sovereignty for your Queen.

CAHAL She can have them and roast. O roast, roast, roast beef, mutton, bacon.

(Monstrous howling)

MAC CONGLINNE To the chains and cables now, my men. I shall hang this cloak upon the warrior stone with this root of the birch-tree underneath. Pichan, your blessing now, for I shall need it, and have all the bishops pray for me and the priests, down to the youngest theological student; and whoever is within a mile of this place, let him go down on his knees. There must be no word of anybody but a prayer.

PICHAN I will see to that.

MAC CONGLINNE Empty the house until there is nobody living in it but the king, the cloak, the fire and myself.

PICHAN I will see to it. I leave my goodwill with you, Poet.

MAC CONGLINNE I shall need it.

(Howling, howling)

> King, I will sit by you now. First, that mouthful I owe you for the cloak I cut it. Mmm.

(Sniff of music)

> I will give you an apple, a mouthful I mean. Do you remember refusing me an apple?

CAHAL Give me to eat, Student.

MAC CONGLINNE Mmm. This is too large for you. I will eat it myself, but first you may smell it.

(A mighty sniff of music, then a vulpine howling)

The Vision of Mac Conglinne   77

CAHAL Give me that mouthful.

MAC CONGLINNE It is too large. I will eat it.

(*Pleasant gulping music*)

CAHAL Oh. Oh. Oh. (*Howl*)

DEMON That was a wrestler's trick, Mac Conglinne. A dirty feint.

MAC CONGLINNE Ha, Demon, have I got your nose out?

DEMON I will be all out in a moment if I do not have food. Then, upon my
word, we will have ructions.

MAC CONGLINNE I do not think so. I am very swift. I go to cut another
piece now. See, O delightful roasting chunk of the year-old heifer, O
paunchy piece, how the poet's gullet goes for you. Mmm.

(*Sniff of music*)

You must smell this, Demon. I will put it to the King's nose, and
then I will race you for it to that pillar stone where the cloak is
hanging. Are you ready?

DEMON By my word, Mac Conglinne, you will run for that piece.

MAC CONGLINNE I will beat you, Demon, for this mass of roasting and
spitting by the fire will delay you. You will never jump that fire
without laying your tongue on everything.

DEMON I can still do that and beat you.

MAC CONGLINNE Here then, sniff.

(*Howl, then trumpets of music*)

Sniff, I said. Now run for it.

(*A blast of things*)

DISTANT VOICES O the world shakes.
Our father who art in heaven.
The great house is rocking.
Hail Mary, hail Mary.
The poet is gone. The King is gone.

MUINCHENN And my cloak is gone, Muinchenn's little cloak, my marvel,
my love, my lifeblood.

STRONG VOICES Not so, the house still stands. It wavers, it struggles, it
recovers. It stands. O the large foundations of this great house!

(*Thrill of music*)

STORYTELLER I end this scene with a shiver of excitement. But where is
the poet? The King is a huddle of chains and cables. He is knotted,
twisted, curled bone on bone. One eye is sunken into his head
until the long bill of a wading heron could not reach it. The other

eye is eight inches out of his head. But he is wild, he is angry, he is terrible.

CAHAL Beggars, brawlers, bosthoons. How comes the King to lie here in such indignity? Release me. I will pull this house to pieces and stamp on the ruins.

(*Majestic music*)

STORYTELLER Well, no lack of life in this King. Outside, threading a way with a retinue through the bowed and frightened people comes Queen Ligach, who used to be of Ailech. Little trumpets go before her and the mass of people before the house of Pichan are even more silent as they lift their eyes to her beauty.

WHISPERS It is the Queen, it is the Queen.

(*Trumpets and herald*)

HERALD Make a path, make a path, make a path. The Queen Ligach to the owner of this house. To Pichan, the Queen orders that she be taken into the presence of the King, Cahal of Cashel.

PICHAN Pichan bows, Queen. I bow to the ground.

LIGACH Take me to Cashel. Now.

PICHAN Pichan bows, Lady, but he regrets that –

(*Rumble of music and falling debris*)

VOICES The sidewall of the house is gone.
No, it is holding, it is holding.
It is returning to its foundations again.
O mighty foundations.

LIGACH What is happening to this house?

PICHAN Lady, the King is within, alone with a scholar and a demon.

LIGACH Do you tell the Queen that you have left the King along with a demon and a scholar? Are you not responsible for his safety, his health, his humour?

PICHAN Lady, the King is my childhood's friend. I do the best for him according to my understanding.

LIGACH You shall account to me later. Lead me, now, to the great door and open it wide for me. I will enter first.

PICHAN Lady –

LIGACH At once!

(*The* King's *hullabaloo in the middle ground*)

That is the King's voice.

CAHAL I will pull this house to pieces. I will stamp on the ruins.

LIGACH What have you done to the King? (*Very loudly*) What have you done to Cahal of Cashel? O Cahal, O little curlyheaded Cahal, what have they done to you?

CAHAL O Ligach, I am cabled, stapled and chained, I am handcuffed, stifled, exhausted –

LIGACH Release the King.

VOICES But the demon, the demon.

LIGACH Release him. There will be a great accounting for this.

PICHAN We will release him, Lady. But you do not understand. There was a demon of hunger in the King –

LIGACH A demon of hunger? I do not believe it. Why, my poor Cahal never ate anything more than titbits. Cahal, are you hungry, my love?

CAHAL Hungry? I would not care this minute if I never saw pick nor plate again.

LIGACH You see?

PICHAN Then the King is cured. The King is cured. MY PEOPLE, THE KING IS CURED.

(*Clamour in music*)

PICHAN Hush now. This is a miracle. Release the King with gentle hands. Take him to the women's sunroom.

LIGACH I will wait on him.

PICHAN No, Lady. Four of you to that litter, the gold litter. Light a fire of octagonal ash in that room, four apertures and with four ridges, and before the fire lay the King on a soft calfskin when he has been washed and combed.

(*Appropriate music*)

STORYTELLER But where is Mac Conglinne? Pichan, busy with the King, remembers him suddenly –

(*Loud chords*)

PICHAN That student, that noble scholar. Has he been seen?

VOICE Pichan, there is no sign of that scholar anywhere. We have searched and searched, for we were anxious to look upon a wonder.

ANOTHER He is not within this house, Pichan.

WOMAN'S VOICE The King is awakening, O Pichan.

CAHAL Who must be found? Who is lost that he must be found?

PICHAN The poet who cured you of the demon, King.

CAHAL I will take your word that I had a demon, but upon my own word I can remember nothing at all about it. Indeed, there is so much that is unkingly about the whole thing that you must take it as an edict that it is not to be mentioned again in my presence. Am I washed enough

to please you, or is the skin to be scrubbed off my poor but responsible back?

PICHAN Still, that poet must be found. We are in his debt. Find him, find
him.

VOICES He is nowhere to be found.

PICHAN I will look for him myself.

VOICE The holy Abbot Muinchenn is asking to see the King.

PICHAN He cannot see him.

VOICE He wishes to pray over him and to ask for his cloak back.

PICHAN It is his cloak no longer. It was given to that noble young scholar.

(*Heavy Abbot music*)

MUINCHENN It is my cloak, Pichan, and it was taken from me by a trick of
the demon.

PICHAN That cloak was yours while you could hold it.

MUINCHENN Possession is nine-tenths of the law. I see it on that pillar and
I will take it.

PICHAN Four of you. Guard this cloak from this Abbot.

MUINCHENN I will put a curse on the man who stops me.

CORK VOICE Abbot, we will not worry much about that. We saw how little
the demon cared for your curse. My God, boys, there is something
inside this cloak.

VOICES There is, there is.

VOICE Pichan, there is somebody inside this holy cloak. Could it be the
scholar?

PICHAN Perhaps it is that scholar, that noble young man. Let me look.

(*Blast of music*)

This is an old man. He is asleep or he has fainted.

VOICE Pichan, he has the face of that young scholar, even if he is old.

PICHAN By my hand, that is true. I will awaken him.

(*Three drum taps*)

You are awake?

MAC CONGLINNE I am awake. I see, by the happy hand of my god, I have
reached the cloak in safety. Have I cured the King?

PICHAN The King is cured.

MAC CONGLINNE Honour and glory to me then!

PICHAN But are you the man who cured the King? That man was young,
he was a student, his face was bright, his head was a glory.

MAC CONGLINNE Am I otherwise? Or is Pichan seeking to evade our
bargain?

PICHAN Give this man a mirror. Put it in his hand.

(Pale and wondering music)

(Strings)

> This is an old face.
> It is a ruin. Some big fire
> Has burned me out of my self. There is no place
> Left in this countenance that will flare again.
>
> Some sad agony has wrung me dry.
> I am a willow-tree without water. My song is sung.
> No queen will love me again for my poetry.
> I am old, I am wiser. But my song is sung.

(Music)

STORYTELLER I end this scene sadly. The poet is washed and combed as the King is washed and combed. Pichan is tender, Pichan is loving. The poet is soothed, he is richly dressed, he waxes in importance in a matter of seconds; for poetry he substitutes pride; for inspiration, self-will; for delight in argument, he substitutes haughtiness. He has arrived and paid all the usual fees for his transportation. Meanwhile there is some matter to be solved between the King and the Queen. The King is in the women's sunroom on a calfskin before the fire. He is morose, weary and utterly without appetite. To him comes a harassed Pichan.

PICHAN King, O my King.

CAHAL I hear you.

PICHAN It is your Queen again.

CAHAL I have pleaded sleep.

PICHAN She carries a cure for sleepiness.

CAHAL I have pleaded weariness.

PICHAN She answers that she will cure that too.

CAHAL I have pleaded melancholy.

PICHAN A sorrow shared is a sorrow halved, she says.

CAHAL Plead coldness.

PICHAN She answers that her presence is warmth in itself.

(Trumpets. Trumpets. Trumpets)

LIGACH O Cashel.

CAHAL This is the King's room, Lady.

LIGACH Wherever the King is, that is the King's room. And wherever the King is, there my heart is too.

CAHAL Was I ever in Ulster? Was I ever in Grianán Ailech?

LIGACH I think you were, my King. I think you are everywhere I go. I think you are a kind of self to me I am always losing and finding again.

CAHAL I am tired of being lost and found.

LIGACH O, but the joy of finding.

CAHAL O, but the lostness of being lost. Why must you leave me? Why must you halve my heart yearly into an Ulster and a Munster? Why am I half a king for half a year, and only a bright and brilliant nonentity for the other half, a suck-a-thumb lover, an apron-string husband?

LIGACH You are my King. O you are my King.

CAHAL You are my Queen, O you are my Queen.

QUEEN I have brought you food by the hands of my own women.

CAHAL I do not want food.

LIGACH It is only a little food, three time nine morsels, each the size of a heath-poult's leg. I will feed you myself.

CAHAL You are a bad woman, but you make me happy.

(*Appropriate music*)

STORYTELLER We leave them at it.

(*Strings*)

> O Woman. She is everywhere.
> An element.
> Behind each quarrel; at the back of every sermon;
> At the bottom of every bad debt.

> And yet I hail her.
> How can I help it? She
> Who divides herself around me like a calendar,
> Who is my twelve climates of feeling,
> Who musters me
> So many shapes, I live like the sun,
> A god within my year.

The End

The Poplar

Dramatis Personae

Commentator
Boy (Jerry), Jerome O'Brien's grandson
Girl (Betty), Jerome O'Brien's granddaughter
Jerome O'Brien, an old Land-Leaguer
Postman
Bernie Haverty, an old friend of Jerome's
Ellen, Jerome O'Brien's daughter
Julia, Jerome O'Brien's daughter
Jamesy, Jerome O'Brien's son
The Poplar
Sadie, Jerome O'Brien's daughter
Larry Hanrahan, Sadie's husband, a wealthy cattle-jobber
The Clock

COMMENTATOR The dim country: What do we love in it
             Who live in it?
             The blank daylight? No. Nor in the daylight
             The bog, its twilight.

             No. And no. And yet a strong man
             May find it kin
             And never know it is his youth he loves
             Till his youth leaves:

             Never know that the woman on his hearth
             Is only Earth
             Good wife, good mother; and the farm he has –
             The lover, never his.

             The great unseasoned unseasonable bitch
             In the last ditch
             Always, and yet in a sudden day of sun
             Almost to be won.

(*In the background vaguely there is an unmusical dissonance of drums and some wind instrument*)

BOY (JERRY) I can get no music out of this.
GIRL (BETTY) You don't blow properly. Show here.

(*Little squeak of fife*)

BOY   Wait. Hear that. Oh blast; it comes and goes. How is it
         managed, I'd like to know?
GIRL   Let me.
BOY   Get one of your own. There are ten of them in the box. How is
         it we never knew Grandfather had those before? Where'd he
         get them?
GIRL   A whole band. Cymbals, too. Oh, look –
BOY   Aw, let me, Betty.

(*Cymbals crash in awkward rhythm*)

         Betty, here's Grandfather across the yard.
GIRL   Grandfather won't mind. HELLO, we're here.
JEROME   Aye, the country far and wide must know that, Girleen.
         They'll think it's Land League days again. Are ye doing any
         harm?
BOY   Oh, no. Is this a fife, Grandfather?
JEROME   That's a fife. Can you do any good on it?
BOY   Hell to the bit.

JEROME	We're an unmusical family, the O'Briens. But your father had always a stave or two –
GIRL	Can't you play?
JEROME	O I was the man with the banner.
BOTH	The what?
JEROME	A big green flag. And a harp of gold on it –
BOY	Where is it?
JEROME	It's upstairs in the chest. Big letters of gold on it, too.
BOY	O show us.
GIRL	What do the letters say?
JEROME	The Land for the People.
GIRL	What people? Everybody – but townspeople, maybe – have land. And Daddy is a townsman and he has land.
BOY	He has an awful lot of land. He has Curskeen and Mount Bawn, Kincullagh and Kiltullagh.
JEROME	Well, the only people with land in the old days were a few landlords –
POSTMAN	God bless the work.
JEROME	And you, Ned.
POSTMAN	I heard you lecturing the young.
JEROME	I suppose, too, you heard them walloping the old band?
POSTMAN	I did. And so did Bernie Haverty above.
BERNIE	So I did, so I did – God bless.
JEROME	Well, glory be to God. I heard you slept till the noon.
BERNIE	They do be wanting to keep me out of the way. And I have to please them. I'll wager, children dear, you got no music of this old hero, this old Grandaddy of yours.
BOY	But he was the man with the banner. I'd love to be the man with the banner.
BERNIE	What good is a banner without a band behind it? Show me that fife here.
GIRL	Can you play, Bernie?
BERNIE	Me? I'd whistle the thrush off a twig. And often I did it.
JEROME	Devil the lie in that, God bless you.

(*A quick fife tune with elaborations*)

JEROME	My soul to you. You've kept the touch.
BERNIE	I'm winded.
GIRL	Bernie, show me the way –
BOY	And I'll bang the drum, Bernie, let us have a march down the road, Grandfather, you can carry the banner –

(*Chuckle of laughter*)

JEROME	Lord love you, Laddeen. My paradin' days are done.
BOY	But why, why?
JEROME	Because there's nothing to parade for any more.
BERNIE	The little holeens are for fingering the notes. Watch my hands, Girl.

(*A quick scale*)

BOY	But we could parade, Grandfather.
JEROME	There must be something to parade for. We got the land off them, and so there's nothing more left.
POSTMAN	I have two letters for you, Jerome.
JEROME	Are you coming in with them?
POSTMAN	Not today. One is the rate-cess. This big lad is from America. The girls aren't forgetting you.
JEROME	No, thanks be to God. Two good horses, Eddy, to drag a plough; long memory and long pocket. Are you off?
POSTMAN	Some of us must work. Good day to ye.
JEROME	God be with you.

(*Fife in bad scale*)

	Are you visiting me or the band, Bernie?
BERNIE	The band was always my glory, Jerry. Off with you and your letter. Do you understand what I mean by fingering, little girl? (*Fading*)
GIRL	Yes, but –
COMMENTATOR	Bands. Banners. There is a time In our lives for them, For the poet and his rhyme, For love and limb.

JEROME	There's a post from one of the girls, Ellen.
ELLEN	Give it here. It's Mary.
COMMENTATOR	O but the days die. What do we achieve But a sleepy agony; We live by leave.

JEROME	Any talk of her coming home?
ELLEN	Hmm. That priest they were talking about always, Father Culleton, he's going to Rome.
JEROME	They'll miss him.
ELLEN	The confraternity is making him a present. Oh, glory be to God, sure we've no room for him here.
JEROME	But isn't it to Rome he's going?

ELLEN   She says – Oh that's different – that if he decides to break his
           journey by way of Ireland – and they're wanting him to break it
           – she'll send us a thousand dollars to make a better house out
           of this one.

JEROME   Is it ashamed of her own home the girl is?

ELLEN   It's not, then. It's room and, and facilities she mentions. People
           used to them, she says, prize them a lot. Sink a well, she says,
           and put in a pump. That'd be grand anyway. Dadda, if we put
           on another room to the east, we'd have both bedroom and
           bathroom.

JEROME   Well, now, what's good enough for us should be good enough
           for her –

ELLEN   Well, if she pays for it. Julia will be in the seventh heaven.

JEROME   Julie is either in heaven or the other place. This house is good
           enough for me as it is.

ELLEN   Good enough for me, too. But they say there's no good that
           can't be bettered.

JEROME   It's the only slated house in this townland.

ELLEN   It is. But this townland isn't much when looked at from over
           water.

JEROME   I built this house with my two hands. And your mother, God
           be good to her soul, and Jamesy and this same Mary slept in a
           hut out there while I put it together. And in between times I
           ploughed the soil and sowed it, but for all that I had a slated
           roof over them before the winds of the winter came.

ELLEN   It was often that I heard her tell the story, Dadda.

JEROME   I ask and I take no credit for it. But your mother thought there
           was no place like it in the country, and ye were all proud of it
           and ye growing up –

ELLEN   Musha Dadda, we're proud of it still if it comes to that. You
           have only to look at it to see, we with flowers walled in and a
           nice garden of apples – anyway, Dadda, you've all the say. We
           can always say NO to Mary.

(Fife splendidly played. Cymbals and an irregular kettledrum)

           It's not Mummers' Day till the day after Christmas. Well, on
           me soul, Bernie, you're only an old gom.

BERNIE   That's right. All dead except the music, remembered only by
           the fife.

BOY   Give us the banner, Grandfather.

ELLEN   What banner?

BOY   It's of old times, Aunty Ellen. He'll carry it, Betty will play the
           cymbals, Bernie the fife and I'll march this way, look, look –

(*Thudding of kettledrum*)

ELLEN	Look, march out of here this minute and put them things back where they belong –
BOY	Aw.
ELLEN	It's parish property, young fellow –
GIRL	We'll do it no harm, Aunty Ellen.
ELLEN	Handle it abroad, then. It's not for a small house like this.
JEROME	There are smaller houses.
ELLEN	Ah, Dadda, I'm not sniping at the place.
BERNIE	Phew. The old wind's gone, Jerome avic. Give us a loan of a lend of your penknife. Had you bad news in your letter?
ELLEN	He had not. He had a lot better than he deserves.
BERNIE	Good enough. I asked only because he looks like a man would be choosing his headstone. Will you have a drag from the pipe?
JEROME	I won't refuse you.
BERNIE	And what had the girls to say?
JEROME	Do you remember, Bernie, the day I laid the first stone of this house?
BERNIE	I remember you putting one stone on another, but the first one –
JEROME	You were driving a young heifer to Callanans above and you called me to the gate –
BERNIE	Bedammed, I do. The red-roan, the finest milker she turned out to be.
JEROME	Was it a bad piece of work I started on that day?
BERNIE	It has stood the test. It has seen time and birth and burial. And stood up to the three of them. I see Julia pushing the bike. God bless her, I hear it won't be long till she gives us the big night. Ha, in the town again?
JULIA	You're great fun, you old angler. Are you responsible for the hurdy-gurdy in our back garden?
BERNIE	I'll take neither praise nor blame for it. How's the big shop-keeper? Do you think he would allow me credit, now, if I said I was your godfather?
JULIA	He wouldn't believe you.
BERNIE	I'd shine myself up and put on my derby. Glory be to God, there was a time when I was something to look at –
JULIA	Is that so?
BERNIE	I didn't maybe hunt a horse – like, hum, some people in the world, big shopkeepers and that like – but I could do better. I could jump over one.
JULIA	Were you running away from anybody?
BERNIE	And your father could jump two horses – and did it. On the

The Poplar

	green of Turloughmore he did it. There's news for you from America, Julia.
JULIA	Was there a letter, Ellen?
ELLEN	From Mary.
BERNIE	She has a millionaire tied up by the shanks for you. He's ready waiting for you to eat him up.
JULIA	This is the best thing that ever happened –
BERNIE	Aye, but you've still to eat him –
JULIA	Dadda, I'll run in to Healy after dinner. He might come out in the morning to see what's to be done. And Ellen, maybe Sadie and John would advise us, too. After all, when the money's there, it might as well be a good job as a middling one. The whole layout of the house needs changing, I think.
ELLEN	I'd ask your father first.
JULIA	What?
ELLEN	He might have a word or two to say in the matter.
JULIA	I know that. But Healy, after all, is the man who should know. Every man to his own trade.
ELLEN	Every man to his own house, too. Will you stay and have something to eat with us, Bernie?
BERNIE	Is it that time?
ELLEN	It is. And there'll be bits taken out of you if you don't go home. Not that you aren't welcome to stay.
BERNIE	Ah, cold shoulder and hot tongue, same one place as another.
ELLEN	They're very bad to you beyond. You're getting so thin, you'll soon want a bigger suit of clothes.
BERNIE	I will, indeed. A wooden one with me name on it. Great heat out today. But all told, I think, a bit of cool shade is a good thing. You were a great man for the trees, Peter. I'm sorry sometimes I didn't plant when you did. Day to ye.
ELLEN	Where are you going, Dadda? Dinner's ready.
JEROME	I'll be back.
COMMENTATOR	From the seed, from the egg; The mystery of it; Will it ever flag? The cock dancing on one leg, And far beyond its range and wit The tree going up like a spray of water, Each serving its own benefit; I too when I begat a daughter. So strange to eyes and ears; Unsought; No self but hers

Inside, no other voice she hears;
The seed always is self-taught,
A self itself and no extension.
Moving into its own thought,
Inhabiting its own dimension.

ELLEN   For the love of God, children, what are you doing in that
         room? Go to bed.

JAMESY   It's a great offer. A thousand dollars, £230. And he didn't
         receive it well, you say.

ELLEN   He was affronted.

JULIA   He's living in the old days. This house was something then.
         But there are ten better now, between here and Galway. Why
         don't you take him in to the next fair?

ELLEN   He'll do no such thing. Do you want to kill him?

JAMESY   Aye, there's still an old crony of his or two standing up in a
         public house –

JULIA   Sadie would see to that side of it.

ELLEN   Do you not know your own father?

JULIA   He was never a drunkard.

ELLEN   And who says he was? But he was never at a fair yet that he
         didn't take drink. It was the custom of his day and he sticks to
         it.

JAMESY   And like myself, he's no stomach for it. I'm sick for a week on
         three bottles of stout.

JULIA   Jamesy, you'll have to get around him. You'll be getting
         married any day. No girl with any kind of rearing would move
         in here.

JAMESY   You've a good eye on my welfare. Should I thank myself or
         somebody else?

JULIA   Oh, it suits me, too.

JAMESY   So I guessed.

ELLEN   Julia, Jamesy, is ashamed to bring out Terry Loftus to see us.

JULIA   That, let me tell you, is not altogether true. I'll bring him out
         when I'm sure of – his mother.

JAMESY   Couldn't he come out without the apron strings?

JULIA   The apron strings are worth a lot of money.

JAMESY   Aye. That's a sound argument.

JULIA   I'd like, too, to impress Terry. Oh, I'm not snobbish, and the
         two of you needn't look as if I had two heads on me. But I'd
         like to start off on an equal footing with the man I'm to marry.
         I haven't his money, so I want at least a show of good breeding.
         Jamesy, you can do what you want with Dadda.

JAMESY   That's because I manage to do what I think he'd like to be

	done. After all, I've only the one father. What the hell are those little devils doing up stairs?
ELLEN	Betty, Jerry, go back to your room.

(Banging of kettledrum, occasional pip of fife)

JAMESY	Glory be to God, did they get at the band?
ELLEN	They did. But I didn't know they brought it to bed with them.
JAMESY	Take it off them at once. If anything started in the parish, it might be looked for.
ELLEN	Who'd start anything here? But I'll go up.
JULIA	I don't think you need to. Here they are.

(Closer drumming)

JAMESY	And the banner.
GIRL and BOY	The Land for the People! The Land for the People!
JAMESY	Ye pair of little divils. Ellen, take it from them – if he sees that banner with them…
ELLEN	Back up with ye. Give me that. Do ye know that I got a clouting myself one time for taking it?
JULIA	Hurry, Ellen. I hear him coming.
GIRL	Ah, no, no, Aunty Ellen.
JAMESY	And here he is.
JEROME	What are ye doing at all?
GIRL and BOY	The Land for the People, Grandfather, the Land for the People!
JEROME	Ah, leave them be, Ellen.
ELLEN	Eh?
JEROME	When their elders go wrong-headed, how could children be wise? Go back to bed with ye. And maybe ye could march that banner in the morning. But only if it's fine. And there's rain in the air. Maybe you'd best put off mowing, James.
JAMESY	I wouldn't say the weather'd break altogether.
JEROME	There's a rainy note in the Poplar.
JAMESY	I told Haverty I'd start in the morning.
JEROME	If you knock that hay you might be paddling round in it for a fortnight. What shopkeeper was Bernie talking of today, Julia?
JULIA	You might ask Bernie, Dadda.
JEROME	I could but I won't. Well, I suppose a father must be content to be the last to hear things.
JULIA	There's nothing to hear, Dadda. If there was you'd be told.
JEROME	Did you bring me that bit of plug?
JULIA	It's on the ledge behind you.
JEROME	Bernie is a great joker. But when he makes a point, he never

fails to lift a bird. Are you going to bed?

JULIA   I am.

JEROME   Goodnight, so. But if there's a man after you, it might be as
          well if you made him known to me. Is he well off itself?

JULIA   He's too well off for me.

JEROME   I see. Well, if he brings good money, you bring the good blood.
          They make good partners.

JULIA   Is our blood better than another's? If it is, we might house it
          better – when we get the opportunity. Goodnight, father.

COMMENTATOR   Goodnight. Goodnight, say
               Goodnight to the light of the day;
               Noon with the burning face
               And all earth in the grace
               Of the tall bright air. The dark night
               Is no old man's delight.

               Who lives in the past? Why, none.
               For who delights in the thing done?
               And the thing to do is future tense
               And the future is silence in every sense
               When a man is old and given to things
               That cannot follow his wanderings.

(*Hoarse old chain-clock strikes one*)

               A rainy promise in the tree;
               To the weather a farmer bows the knee
               And lives in nerves that never stop
               Living the life of every crop:
               Let a tree speak of the weather, I
               Hear and turn to the sky.

JAMESY (*waking with a snort*) Are you asleep?

JEROME   It comes and goes with me.

JAMESY   I'm lighting the pipe. Will I ready your own?

JEROME   'Twould be no harm. We'll have the rain before morning.
          You'll get no machine through that bottom field.

JAMESY   It's not us but the weather owns this farm, indeed. It's a pity in
          some ways you didn't go back to Crarehon when they gave you
          the division.

JEROME   When a man builds a house with his own hands, he stays in it.
          But you wouldn't know that.

JAMESY   I never built a house, indeed. But I see what you mean.

JEROME   You do not. There are some things can't be told. It's only
          when two people pass through them together that they know

	what they mean. And then they don't need words at all. You never heard your mother and myself talking much.
JAMESY	Only when you'd come home from a fair.
JEROME	I was a mouth looking for somebody's ear then. When Chiswick threw me out of Crarehon and knocked down the house I didn't want to go back anymore, though there wasn't a pebble in any field that didn't know me or a bird in the air that wouldn't bid me the time of day. The manhood was ashamed in me somehow.
JAMESY	What could you do? And didn't you do enough afterwards?
JEROME	Aye. Enough to keep your mother praying for my soul till the day she died. I'm giving you sixty acres of Kincullagh, says Chiswick to me. Sixty acres of water, says I. Are you going to take it, says he, or take the road? I'll take it, says I, till I come back here. The Head Constable remembered my words when Chiswick was shot and the first place he made for was here. 'Twas a Sunday morning and I was sauntering home with the rest from the chapel above.
JAMESY	And he was shot in Ruevehagh, eight miles away.
JEROME	Or five miles over the Creggs. He was shot going in the church door –
JAMESY	From inside the porch. 'Twas a terrible thing.
JEROME	If a man is struck, he'll strike back. He struck many. But when that big place of his was split up among us, I had no liking to go back again. Maybe I bought it too dear.
JAMESY	Damn it all, there's only a £20 land annuity on it.
JEROME	Your mother thought it was the place I hankered after, but it was only that I had lost the skin off my pride, thinking that some man could push me out of a place that had been in the family like for generations. The house there was never anything like this house.
JAMESY	It's a kinder place. Now that I haven't your help, I often wonder how you made a farm here at all.
JEROME	It's not made yet.
JAMESY	Them bottom fields cannot be drained any better.
JEROME	They could if you blasted the bed of the river.
JAMESY	The whole country below would be down on me with this law and that.
JEROME	Hah, if we were as careful of the law, we'd be eating boiled nettles to this day.
JAMESY	Go 'sleep, now, with you. You'll ride that old horse to the death.
JEROME	Well, 'tis better put sweat where it's wanted. Could you put

	that money of Mary's to settle with those who won't let you change the river?
JAMESY	Go on out of that. Let me sleep, now.
COMMENTATOR	Words are

> Words are
> The presences of things. They become
> Visible, palpable. There is a river
> Running here and a farm in the room.
>
> Fields flooded
> Half the year. I am sour with the muddy yeast
> And bogged and mired, I am studded
> With rushes and harsh bent hard to the taste.
>
> Relieve me
> Of this water. I am ready for the toil
> Of sowing, I ache towards fertility
> With my heart and all my soil.

THE POPLAR	There is rain in my air.
JEROME (*sleepily*)	I know that; I heard you before, Tree. I told Jamesy.
JAMESY (*drowsily*)	Did you say anything?
JEROME	Eh?
JAMESY	I thought you said something.
JEROME	Eh? Did I say something? Aye, I remember saying there's rain in my air.

(*Tick-tock of old* Clock *fading. Strikes three, fading*)

COMMENTATOR	The next Sunday Jerome had visitors, his daughter Sadie and her husband Larry Hanrahan. Larry was a cattle-jobber who had come on, Sadie was a woman who had gone off. But they met comfortably enough in the middle of their marriage.
SADIE	Where's himself, Nell?
ELLEN	Walking the land. You're welcome, Larry. Is that the new suit? Turn round. It's a great fit.
SADIE	It's likely he'll be down at the river, Larry.
LARRY	Gracious, woman, let me put up the pony. The evening's long.
SADIE	Not if we're to get Benediction at the Friary.
LARRY	The worst of you is that you keep me sweating, running from this world to the next. Give me a peaceful girl like Ellen.
COMMENTATOR	On Sunday the gates

> On Sunday the gates
> Of quiet open and the slow sluices allow the tide
> Of things to go its different gaits;
> And earth shows her other side.

The Poplar

There might be Mass
In the air so peacefully does a country move
Inwards to the bell, slowly to pass
Up, like a smoke sucked surely from above.

Never are colours
More coloured; into them the young drive bicycles;
But the old are contented in their harbours
Of grass and the bright gusts that rise like angels.

LARRY   I'll bet, now, that you have ten pounds of gelignite in your purse pocket –

JEROME   Is that yourself, Larry? You're welcome.

LARRY   Thank you, Jerome. I'll bet, too, that there's a man on every hill between this and Curska watching you. They know you'll do it some day.

JEROME   Haha. I might have done it one time had I the stuff. Is Sadie with you?

LARRY   She's gassing with the girls. I met an old friend of yours last week.

JEROME   Would that be hard for you?

LARRY   They're getting scarcer. I bought two beasts from him. Mikey Quinn.

JEROME   The little place in the Creggs within. I never knew him well.

LARRY   We had a great talk.

(*Intruding sound of drum, cymbals and lovely fife*)

What in the name of glory is that? Well, will you look at the three of them. And Bernie himself another child. Is that the old Land League Band?

JEROME   They found it out.

LARRY   I was asking Mikey if he thought it was Bernie shot Chiswick?

JEROME   Musha, poor Bernie. Weren't we on our way home from Mass together at twenty minutes past eleven? And sure Chiswick was shot at half-past ten eight miles away.

LARRY   Five miles as the crow flies, Jerome. There was always a rumour it was a man from this townland. A good man could have done it in the time – if he knew the Creggs.

JEROME   'Tis an old story.

LARRY   Was the ins and outs of it ever known?

JEROME   What's making you curious at this time of day?

LARRY   Mikey Quinn saw the man making over the Creggs.

JEROME   He did? Did he know him?

LARRY   He did.

JEROME	And did he tell you?
LARRY	He did not. But he had a curious grin on his old gob. Even he couldn't tell me how it was done. There was a man with a guard of four policemen shot at the church door.
JEROME	The Peelers weren't with him at the door. They left him at the gate forty yards away and a clear open avenue up to the church. They used to go for a pint into Harney's then –
LARRY	Aye. Just around the corner of the cross. But they were out at once and no one would have had time to make off before they'd see him. That's the mystery.
JEROME	There was no mystery. The man that shot him was hiding inside the left of the door. He didn't run. He just went up the bell-tower. In five minutes the whole church was cleared and the Peelers were carrying the body back to Harney's. The man came out then and went out the back way of the sacristy into the graveyard –
LARRY	My God. That was cool.
JEROME	It took the man that did it a long time to think it out. Now, poor Bernie is a good man –
LARRY	I see what you mean. What the hell is that banner he has?
JEROME	I used to carry it to the meetings before the band.
LARRY	Hum. The land for the people. Do you know what brought me out today?
JEROME	I do not.
LARRY	I have a prospect for Jamesy.
JEROME	Hah. It's time he made the move. Who is she?
LARRY	Dick Jordan's daughter. We work through-other in the cattle. He has four of them at a thousand pounds a head.
JEROME	Would one with that money come in here?
LARRY	It could be managed. Things is getting too big for me, Jerome, and I want help. Jamesy has a good jobber's eye.
JEROME	Would you take him from the place?
LARRY	He'd be home often enough. Another would do his work for a wage – and do it better, according to Sadie.
JEROME	Aye, that's true enough.
LARRY	The Land for the People. Ye were great men in your day. Ye did a lot. Look at yourself. You must have made this place out of heather.
JEROME	I could work. And I had the heart for it.
LARRY	Jamesy, now, has a heart, too. But it's more like mine. It works in money, and not in the soil like yours. The only crop that interests me is the grass. Jerome, you'll have to give him his head. 'Tis time.

The Poplar 99

JEROME	I'd never stop him, Larry.
LARRY	That's why I'm talking to you. This girl is a nice good plain girl. But there's money where she comes from. And where there's money there's other things. A good big house, and a bathroom. Jerome, I'll talk straight now, for we're the one family. You did your share in your time, it's Jamesy's turn now. Where you built, let him add.
JEROME	It's still the best house around here, Larry.
LARRY	It is, indeed. But you know what Parnell said: 'Let no one put a boundary to the march of a nation'.

(*Drum, cymbals and fife come slowly forward*)

There's old Bernie, now. Living in the past – among children. You're a different bit of work to Bernie, I'll say you are –

(*The band comes very close. Fades*)

JEROME	What are you looking for, Larry?
LARRY	A fork of a twig. Didn't you know I was a dowser? Here we are. Some people think you must have a hazel or a black sally. But there was a time and I could do it with two fingers. This bit of poplar will answer.
SADIE (*at a distance*)	The tea, men.
LARRY	Ah, wait a minute, girl.
SADIE	What are you doing?
LARRY	We have decided that the addition will go here.
SADIE	Nonsense. Put it on the west side. Cut down that old tree.
JEROME	We will not, then. I planted that fifty years ago.
SADIE	You planted a lot of others, too, that needn't be cut. That old thing was always in the way. And dark.
JEROME	It's a good shelter.
SADIE	Sometimes it'd waken you up and the sound of it would make you swear the sky was pouring down on us.
JEROME	That tree will stay.
SADIE	Come in to your tea. For a sensible man you're worse than any babby. That Ellen has you spoiled.
LARRY	You know now what I have to put up with, Jerome.
SADIE	A thousand dollars hanging on an old man's whim. I never heard the like of it. We should leave you the whole place to yourself, and then you could manage, mend and make do to your heart's content – while it lasted and while YOU lasted.
LARRY	Well, well.
SADIE	Come in out of that to your tea. I suppose you know we've missed the Benediction. (*Fading*)

The Poplar

LARRY (*fading*)   Ah, God will forgive us.
SADIE   You may thank Him that he's more forgiving than I am.

(*Fade. The old* Clock *wheezes one*)

COMMENTATOR   Sunday exhausts the land
                      With its tall prayers and the sweet release
                      Of work from the hand
                      And the delicate wonder of bended knees.

                      Gather up the ghost
                      On Monday morning; tackle him to the cart;
                      One long day he was lost
                      In the business of his heart.

JAMESY (*snorting out of sleep*)   Are you awake?
JEROME (*half waking*)   What's that?
JAMESY (*softly*)   It's all right.

(*Pause. Leaf sound of the* Poplar)

JEROME (*drowsily*)   Tree, what is it, now?
THE POPLAR   Soft starlight
                      And I am in the drift. Soaked in the soft I harden
                      And lift sap and shape it all the night.
                      You remember the great peacock in Chiswick's garden
                      And the many pupils of his sight?
JEROME   A big tall tail of a bird.
JAMESY (*more wakeful*)   Are you awake?
JEROME (*deeply drowsy*)   Eh?
JAMESY   It's all right.

(*Pause. Leaf sound of the* Poplar)

JEROME (*drowsily*)   Tree, what is it, now?
THE POPLAR   Vague vast summer in
                      My country. Tomorrow already on its legs
                      And waiting like a runner to begin;
                      You remember the breathless scramble over the Creggs –
                      Vague vast summer, you all the din.

JEROME   The sun and me. I never saw that fellow, Quinn.
JEROME (*awake now*)   What are you muttering about?
JEROME (*wakening more*)   Eh? What is it?
JAMESY   You said something yourself. Who is Quinn?
JEROME   'Twill be fine tomorrow. Maybe you'd start on that bottom
                  field.

JAMESY	I thought 'twas uncertain myself. Will you have a pull out of the pipe?
JEROME	I might as well. 'Twill shorten the night. Do you know what I'm going to tell you?
JEROME (*puffing*)	What is it?
JEROME	An ageing man pays for his life every night.
JAMESY	Damme if I understand that.
JEROME	I don't know, now, whether your mother or myself was the wise one.
JAMESY	I thought it was yourself. The neighbours thought the same.
JEROME	I gave myself to them in their health, but she did it in their sickness. I was where they cheered and she was where they wailed. She was a good woman.
JAMESY	You were a good man yourself.
JEROME	I was too good of a man. That's what I was.
JAMESY	Would you be other if you had to start again?
JEROME	I would not. And that's why I'm not at peace. The things I did were the things that had to be done. If they're on my soul itself, I know in my heart I'd do them all over again.
JAMESY	You should have a talk with the priest.
JEROME	There's nothing I haven't told him long ago.
JAMESY	You're all right so.
JEROME	I'm no better. There are things I'll shoulder out through the door of death. Maybe when I'm there, God will lighten the burthen. Go 'sleep now.
JAMESY	All right.
JEROME	When are you going to throw your eye over that girl?
JAMESY	I hadn't thought about it.
JEROME	It's time for you to think about it. If it's the house that's worrying you, we'll put the job on the short finger. Only leave me the tree outside. It's company.
JAMESY	We could add round at the back.
JEROME	The very place. We could, too, face the outhouses the other way and make a new yard.
JAMESY	That's a right thought. Sure, they could make a garden where the yard is, then.
JEROME	Appletrees. Aye. I'll plant those myself. Maybe Larry'd come out again and look for well-water for us. (*Fading*)
JAMESY	Why wouldn't he?

(Clock *croaks three, distantly*)

COMMENTATOR	I approach You, Soul; you who always watch me with reproach;

Which is the better, I ask,
He who does nothing, or he who takes the task?

He who burthens
Himself each night with a heavy conscience,
And conscious of guilt and pain
Would choose, nevertheless, to do things over again.

To right
Wrongs the hard way and be sleepless all the night,
To catch peace as he can,
A sinner and afraid, who would be all a man.

LARRY	You'd think, now, there'd be more streams here.
JEROME	Maybe, I field-drained them all away.
LARRY	You field-drained surface water. Wait.
JEROME	Cripes, the stick's diving on you all right.
LARRY	There's one here.
JEROME	It's a great gift.
LARRY	I'd nearly swear you had it yourself. Take the twig in your hand.
JEROME	Ah.
LARRY	Take it. Hold it this way. Lightly. Arms close to your ribs.
JEROME	Oh Lord, she's moving.
LARRY	What did I tell you? Walk now at a right angle to this stream –
JEROME	Huup. There she goes again. I can't hold her.
LARRY	Give it here. It's flowing this way. They meet – I can't go further or I'll be into your old poplar. And yet, this is the place you must dig.
JEROME	There's no other place?
LARRY	You have the gift yourself. Do your own walking, now, and try it out.
JEROME	I'll move out a piece further.
COMMENTATOR	O hazel twig, my gift,
	You, a fork of water in my hands,
	More naked than a girl without her shift,
	Find me a bright root under all lands.

Find me the limb I lost
Long ago, the nymph of my garden, my cool
And marvellous one, my water-ghost,
Hidden at the bottom of my soul.

LARRY	There are no more, Jerome.
SADIE	Have another cup, Larry? A cake, Dadda?
LARRY	Have a fill of this.

JEROME	I'll have the old plug.
SADIE	I can't see why you'd let an old tree stand in the way of every-thing. I never found anything soft in you before.
JEROME	I was never an old man before.
LARRY	Every man to his taste, as the fellow said when he kissed the sow.
SADIE	You get more common every day.
LARRY	Aye. We'll meet in some place soon. But as I see it now, Jerome, there are a lot of plans and the interests of a few of us held up by this tree.
SADIE	Julia won't bring out the Loftuses and I certainly won't bring out Ann Jordan till the place is ready for them. And that holds up Larry's plans for Jamesy. Jamesy would make more money with Larry in one year than he'd make here in five.
LARRY	'Tis time for Ellen to be making a move, too –
ELLEN	Don't mind Ellen, Larry. I have my own plans.
LARRY	I never knew a woman yet who hadn't. Who is he, Slyboots?
ELLEN	A gentleman called God. There's no hurry. He'll wait for me.
JEROME	Is it the convent you have in mind?
ELLEN	It was always in my mind.
JEROME	Aye. You were always a bit different. You were like your mother, indeed. As quiet as a prayer.
SADIE	We'll have someone to pray for us anyway. But honest, Nell, I amn't a bit surprised. Though I'll admit I thought it was the idea of leaving Dadda alone that made you refuse Jim Quinlan.
JEROME	Faith, this is a day of news. I didn't hear that before.
ELLEN	You'd have been pressing me to take him. And you'd only have thought what Sadie thought. And from that you'd make out you were a burthen on me, a thing you never were or could be. Go out, now, and show Larry the heifers from Curska.
LARRY	Come on. I'm getting stiff from all the politeness.
JEROME	I've a word to say first of all.
LARRY	Well, say it and come on.
JEROME	It's about the tree. The right thing to do is what suits most people. So, ye can take it down when ye like.
SADIE	Now, that's talking. And only good ordinary common sense.

(*The band again approaching*)

	Glory. Here are those brats again and their band. And old Bernie piping away.
JEROME	And that, too, in its time – I might tell you – was only good ordinary commonsense –

(*Band becomes loud. All slowly fade*)

The Poplar

COMMENTATOR   O tell me, tell me
Where the good ends, where evil delighting in
Its own felicity
Turns good into a sin?

A strong man in his anger
Against wrong is good. Is a woman with a nun's airs
The stronger
Lost in her prayers?

He with blood on his hands
Making a world for her, in which she can live,
Finds she has house and lands
But can only grieve.

And yet he continues
Building, building; there is even a smile on his lip
Though he know he too dies
Like the other on his way to worship.

(*The croak of the* Clock. *Leaf sounds*)

THE POPLAR   There is a fine tomorrow in my arms.
JEROME (*drowsy in his sleep*)   Aye. A fine tomorrow, Tree. I told Jamesy.
JAMESY (*drowsy*)   Did you say something, Dadda?
JEROME   Eh? A fine tomorrow.
JAMESY (*sleeping*)   Aye.

(*Leaf sounds*)

JEROME (*drowsy*)   What is it, Tree?
THE POPLAR   There is a fine tomorrow in my arms.
JEROME (*drowsily*)   I told Jamesy. (*Waking*) But, O Tree, Tree, what of the
     after-tomorrow?
COMMENTATOR   Aye. A dead tree leaves
A silence, a hole in the air,
A space that grieves
For its sounds, for its visible tall green wear.

Not even the ghost of a tree
Remains after it;
But something between me
And the tree will stay a bit.

An Absence come to a Presence,
Drinking me like sap;
I tower among the greens;
I have a tree on my lap.

The Poplar

ELLEN	Where's he gone, Julia?
JULIA	He was mooching out there a minute ago. Ellen, take a peep at this pattern.
ELLEN	He has a sorrow on him, Julia. Will you follow him or will I?
JULIA	You're like a hen with one chick.
ELLEN	Jamesy says he's taken to talking a lot in his sleep.
JULIA	The old are that way.
ELLEN	Well, he's vacant, too. He left his breakfast after him this morning.
JULIA	Look, go to the door and you'll find he's helping with the tree.
ELLEN	If he was there I wouldn't be talking. Here, keep an eye on the dinner. I'll go after him myself.
JULIA	Give me that spool of thread first. Thank you.

(*The noise of a cross-cut saw and men talking comes nearer*)

BOY	The Land for the People. Aunty Ellen, I went up the ladder and there was a little nest, look, but all the birds are grown up and gone.
ELLEN	Did you see your grandfather?
BOY	I did. He went over the style into Middle-field. He wouldn't say anything to me. He was cross.
ELLEN	The devil a cross. Sure, you're his own old pet.
BOY	He's cross now, for always. Why do you want him? It's not dinnertime yet.
ELLEN	Ah, for – reasons. He'll be down at the river. Will you come?
BOY	Indeed, I won't. Jimmy says the tree will be knocked in quarter of an hour.
ELLEN	Well, you'll have to see that. But did you ever see the big trout in the sally-roots below?
BOY	No. Will you show me him if I go?
ELLEN	I'll do my best.
BOY	All right. I'll race you to the stile.
ELLEN	Come on, then.
COMMENTATOR	Sally-trees, upthrust
	Shadows of river-water, green as glass,
	I, too, turned the dust
	On its way upward through my waywardness
	Into a person dressed
	In his own tallness and his manliness.
	But missed your comeliness.
BOY (*far distant*)	There he is by the water. The Land for the People.
COMMENTATOR	Missed the delicate gait
	That is content to stand upon one root,

> Not hurrying to be late,
> Not seeing outside itself the lovely brute
> Who is always the mate
> And always away, evasive, ever mute.
> And I the fool who dances to her flute.

ELLEN   Dadda.

JEROME   Who's that?

ELLEN   Don't you know Ellen?

JEROME   I'm a bit lost in myself. Where am I? Oh, it's Ellen.

ELLEN   Dadda, you're all right, aren't you?

JEROME   Musha, what are you crying for? I'm not a corpse yet. Have they cut the poplar?

ELLEN   I told them they shouldn't.

JEROME   Nonsense. The more the people, the greater the need. Shout up, young fellow. The Land for the People, isn't it?

BOY   Why is Aunty Ellen crying, Grandfather?

JEROME   Because she's good like her mother. She'd let a wasp crawl all the way over her without killing him.

ELLEN   Take hold of my arm.

JEROME   Indeed, I won't. People must always go their own gait and in their own way. That's why you're going to be a nun. And that's why I'm going to die doubtful.

ELLEN   What are you saying, Dadda? Jerry, call your uncle.

JEROME   Leave James alone. He has his own chores and his own cares. Sure, I'll take your arm if you'd rather I would. But I'm doing well enough.

ELLEN   Let us be moving so, in the name of God.

COMMENTATOR   The pity of it. Not to love
> All the love we lean on;
> Always to be at some remove
> And always drawn
> Towards the overwhelming one
> We must meet alone.
>
> O loneliness. We are born to them;
> As mothers they mother us;
> We break the navel chord like a limb,
> That as lovers they love us;
> But recover us
> And leave them for our loneliness.

JAMESY   There's a good drop of the creature in that for you. It might give you a good sleep.

JEROME   Leave it on the chest.

| JAMESY | I will not. Sit up, now, and take a wallop out of it. |

(*A fife and drum band in the distance*)

JEROME	Aren't the children gone to bed?
JAMESY	They're snug this two hours. Why?
JEROME	The band.
JAMESY	What band?
JEROME	Ah, I must have been thinking. That's strong stuff. Barring the night your poor mother died, that's the first doctor was ever in this door.
JAMESY	Thanks be to God for that. How did you get on with the friar?
JEROME	He's a noble man. But the best of them don't understand the old times. They haven't the fury in them, somehow.
JAMESY	Did he give you peace itself?
JEROME	Musha, peace isn't what I'm looking for and I can do without it.
JAMESY	And what are you looking for?
JEROME	How do I know? Maybe it's understanding. I told all of them the same thing one after another down the years. And they could never understand how I had to do it and how I couldn't be sorry that I did it. It puzzles me.
JAMESY	It must be something queer.
JEROME	It wasn't queer, them times. Promise amendment, says the decent holy man. How can I do that, says I? There's no way I can amend the thing I done. By making your life a worthy one, says he. 'Twas doing that thing, says I, that made it worth living at all. If I could be sorry for it, Father, I would be sorry. Do you want to be sorry, says he? I'm doing my best, says I, but it's failing me as it always failed me. And then he tried another tack, God bless him.
JAMESY	Maybe you shouldn't be telling me this.
JEROME	Who else have I to tell? Ye took away the old tree on me. Have a sup of this. There's a band playing in it.
JAMESY	Do you hear a band?
JEROME	'Tis no matter. I know I'm raving a bit. The Land for the People. But how would there be land for the people only for the likes of me? One of the signs of true repentance accepted by God, says his reverence, is a sincere intention not to sin again. I can promise that without any hitch, says I. I've never wanted to kill another man.
JAMESY	Ah. You were the one who – Holy Mary, it wasn't you, was it?
JEROME	Wasn't me what?
JAMESY	Chiswick?

The Poplar

JEROME   Who else? And what's more, I knew what I was doing. I knew
           well I was taking my eternal salvation in my two hands that
           day, for I knew I never would nor ever could be sorry for
           blasting that big bully out of this world.

(*The band comes forward in a ghostly way with crowds cheering vaguely*)

           No one understands those days but the man who lived in them.

(*Fade. The old* Clock *comes forward. Sounds of snoring and heavy breathing*)

COMMENTATOR   Where the tree stood
              And talked, there is a hole in the air,
              A raw void, a tall crude
              Structure without limbs or leaves uttering a nightmare.
              Footless, with no head in heaven, cut away from God.

              O the integrity
              Of a tree. It turns its face up to spray
              Itself wide upon the sky
              And has no knees, no business to pray,
              Nothing to do but live its time away.

              But man, man, old man there,
              You, knotting your thoughts like old rope, who should
              Be only one single prayer,
              Do not be damned by a dream of ancient manhood.
              Nor like your tree be so much firewood.

              Look, the tree has left a place
              Never to be filled with such exactitude;
              A man, too, must take away such a face
              Never to be repeated with such likelihood.
              Can man kill then – and not intrude.

JEROME   Jamesy, Jamesy –
JAMESY   Eh, what's that, what's wrong?
JEROME   Glory be to God.
JAMESY   What is it? Wait, I'll crack a match.
JEROME   It's all right, now. I had a nightmare. I, I dreamed that I was in
           the wrong. I am all right now, I tell you.
ELLEN (*sibilant*) Is it the turn, Jamesy?
JAMESY   Dreaming, he was.
JEROME   Who's that?
ELLEN   Ellen, Dadda. Back on the bolster with you. You'll have to
           make up to your heart for the way you treated it. Open your
           mouth, this is brandy.

JEROME	The little nun. Do you know, I think your mother was always something annoyed with me because I was never sick.
ELLEN	Aye. You must congratulate me so on my good luck.
JEROME	What sort of night is in it? I've lost my gauge, my weather gauge.
JAMESY	Quiet enough. I'll do the rest, Ellen. Go to bed.
ELLEN	Good night now, Dadda.
JEROME	Lord and dear me, but 'tis you are like your poor mother. Good night, girleen, and God bless you.
JAMESY	I'll put out the candle. Are you resting?
JEROME	Somehow I keep waiting for the poplar. We were a pair of old cronies.

(*Croaking of* Clock *begins*)

JAMESY	When you spoke of being wrong tonight, what did you mean?
JEROME (*drowsy*)	Eh?
JAMESY	It's all right. Go 'sleep.
JEROME (*drowsy*)	How could I be wrong? If I'm wrong, everything in the world must be wrong. That couldn't be. If there's no justice in the world, we must make justice.

(*Tick-tocking of old* Clock *seems to come forward*)

THE CLOCK	You never noticed me before.
	I am the clock tick-tock tick-tock tick-tock.
JEROME	It's a terrible silent night.
COMMENTATOR	Aye, but there are still greater silences.
	There is the hole the poplar filled.
	And the void where a man lived in all his senses.
	A body is a voice of God, can it be stilled,
	Cut down, killed?
	The place it owned, you know, must still be a Presence
	By its very absence.

JEROME	Oh, if it be that way –
JAMESY (*wakening*)	What is it? Did you say something, Dad?
JEROME	Eh? What's that?
JAMESY	You were groaning in your sleep. Will I light the candle?
JEROME	The candle?
JAMESY	Will I light it?
JEROME	No. I must grow accustomed to the dark. I was thinking, Jamesy, that Chiswick was like the tree, leaving a silence after him –
JAMESY	I don't understand you at all.
JEROME	A big hole where he used to be, a hole in the air –

110   *The Poplar*

JAMESY	Would you like another drop from the bottle?
JEROME	No. I'll die game. His absence can haunt me by its presence –
JAMESY	Glory be to God –
JEROME	But I'm brought up to the point when I'm standing there in the porch of the church –
JAMESY	I'll go for the priest for you, Da. He'll be some comfort to you –
JEROME	There's no comfort. I'm standing there and he's down and I'm only sorry for myself, watching him, knowing that if he was a sacrifice to the times I was a sacrifice myself as well.
JAMESY	I'm off, now. Would you like Ellen to stay with you?
JEROME	Eh?
JAMESY	Would – you – like – Ellen to stay with you – ?
ELLEN	Is there anything wrong, James?
JAMESY	He's troubled in his mind over some old thing. I'm slipping away for the priest. If you're quiet, he might sleep. Don't make a light.

(*The tick-tock of the old* Clock)

JEROME   Aye, there is a terrible silence in this porch.
ELLEN (*agitated whisper*)   What did you say, Dadda?

(*The old* Clock *comes forward and suddenly the clock stops ticking*)

ELLEN   Dadda, (*shouts*) JULIA, JULIA.

(*Bang of door. Silence for a long moment*)

COMMENTATOR   A silence here, too.
Leave it on the old wooden bed. Tomorrow
It will be washed and shaved, an old corpse made new
And buried with some sorrow.

And whether he was right or wrong
Only God knows; but in the middle of an action
He surrendered his balladry to the Soul's bleak song
And became a conviction.

He stands there in the porch
Maybe eternally. He knows what he's done;
It's all there in his heart for you, a murdered man in a
church.
Accept him, O Mary's Son.

The End

The Hags of Clough

Dramatis Personae

Commentator
Landlord of an inn in Connacht
Buller Clancy, a pedlar
Marty, his mate
The Scholar
The Jockey, the Scholar's twin brother
Mephistophilis
The Hags of Clough, local witches or folk demons
The Earl of Leitrim
Old man
Master of Ceremonies
The Vicomte, a suitor to the Lady
The Lady, daughter of the Earl of Leitrim
Blake, footman to the Earl of Leitrum
Girl
Guard
Bishop of Elphin, uncle to the Scholar and the Jockey
Housekeeper to the Bishop of Elphin
A folksinger
Innkeeper of an inn in Athlone
Dilly, a servant at the inn
Gamekeeper to the Earl of Leitrim
Betty, maid to the Lady
Butler to the Earl of Leitrim
The Countess, the second wife of the Earl of Leitrim
Raoul, nephew to the Earl of Leitrim
Woman
Coachman

Voices of crowd, courtiers, drinkers, etc.

COMMENTATOR   Gods who died
                Will linger on;
                Old shells take fire
                At the full moon;

                Old crones survive
                Death smells; a body
                Dance on Hagshill,
                A religious body –

                But widdershins, widdershins,
                Turned round and back,
                The fertile thing
                Gone off the track.

                The old shells shake,
                An old dry mouth
                Sing the bellyache
                Of wanton youth.

A roadside inn in Connacht, under the Seven Standing Stones at Hagshill.
Two pedlars arriving after dark. They knock –

LANDLORD Who is it? Buller Clancy, Marty too.
                Come in, come in.
                        Why, Marty looks a bit
                Aback –
BULLER (*jovial*) He heard a tomcat squall
                On Hagshill –
MARTY   No cat, no cat. The Hags. I saw the moon
                Squint on bare skin, I say.
BULLER   Whiskey now
                And a bit of butter in it –
MARTY   It's no good luck
                To see the Hags –
BULLER   Cats, that's all. Creeping into the shine
                Of one another. Whiskey and butter now –

        (*Phrase on piccolo*)

                Hah, is the Scholar here? Is the one
                And only velvet fellow in these parts?
LANDLORD You know the Scholar?
BULLER   The piccolo, the little piccolo. Has he
                Cured anybody hereabouts?
LANDLORD My wife. And it's a miracle.
                        A heap.

Of dirty duds in the backroom, that's what she was
This five years past, without a word.
                              Till he
Sat down and looked at her.
                       And now I have
A woman in the house, peep in, in here,
The kitchen spick and span. My sons at ease
With their own mother once again –

BULLER   He cured the mad priest
At Manorhamilton –

LANDLORD A man again,
That's what I am.

BULLER   Now he'll discourse
The night away –

MARTY (*complaining*) Keep working men awake,
And Buller here will break out on the beer
Again.

BULLER   I love a learned man. Here, put
Away the packs –

LANDLORD No, bring them in. We're full,
You'll have to sleep on them –

BULLER   Mart, open up
The door.

(*The* Scholar *forward. Drunken*)

SCHOLAR   The acorn drops
But keeps the image of the oak. An egg
Hatches its kind. Everything that lives
Aches after its own vast original.
Sus sui, canis cani, bos bovi, et cetera;
The first and perfect image of each one
Exists in God and is reflected down
The line
            Quote Plato here.
                    And Homer's golden chain. (*Hiccup*)
Cite authorities.
                Primordial
Contemporaries, that's what we are.
One, all one
            In God all one. So on
Some level we are comprehensible
To one another.
             (*Hiccup*) Open secrets. We

Are music on a single instrument. (*Hiccup*)
I hope.
                Give me another drink.
                                We share
A common factor of divinity.
Ergo, ergo, give me another drink. (*Hiccup*)
You follow me, I trust.

AWED VOICE Mister, it's a noble monologue.

BULLER   The discourse is familiar, Scholar.
                                        Don't
You know me, Buller, pedlar of all, of all
And sundry –

SCHOLAR (*vaguely*) Where was I?

BULLER (*merrily*) Cavan, Cootehill, Belturbet,
Manorhamilton –

SCHOLAR (*loudly*) Bodies, musical bodies, made
Long before the world began, each soul
A paragon, unique.
                        That's what we are.
A balanced being, each of us.
                                And oh
Most precious for all the fall of flesh.
                                    The flesh
Has meanings too.
                        Darkens they say, but never to
Obscurity. The glory stays. And we
Divine the skeleton, which is, as I
Assert, a preconception of its first
Ideal form
                (*Hiccup*) Quote Plato here. Give me
Another drink.

LANDLORD (*low*) Pass on this jug.

SCHOLAR   All illness is
A jarring of that skeleton. To cure
It we define the skeleton anew,
In all its early glory. So we seek
Obstruction out, discover the Gorgon's head,
Uncover it.
                The Devil will be there.
God's work, you say.
                        A drudgery
For tonsured heads? And holy hands, the pious and
The oiled?

    (*Roar*) Give me another drink. *Homo sum,*
  Humani a me nihil alienum
  Puto.
BULLER The Latin, boys, the lovely and
  The lettered.
SCHOLAR (*loudly*) Souls are the care of all.
  The cure is everyone's who can. That's what
  I do assert, you learned baldheads, tonsured pinheads –
  Who knows can cure, and must.
        To know is all
  The cure.
      But one must know, know all.
           I say
  That people on some level are quite plain –
  Visible to one another. Pictures come
  In waves, we talk, confide our souls to one
  Another, love, and pity, see the ill,
  Discern the distortion,
        Uncover the Gorgon's head.
  Galen cast horoscopes. Ficinus, Crato too;
  And Paracelsus would unite the heavens
  In one gigantic bright nativity
  To find the source of toothache in one mouth.
  I cite authority, *homicidas medicos,*
  Astrologiae ignaros. Socrates, too,
  Would not prescribe for Charmides'
  Sick headache, first he needs must learn the ill
  Within the mind.
      Quote here, quote here, *Oculum*
  Non curabis sine – et cetera.
  See Leo Suavius, Pistorius – there's
  Citation, sirs. The art is true, he says,
  But few have skill in it. *Ars vera est –*
  Et cetera, meaning the devil does
  Not diagnose.
      Give me a drink. I am
  Shaking a synod down.
LANDLORD (*hushed*) Pass on the jug.
  Lord, he looks sick himself.
BULLER (*low*) That's the way with him
  When he cures anyone –
SCHOLAR You'll call on Nicholas Taurellus. I
  Expected that. Common experience

             The Hags of Clough

He states, confirms that the Devil can
Without impediment penetrate through all
Our bodies part by part, and after heal
By means unknown.
                              Erastus holds with him
And most Divines agree.
                              So Sorcerers are banned,
The Servatores, rightly too.
                              But who
Shall know them by their works, the lost who league
Themselves with demons yet do good?
                              Give me
Another drink.
                              Question, do I belong
To that category?
                              Have I the wheel
Of Catherine in my mouth? Or otherwise
Inscribed upon my person?
                              (*Hiccup*) The answer's negative.
I have been stripped –
                              In France, low Germany
And other places,
                              lost a little of
A scholar's dignity –

(*Piccolo bright a moment*)

                              Displayed my parts
Of manhood in great council chambers, been
Admired, alas.

(*Piccolo again*)

And here is Master
Paracelsus. It matters not, says he,
Whether it be God or Devil cure
If I be troubled with a malady.
Solomon cast out devils, before
Vespasian Eleazar did as much
And David tenderly would pipe for Saul.
The primitive church did recommend us too,
The fools of God.
                              Yet evil is not done
That good come of it. Much better die, says one
Delrio, much better die than be so cured.

The Hags of Clough   119

A quandary, a case of conscience, one
I argue, sirs, continually.
                              Afraid
At night. Unhorsed. Cursed by a talent I
Find all too cumbersome.
                              Give me a drink
And blot this scholar out a while. *Odi,*
Nec possum cupiens et cetera.
I hate what I am; and yet no matter what
Can only be the being that I hate.
Pass on the barrel –
                              Finis the one-man show.

(*A buzz of voices*)

BULLER   We meet again. Dear lord, you are
In spate tonight –
                              Don't you know me? Ah,
Come out of Devil's Island – Have a jar
With Buller.
SCHOLAR   The bully pedlar –
BULLER   Himself, himself.
SCHOLAR   You had a mate who prayed for you –
BULLER   Marty, you mean –
MARTY   I'm here. We came round by Elphin.
The Bishop, your uncle, talked about you. He
Implored me to advise you to come home.
SCHOLAR (*hiccup*) *Civis Romanus sum.* I am
A pothouse fellow. Where a barrel is
I am at home.
BULLER (*jovially*) By God, we'll pull a bung
Or two tonight.
                              (*Roar*) Landlord, here.
LANDLORD It's on the house –
MARTY   Your reverend uncle –

(*Piccolo background*)

SCHOLAR   A Pauline product. He
Believes in a LITTLE wine. And bears the brunt
Of poor affronted flesh.
                              Never mind. I see
A sermon in your face.
LANDLORD A jug for two.
BULLER   Butter in mine.

        The Hags of Clough

SCHOLAR   How is
           The good old man? Never mind. I know
           He's praying for me. Sad. I lost a hat
           Along the way, a bright biretta, boy.
           For I was very pious once. Louvain,
           Strait Heidelberg, and Paris too. Logic on
           Tall stilts, and that was me, with Reason on
           Its last poor legs.
                              Hah, here we take
           A holiday from pain –
MARTY (*petulantly*)   Lord, if he saw you now,
           Soaking home-made brew.
VOICES (*annoyed*) Shut up, Pedlar.

   (*A light phrase from piccolo*)

SCHOLAR (*merry*) *Pax vobiscum*. I'm away, Two shoes
           Are ready for the road.
LANDLORD (*Hurt*) Leaving, ah it's late.
           It's night and dark –
MARTY   And the Hags out –
           I saw them on the hill –
BULLER (*jovially*) A squall of cats,
           Festering with the moon –
MARTY   Belie me if you like –
LANDLORD (*low*) Scholar, stay
           The night.
                      Well, take this last drink so?
SCHOLAR (*hiccup*) Summer delights the scholar;
               His knowledge is out of season;
               He takes his task to the air;
               He wanders by the river;

               He reasons with rook and finch,
               The thrush, the blackbird, sing for him;
               His sober blacks turn green;
               He chews a daisy chain;

               Amply from his twig
               He may admire the dawn;
               See Lyra strung each night,
               And praise the sweet musician;

               Thus hedge-schooled he will find
               A theme in what occurs,
               The sylvan speech of God
               Who sings the simple verse.

The Hags of Clough   121

But back in candlelight again,
The pain of man will rear its head,
His vellums glow with fire and hail:
He hears the choirs sing for the dead.

(*Murmur of men. A piccolo phrase*)

(*Hiccup*) For the dead.
                              Day's done, the well is dry;
Let's out of doors, and milk the moon –
LANDLORD Scholar, you've a visitor, a man –
SCHOLAR (*hiccup. Orating still*) The pain of man –
LANDLORD Waiting at the door –
It's Leitrim's jockey, won't come in, the best
Horsemaster –
SCHOLAR (*loudly*) Will rear its head –
LANDLORD (*louder*) It's Leitrim's jockey –
JOCKEY (*coming forward*) Leave him to me.
LANDLORD (*low*) He's far gone tonight.
JOCKEY (*at hand*) A bright sprig. And drunk
As Bacchus.
                      So you're the puff, the blade,
And Mister Notoriety himself?
Remember me?
                              Here, look up –
SCHOLAR   Your face is most –
Familiar –
                      Most unloving too, I think.
And yet, without the horse, it could be mine.
Wait –
JOCKEY   Aye, we share the face –
SCHOLAR (*loudly*) Brother.
JOCKEY   The twin
Who ran away. I want to talk to you.
Hold on, no soft words, friend. I do not feel
Affectionate tonight. Indeed, I spit
On shapers like you – ne'er-do-wells – is this
What education does? Have you come home
To teach them how to drink in Connacht?
Thank God, I slung my hook –
SCHOLAR (*hiccup*) Brother, there's so much horse
In you, what happened to the man?
JOCKEY   Easy, lad. Hold there. If one of us
Must mock, it's me.

The Hags of Clough

I look at you, a mess,

By hell.

SCHOLAR (*sigh*) A mess.

And you, you ran away

To find great horses, ride –

JOCKEY (*complacently*) Brother, I found them. And I ride.
I found them.

I was starving when I crept

Through Leitrim's wicket, weak from the road, a child
Blackberry-blue and sleeping wild – I had
As many bedrooms as the hare.

I found

My horses, crept in with the grooms, an imp
Unwanted; chased away I'd slink, return
And fawn –

Times creeping round the cooks I wept;

And times in the straw –

No matter now.

It's done. I'm master, brother, honoured. I
Am Leitrim's horsemaster, a name in all
The land; in Europe too.

And you, and you

The bright fellow, the cherished, look at you
The family halo, Mama's innocent,
My uncle's choice, you were to shine, I believe,
In some great diocese, deliver law –
And look at you.

SCHOLAR (*sigh*) A mess, indeed.

JOCKEY (*complacently*) A mess.

SCHOLAR And yet you're here on business, not out
Of love.

JOCKEY (*violently*) Love – brotherly, eh? And when did we
Two love? You stole it all, my portion of
Attention, every eye, the merry lad
Who tootled on the piccolo; the old,
The sick, the silly, beasts of the field –
Were yours –

SCHOLAR (*mildly*) What do you want of me?

JOCKEY (*deeply*) I want you.

Yourself – in person too.

I am accused of being you.

(*Anger*) God's truth.

Imagine it. Me – you. The Jock in duds

Like yours. The velvet boy. A tavern suck,
A bung, a bottle, carousing to cockcrow.
I am accused of it, of blowing the froth off towns
I never heard of –
                    me, the trusted, sober
Horsemaster, yet Leitrim must accuse
Me, threaten –
                    (*Loudly*) As if I were a shambler, some
Strawfellow –
                    Me with years of service, of
Achievement, fame –
                    Accuses me. So I
Produce the real culprit, silence him
Without a word.
                    See.

SCHOLAR (*sigh*) I see – much more.
JOCKEY (*uncertainly*) You do. (*Loud*) What do you see?
SCHOLAR (*sigh*) You know as well as I.
JOCKEY (*uncertain*) I do?

(*Faint peep of piccolo*)

SCHOLAR   What keeps you there –
                    So disregarded?
JOCKEY (*loudly, angrily*) What keeps me? Horses, horses. None
                    Like them anywhere
                              And if I am
                    So – disregarded, I'll put up with it
                    While I've such horses.
                              Now, get up, get up.
                    I say get up.
                              There's dancing there, a ball
                    Tonight, my lady's birthday; every cock
                    And hen with quarterings; carriages
                    Are in and out, and nobody knows who's who.
                    You'll pass with me, some velvet fellow I
                    Was sent for, see. And then confront him in
                    The crowd.

(*Pip of piccolo. Mocking*)

                    Put up that instrument.
                              Tonight's
                    The only time you'll have a chance to meet
                    My lord. He's down on company, he lives

The Hags of Clough

Secluded, walled away, sees nobody, is strict
On gatekeepers –
                 Tonight's the chance, a ball
To all and sundry – she's eighteen, of age
Tonight.
            (*Low*) Of age tonight. A child I watched
Grow up. A child no more.

SCHOLAR She keeps you there?

JOCKEY She?
           That's good – a child,
And sickly nowadays, avoids my yard
And rides no more.
                 No need to mention her.
Get up, get up. A child I taught to sit
Her pony, headlong, a difficult child I watched
Grow up.
           And ailing now I think – what's that
To you or me?
             I want you to confront
This lord and set me right.
                    Come on, come on.

SCHOLAR (*quietly*) Sit down,

JOCKEY Sit down.

SCHOLAR You have some need of me.

JOCKEY I have?

SCHOLAR (*sigh*) It's not to lull that lord of yours –

JOCKEY Then what, what, tell what?
                  By hell, you have
A piercing pair of eyes.
               Pry into me and I
Will strangle you. We are not children now.

SCHOLAR (*sigh*) And not too happy, you and I.
                    You love
This girl –

JOCKEY I what, I what?

SCHOLAR *Remedium amoris*, I know none,
No cure but marry –

JOCKEY By hell –

SCHOLAR You're man enough –

JOCKEY A child I saw grow up,
A difficult wayward piece, a headlong girl,
And if a woman sometimes – still a girl,
A child, a very child.

Cubbing the gorse
Or jogging from a meet, in failing light,
November light, the sun low on the ground
As my bull-terrier, she'd make up some
Excuse to stop.
                    Jockey, pinch up my girth
Another inch –
                    A woman in the child,
But that's the way they grow; they soar before
Their legs are made.
                              Her servingman, that's all
I am; and man enough elsewhere – I've shed
Some seed where needed. Golden nurseries
Shall see it thrives.
                    (*Loudly*) But this girl is pure gold,
Too young, too young for this old scavenger
Who takes his snatches as they come.
                                        Up on your feet.
I want you to confront a lord, that's all
I want of you –

SCHOLAR (*sigh*) You want much more.

JOCKEY   I do?

SCHOLAR   Come down to it, or let me drink in peace.

JOCKEY (*violently*) Drink –

SCHOLAR (*quietly*) You need me to heal someone, brother. Who?

JOCKEY (*deep breath*) You always saw too much of me. I feel
                Exposed, by God. I'm like a glass of water in
                The light –
                              (*Loudly*) You see so much of me, then tell
                Me what I have in mind.

SCHOLAR (*sigh*) I'd rather be left
                Alone –

JOCKEY (*roar*) To drink?

SCHOLAR   To drink, collect the sensible and drown
                It. You and I are opposites, I have
                No shell –
                              Now talk or go.

JOCKEY (*quietly*) I'll talk. Your face
                Is sadder than Good Friday and the bell.
                I'll talk.
                        It's hard. I could be slandering
                The lord I work for. Here's the gist.
                                        I think

The old cock's crowing in the daughter's coop,
Or near as makes no matter.
                              Do you get
My drift? The sin of kin. A shameful thing.
And I've no real evidence.
                              Except
Those horse-matches I ride for him.
                              (*Whisper*) Listen now.
I've ridden seven matches, all in a row
Against the young sprigs who came courting her,
Her suitors, lordly fellows.
                              Some she liked,
And all she favoured, she'd have married one,
I think, if left alone; have married any
One of them, maybe, a nubile maid
If daunting, high and mighty –
                              Do you hear
Me, are you listening?
SCHOLAR (*low*) I hear. You love this lady too.
Why not elope with her –
JOCKEY (*low, harsh*) Elope, says he?
That day is gone. I'm Jock the servingman
This four years past, downgraded, brother twin;
And that's the way I like it nowadays –
I could have had her, yes, – and ruined a child
That I respected – ah, let be, let be.
                              Come back
To old mad Jack, old Guts-and-gaiters, Leitrim's lord.
I think he challenged those young fellows, staked
His daughter on the match, the colt and I
Cannot be beaten, see –
                              And when I won
A suitor disappeared, said his goodbyes
And left forever.
                              (*Whisper*) One young fellow tried
To bribe me too. And there's another now,
A forward Frenchman, gently touching me,
A gallant youngster, one I'd like to see
Well-married to the child.
                              Now I must ride
And beat him, we meet at Castlerea, he stands
No chance with me.
SCHOLAR (*weary*) Is she in love with him?

The Hags of Clough   127

JOCKEY	In love, in love, what's love?
	A variable. What girl is not in love –
SCHOLAR	Then let him win the match.
JOCKEY (*aback*)	Let him win? Beat me
	Who never was beaten, who never will be beat?
	I live in every horse I ride, together we
	Discover what's beyond the bit.
SCHOLAR	I'll hear no more.
JOCKEY	You'll hear no more?
SCHOLAR	You bring me homework you can do yourself.
	So simple on the face of it –

You lose

A match, the girl marries –

JOCKEY (*low*)	Brother –
SCHOLAR	Brothers, yes. Yet any horse
	Would know the difference –
JOCKEY (*low*)	She's lost her spirits, sits
	Upstairs in a big window staring out
	When there's no company; she's taken rooms
	In the old wing, remote – I have bad dreams
	Considering it –
SCHOLAR (*low*)	You speak of her – and light
	A lamp somewhere. That's love.

Tonight the Jock

Has all the radiance. I never loved
At all like this.

But if the glory came

About – I think I'd lose a match –

JOCKEY	I cannot cheat
	The thing I am, I cannot rob a horse.
SCHOLAR	You have integrity – of sorts, indeed.
	Give me a drink –
LANDLORD (*a little distant*)	They're lined up here,
	A dozen jugs –
SCHOLAR (*loudly*)	Integrity. What's that
	To love or pity? I would lose a match.
	Pull Daddylonglegs off your back, the jock
	Who rides you –

Man's ridiculous to trade

His freedom, his personal conscience, to
Some great Imago he creates, some pride
He feeds out of his guts. I'd lose a match
And be a man. If I could love I'd die

For it, and simply be God's fool —
                                    But I'm
A broken kind of fellow, I can love
Enough to heal an injury, to give
Myself to some sick person like a lover,
And afterwards be this, a sot, a clown,
Sucked dry and craving company.

JOCKEY   I'm damned if I understand
A word you say — except this 'lose a match' —

SCHOLAR (*hiccup*) Brother, you're two. One loves a woman, and one
A Jock, a silly jock, an acrobat
On some quadruped, tailoring a trick —

JOCKEY (*wounded*) No more of that.

SCHOLAR   I'd lose a match.
                              She sits
You say, in a big window.
                              Lost.
                                    Now there's
An image that could move a silly soul
Like me —
                But not tonight.
                                    The girl is yours.
Climb up and comfort her — or lose a match
And marry her off to some escutcheon —
                                            Drink,
Get drunk tonight. You were not always Horse
The servingman. In all my childhood you
Were number one, a vigorous fellow who
Could strut. I did admire you, aped you too.

JOCKEY (*incredulously*)   You — did? Me, the sullen foal?

SCHOLAR (*low, weary*)   You were so natural, and I too old
For one so young —
                          And now it's the other way
About.
          I am the child.
                              I have no shell,
The ill, the sick move me too much. Too much —
So life's disordered — shall we say. And yet
I rather me than you.
                              The girl is yours,
If only in a father's way, she's yours —
Your love makes you responsible. So lose
The match at Castlerea —

JOCKEY (*loudly*)   I couldn't do it. That's enough.
SCHOLAR (*wryly*)   The Jock wins. The Jock will always win.
　　　　　　　Poor Jock the funnyman –
JOCKEY   Easy now.

　(*Piccolo*)

SCHOLAR   I mock the Jock,
　　　　　His hide, his four legs, he
　　　　　Forever set
　　　　　On victory.
JOCKEY (*loudly*)   Shut up, or by the lord above –

　(*Piccolo*)

SCHOLAR   Mock, mock the Jock.
　　　　　Cedit amor rebus, he
　　　　　Must wear the mad
　　　　　Set face of victory.
JOCKEY   By hell, I warned you.

　(*Sound of a blow. A fall*)

VOICES   Oh.
LANDLORD (*after a silence*)   You struck him, Jockey.
　　　　　And in my house.
JOCKEY   Leitrim's house. A word from me
　　　　　And you'll be out of it.
　　　　　　　　　　　Look after him.
　　　　　Goodnight to you.
LANDLORD (*pause*)   I let him go –
BULLER   What else was there to do? We live
　　　　　Like woodlice in the shadows of the great.
LANDLORD (*low*)   He's bleeding, Buller.
VOICES (*low*)   How is he, how is he?
BULLER   Stirring. Many a drink will stream
　　　　　Down that bright gullet yet.
　　　　　　　　　　I'll wash away
　　　　　The blood.
LANDLORD   I'll call the wife.
BULLER   No need. Give him a pallet here
　　　　　Beside the fire.
LANDLORD   I'll put gruel on.
BULLER   Whiskey and butter is the best.
　　　　　Hah, Scholar, looking up.
　　　　　　　　　　As innocent
　　　　　As curly Cupid in a picture book.

The Hags of Clough

SCHOLAR (*drowsily*) Aquinas so defined it,
                A niggardliness of soul, a miser's sin –
                That's incest.
LANDLORD (*low*) Raving.
BULLER   The blow was heavy. He struck stone.
SCHOLAR   A parsimony of the Being. All that I
                Beget is mine –
LANDLORD (*low*) Move him softly over.
SCHOLAR (*testily*) A peevish sin.
                                        Yet everywhere
                The old are silly souls, the great are small –
                I tell you, brother –
                                There was Sophocles
                When old, bareboned as January, cold,
                He doted on Archippe.
                                        Not a peck
                Of corn in pantaloon, and yet he bought
                A mill.
LANDLORD (*low*) Scholar, sip this.
SCHOLAR (*drowsily*) The bully pedlar.
LANDLORD How do you feel?

(*Pip of piccolo*)

SCHOLAR   Not – too lascivious. *Nec*
                Mihi cincta Diana placet, nec
                Nuda Cythere.
                                Give me a drink,
                No pap tonight.
                                And help me up.
                                                I was
                Developing some theme with clarity.
                Whatever it was...
                                Has Brother Horse gone home?
LANDLORD (*hard*) I threw him out.
SCHOLAR (*drowsy*) He's in the air, poor fellow, his front hooves
                Are in the air.
                                (*Yawn*) I told him lose a match,
                I think –
BULLER (*sharply interested*) To lose? Heavenly Lord, I know
                I'd get a hundred pounds to one –
SCHOLAR (*tired yawn*) He won't, he can't.
BULLER (*low*) A hundred to one in Castlerea
                The French horse doesn't win.

(Pip of piccolo)

SCHOLAR　Trip the other then,
　　　　　Be *Deus ex machina*, easy money for
　　　　　The pedlar, save the situation.
　　　　　　　　　　　　　　　　　　　I
　　　　　Must think of it.

BULLER (*whisper, awed*)　A hundred to one.

SCHOLAR　Why, that's how great deeds come –
　　　　　Cupidity, commodity, what empire's raised
　　　　　On charity?

LANDLORD　Drink this, you're shivering.

SCHOLAR (*drowsily*)　What ails my head?

LANDLORD　You took a dunt from brother Jock.
　　　　　(*Whisper*) He's looking bad. (*Louder*) Another sip.

SCHOLAR (*drowsily*)　Twins. In all
　　　　　The tales one kills the other, that's the way,
　　　　　And takes the wife. Midsummer Night and John
　　　　　Must dance without his head.
　　　　　(*Sighs or yawns*) The bride goes on
　　　　　Around the merry year.
　　　　　　　　　　　　　　　Tradition, Sirs. (*Hiccup*)
　　　　　Old allegories, we.

LANDLORD　Another sip.

SCHOLAR (*drowsy*)　I take the dunt, yet brother twin
　　　　　Resigns the lady.
　　　　　　　　　　　　So she'll sit up there
　　　　　And fade –
　　　　　(*Loud*) *Multi fascinantur in*
　　　　　Melancholiam – they must exude
　　　　　A sort of odour too, the Furies come –
　　　　　They nose the thing, they sniff it out, they'll quit
　　　　　Only when the coffin comes.
　　　　　　　　　　　　　　　　What's that to me?
　　　　　My brother's business.

LANDLORD　Drink this.

SCHOLAR　In a big window, sick –
　　　　　　　　　　　　Where others would
　　　　　Receive young goat-legs on the windowsill
　　　　　This maid will water the geraniums.
　　　　　Yet flesh has rights in all.

LANDLORD　Scholar –

SCHOLAR　Give me the jug.
　　　　　　　　　　So many are oppressed.

　　　　　　　　　　　　　　　　　　　The Hags of Clough

And what is that to me?

Physician, heal

Yourself. My own dogs nip my heels. Tonight,
Let God or Jock go into business.
I'm spent, spent.

LANDLORD (*low*) He looks bad.

SCHOLAR (*drowsy*) Saturn and Mars, one culminating, one
In the fourth house, when he shall be borne –
And that is me, that's me, he shall be mad
Or melancholy.

But present there,

Beholding me, was Mercury, a sprite,
A brilliant imp. I may be saved.

But she,

Who'll save?

BULLER (*low, almost anguished*) A hundred to one.

SCHOLAR (*drowsy*) The pedlar.

Why, just trip the horse.

Riches for you –

And for the lady – life,

Another life.

Out and – trip – the horse. Out – and – trip.

(*Snore. Sigh. Snore*)

LANDLORD (*low*) Asleep.

BULLER (*pause, low*) A hundred to one.

SCHOLAR (*muffled in snores*) I'll have to go away. Away.

LANDLORD Ssshhhh. Pass that rug.

SCHOLAR (*low and fading*) Away.

(*Nightsounds. Plover near*)

COMMENTATOR Away, this way, that way.
What suffering man has walked those flints
Before me, leaving such
Enormous footprints?

Follow them
Till earth move heaven. Where's the loss
Since all will bloom again
Upon the cross?

SCHOLAR (*hiccup*) This road, and the Devil take all roadmenders,
Is puddle alley. Back, dyke, don't ambush me,
Ditch, keep away. Ah. (*Falls on wet road*)

Thus students come

The Hags of Clough   133

To earth. The righteous stumble. Poets drop
Dear rhymes into the gutter.
                                A problem here,
Dynamics, ecstatics, aesthetics, how to lift
This poet upright, how acquire
The perpendicular –

(*Distant howling of cats*)

MEPHISTOPHILIS (*suavely*)   If I may lend
           An arm, sir?
SCHOLAR   Ho, a nightwalker. A silent mover too,
           And not too evident, not apparent –
                                        Where
           Are you, Sir?
MEPHISTOPHILIS A little to the rear, upon
           The sinister side of course.
                                Allow me, Sir.
SCHOLAR (*vague tremor*) No.
MEPHISTOPHILIS No?
SCHOLAR   I can't distinguish you, and that is odd –

(*Surprise, disturbing*)

           But who blots out the moon?
MEPHISTOPHILIS (*Soothingly suave*)   A cloud
           Passed over.
SCHOLAR (*vague tremor*) Diana, too,
           Accoutres men with shadows. You cast none
           That I could see –
                        But I am drunk.
                                Yes, I
           Am drunk. Reeling.
                        Why do you nightwalk, Sir?
MEPHISTOPHILIS (*jovial*) The dark's commodious. And, friend, you've had
           Your lady assignations too.

(*Cat music near suddenly*)

           My dears, my darlings. There they go.
SCHOLAR (*hiccup*) Cats
           In plural and in heat, that's all I can
           Distinguish.
MEPHISTOPHILIS Oh, form is metaphysical,
           And matter something we adopt at will.
SCHOLAR   My words, my very own –

MEPHISTOPHILIS (*jovial*) All taken down,
            Recorded. It's good business, I find,
            To use a man's convictions when I come
            To bargain.
SCHOLAR (*low*) Ah.
MEPHISTOPHILIS The cat was worshipped here,
                                    Long, long before
            My ladies took him over.
                            I use old forms,
            Abandoned gods and such. The empty shells
            Hang round, and still have some traditional
            Significance.
                        Most useful too.
                                    Do I
            Disturb you, Sir?
                            O, have no fear. The Prince
            Of Darkness is a gentleman.
                                    Really
            I fence quite fairly too. Don't be afraid.
SCHOLAR (*choking*) Mother of God.
MEPHISTOPHILIS Dear boy, no prayers, please.
            I'm well within my extra-mural rights
            In offering my point of view.
                                    I am
            The great alternative, you know. When all
            Questions are answered satisfactorily
            I still remain, the last, the little doubt.
            A sort of residue that must in time
            Collect itself, and work the yeast again.
            (*Orating*) Life, that's me, and alteration, change,
            No dominance of One –
SCHOLAR No.
MEPHISTOPHILIS Hah, you find your tongue.
SCHOLAR God is creation, all
            Exists and moves, has being in Him. He
            Is all the stir, the music. Matter falls
            About him into place, most various –
MEPHISTOPHILIS Hah.
SCHOLAR Created, we
            Display Him –
MEPHISTOPHILIS (*jovially*) For fornicating in
            Low Germany and France? For wading in
            The Hook of Holland after a larded wench

That lurched on tall stilts like a crane –
SCHOLAR   *Mea*
            Culpa, I
MEPHISTOPHILIS Caught up in images,
            Seduced, a traveller from one poor place
            Of woman to the other –
SCHOLAR (*low*) An honesty of flesh –
MEPHISTOPHILIS (*arrogantly*) Not so. All wenches move
            Most amorously through my hands, it's I
            Who must endow them, puff the flame –
                                         so souls
            Fall my way,
                    Vel in puellam impingunt
            Vel in poculum –
                        Humhum,
                                And poets bless
            My dispensation.
                            Eustathius, Tatius, Achilles,
            Heliodorus, Ovid, Catullus,
            Lucian, Tibullus, dear friends, my pot
            Companions –
                        I put the words, endowed
            The mouths –
                        Propertius, Gallus, Petrarch too,
            But first I introduced the lady.
                                Lechery, she is,
            And lost? Cynthia, Lesbia, Lychoris…
            So, my dear boy, tonight, tonight – in turn
            About you see – I bring your paragon,
            Your Muse, your Muse, your death as man.
                                            Your life
            Forever as a poet.
                        You do not answer me.
SCHOLAR (*low*) I wait.
MEPHISTOPHILIS You wait.
SCHOLAR (*low*) To catch your drift. I am
            No poet. I require no Muse.
                            (*Louder*) You lead
            To something else, to something that I am.
            The master of lies, and shifts, of stratagems.
            A poet, no. I love no woman, none.
            And as a lover – *Nescio quid sit*
            Amor nec amo – I am none. I lie
            With any –

MEPHISTOPHILIS (*jovial*) That miller's wife –
                In starch and blue she meditated on
                The watergate –
                                She proved to be too fat.
                That tutor's wife, her bodice hung too low;
                '*Ah, si liceret?*' says you, a reader of
                Antonius Caracalla –
SCHOLAR (*low*) Toys, my youth,
                Exuberance of flesh –
                                You'll try me on
                Another level, hold my eye while you
                Unpick the bolt behind my back, surprise
                The fool…

    (Mephistophilis *laughs jovially*)

MEPHISTOPHILIS I am not at all above the board. Indeed,
                My feet go down some fathoms, down below
                All flesh, all origins –
                                Come, I'll not be hurt.
                Come, see my ladies –
SCHOLAR (*low, harsh*) You've lived on my
                Periphery awhile –
                                Those nights I've groaned,
                Drunken, in prayer too –
MEPHISTOPHILIS (*arch*) Debauchery becomes
                The scholar, but in youth, mark that, in youth.
                Hymen O Hymenae? Marry while able, stop
                The ass from kicking. Young men die, but old
                Men dote, swell Fiddlers' Alley – Niphus once,
                A public figure with more toes than teeth,
                And Jovianus Pontanus –
                                I see I'm not
                Amusing you, my dear.
SCHOLAR (*low, harsh*) Those nights, after I healed
                Somebody –
                                You were the doubt inside me, all
                The questions raised –
MEPHISTOPHILIS (*jovial laugh*) Dear boy, here are
                My ladies now. I am expected here –
SCHOLAR (*low, harsh*) You filled me up
                With doubts, with scruples –
MEPHISTOPHILIS (*angry*) Yet you healed
                And went on healing, what I latched you loosed –

The Hags of Clough   137

(*Change to easy tone*) Well, well. We'll talk again. My ladies
                                                                    first.
        What do you see?
SCHOLAR (*angry*) A mummery. No nunnery this.
        Seven cats in heat, their bellies to the stone.
MEPHISTOPHILIS The Hags of Clough, dear boy. My Specials, my
        Sweets prompts, familiars.
                              My place is on that stone.
        Excuse, excuse. I'm late. My darlings are
        Exhausted, conjuring me.

(*An odd rhythm of music forward*)

             And now I'm here. You see
        My eyes shine from the stone.
SCHOLAR (*angry*) Hallucination. Devil me
        With something to my size.
MEPHISTOPHILIS I sit upon
        A stone and shine. My darlings dance.
HAGS (*a little distant*) Dance.
SCHOLAR (*low*) Lord in your Trinity, O most
        Powerful Father, Son, and Holy Ghost,
        Treat this straying student as your own.
        Let me not be surprised.
                     (*Loudly*) This drollery is
        For children, for poor peasant souls.
                              Silly wives,
        Will even the lecherous cat's nine lives
        Be recompense for evil done?
        What can you value under the sun,
        You who must be nondescripts
        Between two worlds for all your shifts?

(*The music ends in background*)

HAG 1   Our Lord is here.
MEPHISTOPHILIS (*jovial*) Indeed. And truly *de facto*.
HAG 2   Another too, some other I
        Can scent.
                (*Furious*) Search round about, all you.
MEPHISTOPHILIS No.
HAGS ALL   Master says no?
MEPHISTOPHILIS Master says no. (*Jovial*) Now tell your news,
        What's best? What's first?

(*A gabble*)

Ladies, one
Must speak for all. Let seniority
Decide. (*Pause*) What, is none the eldest here?
(*He laughs jovially*) Well, let the worst give tongue.

(*All gabble*)

Ladies, one
Must speak for all.
You, sister, you.
Begin.

SCHOLAR (*low, intense*) Lord, let me not be
Surprised.
Now that I believe my gift is yours,
Let me not be surprised.

MEPHISTOPHILIS What's best, what's first?

HAG The earl, Lord, the one we haunt.

MEPHISTOPHILIS The Lord of Leitrim, eh?
Ah, yes.
You put in his head that he had killed
His lady wife.

ALL (*madly*) Yes, yes.

MEPHISTOPHILIS A stallion savaged her.
He tried to save her – if I am correct –

ALL (*madly*) You are, you are.

MEPHISTOPHILIS Ladies, please. One tongue for all.
Sister, you, tell all the story –

HAG (*protest*) But you know it, Lord.

MEPHISTOPHILIS Tell me again.

HAG She was about
To leave him, Lord. That earl is vain, he would
Not believe her –

HAG (*cackle*) So vain, so vain, he could not believe
His woman would affect another man.

(*Cackle of* Hags)

MEPHISTOPHILIS Ladies, please. One speaks for all.

HAG When she convinced him, he
Took down a whip –

ALL (*madly*) She ran, she ran. The stallion was
Rampaging on the lawn.

MEPHISTOPHILIS Ladies.

HAG Seek round about.

MEPHISTOPHILIS Darlings, my very own.

My mantle.

HAG   My Lord, I felt –

MEPHISTOPHILIS My love, all hell's on guard. Our councils are
Most private.

Ahum.

Continue, Sweet.

HAG   He festers for her.

HAGS (*madly*) A boil, a boil.

HAG   A boil that's coming to
A head.

HAGS (*madly*) We'll break the head.

MEPHISTOPHILIS A private sin
Can be concealed. Crimes in great places are.

HAG   We know, we know. But we'll spread rumours round.
And scandal is enough.

We start at Castlerea.

HAGS   Another suitor will match a horse
Against the earl's –

MEPHISTOPHILIS Does that mean anything
Except a friendly play?

HAG   My Lord, you know, you know.

MEPHISTOPHILIS (*jovially*) Refresh me, Sweet.

HAG   The earl will win the match,
The suitor will leave.

Nobody knows

The lady-daughter was at stake. Six times
We've watched it happen –

MEPHISTOPHILIS Is there no horse
To beat this earl's?

HAGS   None, not in this world. No jockey like
His jockey, Lord.

HAG   A man compelled to win,
And incorruptible.

Suitors

Have tried him.

MEPHISTOPHILIS And nobody knows
The daughter is at stake in every match?

HAG   Nobody, but soon shall.

(*Cackle*) We'll spread the tale,
We'll bruit the thing. We wait for him to win
At Castlerea.

MEPHISTOPHILIS And if he doesn't win?

HAG (*low, aback*) My Lord, he must. The horse –
MEPHISTOPHILIS The horse, he could be tripped.
HAGS (*madly*) Tripped, tripped.
MEPHISTOPHILIS It's possible. I heard it broached
     In some low public house.
               A velvet boy,
    A drunk, a turbulent.
            And that last fence
    Is hidden in a hazel clump – if I
    Remember right.
            A rope, he said. A rope
   Could do it.
        And I heard.
HAGS (*madly*) We'll seek him out. We will
    Destroy him, Lord.
MEPHISTOPHILIS Leave him for the moment. I will see
    To him.
       You, sister, answer me.
              This earl,
    Can he be cured?
HAGS (*madly*) No. No. No. No.
HAG (*low*) Our master must have the truth.
              He can
   Be cured.

  (*Murmur*)

    And there's a healer loose.

  (*Murmur*)

    We learn
    Of cures impossible.

  (*Murmur*)

    Tell Master all.
TWO HAGS (*sullen*) Some presence, some power in
    The neighbourhood beyond us.
ALL (*madly*) We cannot trace. We scour the place,
    Nose this and that.
           We cannot trace.
MEPHISTOPHILIS (*calmly*) I'll see to him.
HAG We've taken some precautions, Lord. We've made
    Our earl suspicious, he allows
    No strangers near –

HAGS IN TURN   I stopped his ears.
              His eyes, I.
              I in his mind,
              His flesh, I.
              I titillate
              And I subdue.
              We guard, we guard.
ALL   And direct him on the girl.
HAG   Besides, O Lord, this healer too
              Must know the cause, if he's to cure.
                   Even if he gain access
              Where every wall is sentry-walked, he must
              Know the secret thing, the cause of all.
MEPHISTOPHILIS   Well done, or should I say ill done.
              I take it, then, this earl cannot be cured
              Except I take a hand –
                        (*Jovial*) Turn healer, I
                                  Myself?
HAGS (*madly*) My Lord laughs.
              Smiles,
              Is merry.
MEPHISTOPHILIS   I woo you, ladies, and now must take my leave.
              A kiss for each sweet catskin first –
HAGS (*muted*) I swoon.
              The ecstasy.
MEPHISTOPHILIS (*ominous*)   Aye, make it last. Time's such a variable
              In hell.
                   Away now. No, not this way. That.
              Well, all away, away. Broomstick it, friends.
              Tuck up your tails, and fly.
                             Small souls. I see
              My scholar's not impressed.
                                  Yet we can do
              A cure together.
                        No?
                             A Christian chore
              That can't be done without me.
                                  No?
SCHOLAR (*low*) You're building up
              Another thing.
MEPHISTOPHILIS   Dear boy, I made a point. I've shown you how
              Your earl may be cured –
SCHOLAR (*angry*) My earl? –

142   *The Hags of Clough*

MEPHISTOPHILIS (*ignoring him*) Deceived my sweet
                    Familiars in doing so.
                                        Ahum.
          A Christian chore.
                              My daily dozen.
                                                Now
          Heal the old goat, if you wish. I give
          You my permission, Sir.
                                        Well, heal him then
          Without me.
                        No?
                              A noble earl, two feet
          In court. He'll make you. Royalty
          Ennoble you, I'm sure. You'll sire a new
          Blood-line, a gilded stock, have towers, towns,
          Incomes vast, a palace, ladies you
          May woo in broken French –
                                        if you refuse,
          A fool, a learned man who cannot see
          His nose.
                    A doting student, churl, an ass
          Without preferment, without a friend
          Among the great.
                              A silly scamp who airs
          A few bare Latin tags in taverns, who
          Being shown most uncanonical was condemned,
          Expelled from school –
                                    Thrown out,
                                            With half a tonsure still
          Unhealed upon his nob,
                                    The itching scab
          Of spoiled divinity.
                                Marsilius
          Ficinus had it right. All scholars have
          Soft heads. Who values them?
                                        All sophisters,
          Historians, rhetoricians, all those poor
          Et ceterae, grasshoppers once, if we're
          To believe your Socrates.
                                    He told the tale
          To Phaedrus
                        On some riverbank.
                                            They sat

Under a planetree's shade.
                              Grasshoppers chirred
With anger all that afternoon to be
Miscalled.
               Hos populus ridet.
                              Well, well.
I wander, eh.
                    You'll heal that earl, of course?
No?
          Still negative.
                              Well, the Devil's done.
                                        I'll take
My beating in good part.
                              Integrity
I do admire –
                    But paupers, Sir, wear out
Their lives for provender.
                              Homer must beg
If he want means – O, the fine future you
Deny a scholar.
                    I leave you now – as far
As I can leave a soul.
                              Goodnight, goodnight.
And no more nightmares, eh?
                              You've met the Prince
Of Darkness, and in simple silence talked
Him down.

(*An orchestra playing dance music in the background*)

SCHOLAR (*softly, hurriedly praying*)   Deliver me, O Lord.
          Out of the depths I cry unto you.
          The night is not done. Not yet is the night done.
          Temptation has not yet begun, deliver
          Me, O Lord. Let me not be surprised.

(Mephistophilis. *Heavy slow laughter*)

MEPHISTOPHILIS   Towers, turrets of
          Some castle. Rabbits on the lawn.
                              There's Tom
          The badger snuffling by the oak.
                              Sweet smells.
          This limetree droned all day with honeybees.
          O Summer world.

                (*Laugh*) A rout in progress too.
A chain of lamps along the terraces.
And music. O night of love.
                       Why, this, if I
Make no mistake, is Leitrim's lordly seat.
And someone is eighteen tonight.
Dear me, how time goes by.
                     I entertained
That whippet when she loved a Jock.

(*Music forward a bit*)

                       They go
To it young, those lasses of mad Jack's.
                    They fly
The kite, they hold court in the cot.
               My, here's beauty in
A night of garters. Lords, and soldier sons.
Stars, constellations.
              And ladies, ladies in
Sweet exhalations.
                 Whaleboned stuffs.
                   Ah, how
The delicate bubbles find the top.
                   Cry now
Si liceret, et si liceret.
              And yet
Not much, an honest show, poor country flesh.
No greater sinner there. No one that I
Inspire.
          Walk round, walk round.
                   No one
Inspired. No one beautiful accordingly.
And here's Mad Jack himself.
                 Ahum.
                 How he
Endows a chair, and glorifies it. Hum,
How goes it, Sir? How does the carcase feel
To be both sire and lover?
LEITRIM (*high*) Somebody spoke to me.
AN OLD MAN   None here but you and me. You were
       Expatiating on stud values, Sir.
       Most interesting.
LEITRIM (*normal*) Ahum. I thought, well, well. A stud.

The Hags of Clough

Three things required, sir, mark this well,
Ahum –
MEPHISTOPHILIS Ahum, ahum.
LEITRIM Ahum. The first –
MEPHISTOPHILIS Ahum –
LEITRIM Ahum, is soundness in foundation stock.
MEPHISTOPHILIS Ahum.
LEITRIM Ahum. The second is soundness. And the third –
MEPHISTOPHILIS Ahum.
LEITRIM Ahum, is soundness too.
OLD MAN You inbreed, Sir. You believe
In the close family –
MEPHISTOPHILIS Ahum.
LEITRIM Ahum. The major bloodlines are
Most inbred –
OLD MAN But don't you find incestuous linking makes
For poor fertility –
MEPHISTOPHILIS Ahum.
LEITRIM Ahum.
MEPHISTOPHILIS A sire to filly-daughter –
LEITRIM (*high*) Who mentioned sire and daughter?
OLD MAN Not me, not you.
LEITRIM (*normal*) Ahum. Well, perhaps, I had
Something like that in mind –
OLD MAN Too close, the kin's too close.
LEITRIM Well, well. Well, well.
MEPHISTOPHILIS (*low laugh*) O sweet small hymn of man. I pull
Sheepstrings apart.
And this is the body politic,
The sum of fifty thousand souls. Towns mark
Him with a monument. The steeples chime
When he's in progress.
Pastors peal his name.
Ahum.
LEITRIM Ahum.
MEPHISTOPHILIS He owns the house and the inhabitant,
The field, the grain, the orchard, the poor ass
That jogs to market.
He's Lord Keystone, he
Is King and Parliament, custom, he is law,
Observance. In this person is the whole
Platonic mirror of the universe –
So ordered, Sir, that if he falls,

The Hags of Clough

A world is shattered too.

                A local world,
I do admit.

           My oratory, Sir,
Does not impress.

                I fail again. You have
No interest in the body politic
Alas.

        And yet for a moment – almost you
Were visible.

             The healer moved.

                    I felt
The pity well.

            (*Heavily*) My ladies have
Distorted that poor brute.

                 Why not?

                  Sins of
Distortion are in pattern, they make up
The plan,

         man's portion too, his trial by
The very matter he assumes.

              And I,
What room have I in this? What part is mine?
(*Loudly*) I am distortion, Sir. I am the act
Of God that bleeds. I am the eternal flaw
In all, in all, the opposite, I am
The death in every birth, the fall, the fall
In all that flowers, tension I am in things,
Contention too and limitation, I
Am hate in love and I divide the seed
In two and set them on each other.
(*Pause. Heavily*) I have my place. I am an absolute.
And yet a Fakir with some holy lamp
Sets me awry, disturbs the balance which
Exists in all.

          Work in with me and you
Do lawful work.

            Hermes Tresmegisthus,
Your Paracelsus, mumbling mouth, had yet
Some divination. Neo-Platonists –
I figure in all discourses being there
Before discourse began.

             Indeed, I trimmed

The quills.
                    Invented alphabets. Ovens
For tables –
                    Ah.
                         I see you wear
Your armour against argument.
                                        Well, well.
I fail again.

(Music gives way to an Elizabethan folksong in background. Faint buzz of voices)

MEPHISTOPHILIS *(jovially)*   Dancing, wine, arrays
Of lovely ladies, perambulating Toms
Of course.
                    Shall I make you visible
To take potluck?
                         No?
                              Not lawful, eh?
Not lawful, eh?
                         A chamberer and so
Collected. Why, you'll live to moralise
To ladies past their best.
                                   Take offerings
On Sundays, Catechism classes, preach
From stumps of trees –
                              Then take a fall or two
From nature when you're good for nothing, old,
Unable.
              Walk around, dear boy. And take
Your pick. I shall arrange it.
                                        This? Or this?

(Low, breathless laughs of women)

Here's cream that floats a rose, here's gold
And cupid's mouth. Here's a tall tartar you
Could tame, a noble dame she is; and this
With the black brow, some devil here, the nose
Is Messalina's. Here's a pious mouth
That needs a tilter. Here's tamed tiger too
But burning bright in patches. Daphne here
In flight, ah pinch her, boy – like this –

(Girl's sudden half-scream, half-giggle)

                                              This one
Would bring Leander swimming, pinch her too.
Come wench it, boy, with one or all. I shall
Arrange it. Dinah, Esther, Judith, all
Will have a fling with you, Psyche drop
Her candle.
                        Caligula gave
One hundred thousand sesterces, his whore
Bought pins to hold her hair while Roman walls
Fell down.
                        Let lechery thrive.
                                        I see
We make a stir, our presence felt.

(*Muted merry laughter in background*)

                                    Come now,
Let us be visible. This is our night.
A balcony for Romeo. I'll not chalk up
The deed. No compliment. No payment asked.
Let us be visible.
                        They ask it of us
Now we've worked upon 'em. See. They wait
In pretty gaggles.
                        No?
                                That negative
Again.
(*Ominous*) Yet in a moment, lad, you'll wish
For flesh.

(*A gong. A hush*)

MASTER OF CEREMONIES Ladies and gentlemen, midnight comes.
                Upon the stroke my Lord would have you drink
                The birthday toast.
                                    Those wishing my Lady well,
                Please gather here.

(*Clink of glasses. A great clock chimes*)

MEPHISTOPHILIS (*jovial*) My hour, my boy; my boy, my hour.
                God steps from the machine.
LEITRIM   Ahum. Where is my daughter?
VICOMTE (*faint French accent*) I yield her, Sir,
                With great reluctance.
LEITRIM   Ahum. Please, step

Up on the dais, my love.
                                Your father first
Presents his compliments.
LADY   I thank my father.
LEITRIM   And for my present.
                                Throw open the great doors.
But first the toast. Ahum.
                                To my daughter, my
Dear daughter.

(*Clamour genteely muted. A colt neighs*)

Now bring my present in.

(*Horse hooves resound on the board floor*)

VOICES (*shrill women but muted*) The colt.

(*Colt neighs*)

O lovely animal.
                                A present for
A queen.
                                Majestic.

(*Colt neighs loudly*)

MALE VOICES (*disturbed*) Keep back.
LEITRIM   Ahum. A little room, more space. No need
For worry.
                                Jockey, let him come.
                                                My dear,
A loaf of sugar. he will nibble it –
LADY   This – animal, Father. Mine?
LEITRIM   My dearest possession, child.
LADY   But I hate him. I told you so.
I've nightmares –
LEITRIM   My dear, what nonsense.
                                See,
He answers to a word.
        (*Gives a small, sharp whistle*) See, Beauty, Beauty, worth
A ransom.

(*Colt nickers*)

Touch his nose.
                                You loved a horse,
Prayed me for bigger, faster ones when you

Were still knee-high.

And now, and now –

the most

Prized of all I have. Of everything.

LADY (*low. Pause*) I thank you, Father, for the colt.

LEITRIM Take the halter, child.

He's yours. Now lead

Him to the door.

He'll know you, and from this on,

He'll only follow you.

The halter, sweet.

LADY (*low*) Father –

LEITRIM (*authoritative*) Take it, child. Do as I say.

He's yours to lead.

(*Low*) Before the county to behave

Like this.

I have thrown in a town or two,

And you'll find jewellery in your closet, but

This – animal, as you miscall him, is

The very gem.

LADY (*low*) I dread him, Father. He is in

My sleep each night –

Yet.

Jockey, the halter, please.

(*Chorus of admiring guests*)

JOCKEY (*low*) What the hell are you afraid of? You're

His master now.

He knows it.

LADY (*cold, imperious*) The halter, please.

And follow me.

(*Clapping guests, climaxing in an acclamation. Suddenly, the wild savage neighing of the colt. Uproar*)

VOICES Hold him. Hold him.

(*Piccolo heard. Uproar dies. Piccolo in background. A sweet air*)

JOCKEY (*shaken*) By hell.

Unmanageable, yet

You held him.

LADY (*shaken*) I – held him.

JOCKEY Tamed him too.

LADY (*shaken*) I – I don't know. And yet – he is – obedient

If nothing more –

The Hags of Clough

LEITRIM (*shaken*) My child –

LADY   Hates me, I him. But – thank
     You for your present, Father

(*Hooves fade. Buzz of people moves into background*)

LEITRIM (*jovial*)   In a dream, Scholar?
                  Yet you calmed down
The colt, the visible colt.
               But there's the colt
She dreams of in the night, a stallion all
His molars showing.
            Forty-four teeth has the horse,
Incisors, canines, molars and pre-molars,
And he displays the mouthful every night
She sleeps.
       He roars upstairs.
              A nightmare
I foster fervently. She does not know
The creature is her father.
           His shadow thrown
Across the daughter, a future event that she
Unconsciously foresees.
          We are, of course,
All consciousness below, all timeless too –
But that's old hat –
         The devil can't instruct
The scholar.
      (*Laughs jovially*) Why, we're following the lady.

(*Faint hoof beats of a walking horse*)

How does this come? It's not my wish. And yet
We follow the lady.
       (*Arch*) Powers that be,
You have not fallen?
        A most imperious piece,
A head out of antiquity – but whose?
Lais of Corinth? Phryne of Thebes, which?
What jouster, what?
      That delicate jut
Of mouth, those nostrils in a flare, such brows,
Cupidinis arcus, Oh, that Roman, what's
Her name, she's dead, she's dead, Aretine's
Lucretia.

             The Hags of Clough

How matter does aspire
To be a healthy wench.
JOCKEY (*a bit distant*) I'll see to him, I say.
No need to trail those silks in dust. I'll see
To him, I say.
You've mastered him, now let
Me do the chores.
I'm paid for them. I'm Horse
The servingman. I tug my forelock to
Your ladyship.
Now let me do the chores
And save your silks.
You needn't put me in
My place. I know my place.
You mastered him,
Now let me have his head.
What's wrong, what's wrong?
If I said anything –
LADY (*quietly*) This brute, I did not quiet him. I was
Afraid, afraid.
But there was someone there –
Such quiet eyes, I felt them on me,
This
Mad brute and I –
And certainly I heard,
No, not heard, divined, some instrument.
A – piccolo –
JOCKEY (*loudly*) Piccolo? Piccolo, by hell, he came.
(*Loud sigh*) So, after all, he came.
And he could do it.
There was a covering stallion once I've seen
Convulse a fairgreen, he could do it, he
A mere child then –
My brother, lady, twin
To me.
A flip, a disappointment. He
Was born for great things.
(*Loudly*) So he came,
The pup, but how, but how?
LADY (*quietly*) Jockey.
JOCKEY (*loudly*) But I didn't see him. Yet
A piccolo, you say.
LADY (*quietly*) Tell me of your brother.

JOCKEY   A twin. He the bright, and I
          The glum. He towered over me. I left
          To find more room.
LADY   Continue.
JOCKEY (*heavily*) He had some power over things –
          Like birds, or beasts.
                            Sick people too – you know,
          The daft or half-daft –
                    (*Loud*) Even as a child,
          And now the country's creeping with queer tales
          Of things he's done.
                    But he's a bowsy now,
          A drunk. Tonight I floored the fop. I floored
          Him, floored him –
                    Gifted with everything
          He boozes it away. Great colleges
          Have thrown him out.
                    Well, here we are.

  (*Colt clops on cobble*)

          I'll bed him down.
LADY (*simple sigh*)   Smell of sweet straw.
JOCKEY (*busy*) Among
          Some other things. I'll lift the scalp
          Of that red whelp who does this box –
                    (*Suddenly in wonder*) But how
          Could he have come among the guests? That's what
          I want to know?
LADY   Tell me more.
JOCKEY (*rubbing colt down*) You've all the gist. And yet
          Not all.
               He's two in one, I think.
                          A capering drunk
          And then next moment starched, starched stiffer than
          The priest on Sunday.
                      Whoa there.
                              There, in
          The lantern you're like a child I knew.
LADY (*suddenly*) Why did you hit him, Jockey?
JOCKEY (*surprised*) Why – that's another tale.
LADY (*pause*) It's very peaceful here.
                    When that
          Colt tore the rein –

JOCKEY (*busy*) Forget it now –
LADY (*low*) And then the peace that came.
        A presence, but inside, inside me.
                          How could
        That be your twin?
JOCKEY I don't know, I don't know –
        But there's the piccolo –
LADY (*quickly*) And why should he come here?
JOCKEY (*flustered*) Well, I, well, I – asked him, do you see?
LADY Against all rules? My Lord will have your hair.
JOCKEY He's kin. I'm trusted.
LADY Jockey!
JOCKEY (*flustered*) I thought to save
        Him from himself.

  (*Peep of piccolo*)

        Did you hear a – noise?
        He's here, somewhere, by hell.
                      We'll look for him.
LADY (*calmly*) No.
JOCKEY No?
LADY I am of age tonight, grown up; a person now –
        Who must be sought.
                If Mister Piccolo-player
        Has forced his company on invited guests –
        Foisted himself –
                (*Lower. Another tone*) I see nobody in
        The yard. And not a sound.
                 Wait, there's a step,
        A footstep in the arch.
JOCKEY By hell.
LADY Jockey, if he has dodged
        The keepers, forced the wall, and sidled through
        The woods –
              I think most probably I shall
        Give him in custody.
JOCKEY And have the skin
        Stripped off his back?
LADY (*grandly*) I'll think of it.
                  There is
        Some question of impertinence. I could
        Have calmed the colt, now that I think of it,
        Now – that – I

The Hags of Clough

                          (*Low*) Jockey, shut the door.
                 Blow out the lantern. Quick.

VICOMTE (*distant*) My Lady – where –
JOCKEY   Suitor number seven.
                 And not too welcome. Why?
LADY (*coldly*) Is your twin like you?
                 A forward fellow?
VICOMTE (*nearer*) My Lady – where –
LADY (*sigh*) I do not know myself too well, it seems.
                 A boy who has bowed in many courts, a wit
                 And bright today, acceptable.
                                      And night
                 Has brought the moon, and gallantries, I am
                 Beamed upon by all –
VICOMTE   My Lady.
LADY   Yet here I huddle from a husband, steep
                 My gown in stinks of horse,
                               A jockey too
                 Who niffs of the animal.
                         I loved you once.
JOCKEY (*surly*) I know.
LADY   Eloped with you so often I grew tired
                 Of sitting on your crupper.
                         But you whored
                 It with my elder sisters.
                       Am I like them?
JOCKEY (*surly*) No.
LADY   What did I lack?
JOCKEY (*surly*)   A certain rot.
LADY   Oh. But I was willing – then.
                 I wanted you to be the first.
JOCKEY   The first?
LADY (*sigh*) Some sort of trial horse. Then I'd go on –
                 And on and on and on.
                       I'm beautiful
                 And well aware of it.
                       But quite corrupt,
                 Alas.
JOCKEY   Alas.
LADY   And so you spared the child
                 And spoiled a rod.
                 (*Affectionately*) Dear Jockey, thanks.
                            Now let us go.

JOCKEY   Us?

LADY   You'll sit up on the balcony – and if
           Your curious brother – well – you'll point him out
           If he is there.
                     But really, I shall –
           And certainly – feel, nose him out.
                               Come on.
           Unlatch the door.
                          Really, the night
           Seems most unaware of us.

JOCKEY (*low, with an effort*) My Lady.

LADY   Lady, yes. Back to formality
           We go.

JOCKEY   If you ever love, if – you take the dunt
           From some young sprig, I mean feel all that should
           Be felt –

LADY   Well?

JOCKEY   Well – indicate it, let
           The Jockey know.

LADY   Well, well.

JOCKEY   There's something – he would do, some help
           Some aid he'd render –

LADY   Would that be necessary?

JOCKEY (*swallowing*) Indeed, I – I – ah, forget it, Lady, I
           Am not myself tonight.

LADY   I've never seen you in this state before.

JOCKEY   Aye.

LADY   Your bad brother, meeting him –

VICOMTE (*near*) My Lady, Lady.

LADY   Bother.

VICOMTE   I thank the night
           That you are in it. I feared you had eloped
           With some moon-man, that some rosetree had snatched
           You up –
                     Oh, Jockey, you.

JOCKEY (*surly*) Myself.
                     Lady, I'll go ahead
           And take my place.

VICOMTE   My arm, Lady. It
           Has missed you very much.

LADY   Surprising.

VICOMTE   Surprising, why –

LADY   I mean the night, surprising night. I feel

Everything happening –
VICOMTE (*grimly*) Here's one intrusion, Ma'am,
　　　　　Not unexpected.
　　　　　　　　　　Father's footman, see.
　　　　　As usual.
　　　　　　　　　How many moments have
　　　　　I had alone with you?
LADY　　　You twittered on
　　　　　My windowsill one night. You lost me too
　　　　　In my own shrubberies, for bits of gold
　　　　　You bought my gillie and all but drowned me in
　　　　　Lough Derg.
　　　　　　　　　What is it, Blake?
FOOTMAN His Lordship's compliments, Ma'am –
　　　　　　　　　　　　　　He'd be obliged
　　　　　If you'd attend him in the drawingroom.

　　(*Pause*)

VICOMTE Dear Papa.
　　　　　　　　　Great Argus has a hundred eyes
　　　　　And all on one small daughter –
LADY (*sharply*) Sir.
VICOMTE Forgive me. I'm bitter, yes,
　　　　　But puzzled more.
　　　　　　　　　I'm eligible, I
　　　　　Can match you in acres, manors, towns;
　　　　　I'm recommended here, I have a tree
　　　　　To Charlemain –
　　　　　　　　　And you have looked on me
　　　　　With kindness too –
　　　　　　　　　(*Urgent*) Lady, elope with me,
　　　　　I've laid a chain of horses to the port,
　　　　　Forgive me, there's no other way. I love
　　　　　You, all the rest will follow. Believe I love
　　　　　You honourably –
　　　　　　　　　Here's a great moment now
　　　　　And I must choke.
　　　　　　　　　(*Low*) Tonight your eyes lit up
　　　　　For this poor fellow – now, I'm bold, but there's
　　　　　No time, no time – you favoured me, I say,
　　　　　With looks that must belong to love –
LADY (*calmly*) Wait, Sir.
　　　　　　　　　You're further than

　　　　　　　　　　　　　　　The Hags of Clough

I wish to go. Love is another thing –
I think, though what it be, or what
It means to me or any woman, I
Don't know.
                    I hoped you were the man to tell
Me – but –
                    I sleep as usual. I do. My head's
Not turned, not yet. And you must show me if
It can, and make me mope and sigh and all
The rest. In time you might, indeed,
In time, how do I know?
                                   But there's no time.
Elope with me, you say. Tonight.

VICOMTE   It must be tonight. My love, my love,
Don't fail me now. Love will follow, love
Will come.

LADY   A moon, a gallop of horses, father's men
Behind us. Once I could have thrilled to it –
And now – the ballad's for another.
                                          There's
Some dignity involved.
                              It seems I am
Grown up.
                Grown up, that's it. And to be wooed
Again – I fear.

(*The ballroom in the background growing*)

Grown up. And in an hour.
Surprising night. All things are happening
At once, I can't tell how.
                              I'm eighteen, Sir,
Since midnight struck. Do I look different?

VICOMTE (*groan*) Most beautiful.

LADY   Now let us in.

LEITRIM   Ahum. You're late, quite late. You were –

LADY (*lightly*) Nightwalking, Sir.

LEITRIM   In, my Lady. We
Will follow.
                (*Pause*) Ahum, if I understand
You've horses stabled in some towns, my Lord,
Towns that go seaward.

VICOMTE (*calmly*) What of it? No matter now;
The lady has refused. And so our match

Still goes.
                    It's folly, I've no horse
            To cope with yours.
LEITRIM   Ahum, you can withdraw.
VICOMTE   And leave, as per that compact you
            Compelled.
                    I have a week.
                            That match is mad,
            The custom barbarous. Some fool stud-raised
            May win her in the end, some fellow with a mane
            And tail, who'll neigh, Sir, neigh.

(*The music fully forward a moment*)

            She should have Wits
            Around, great men with names. And boys with harps.

(*Fading*)

            And poets, oh, goose-quills in libraries
            Would labour for this ladyship –

(*Fade*. Mephistophilis' *jovial chuckle*)

MEPHISTOPHILIS They thronged the gates
            Three-fold to see Lucretia. This, too,
            Could be a famous saunterer. She'll sail
            The seashell yet.
                    Go in and dance. I'll make
            You visible.
                    No?
                            Not even for this?
                                    And yet
            You're moved, you're moved.
                            (*Chuckle*) I'll leave you now.
            Poor soul, she's fallen to your ghost; see how
            She searches,
                    Dances, finding, filling up
            Some drifting footprints that Herodias
            Left on a marble floor.
                            The head was on
            A silver dish, her little feet red-soled;
            She danced into a deadman's gaze.
                            (*Loudly*) You're moved,
            You're moved.
                    (*A vast chuckle*) Enough tonight. At Castlerea

The Hags of Clough

We'll end the joust.

     (*Ominous tone*) First, let me make it plain.
You cure this earl at your peril; now
I've shown the way, I am the healer, Sir,
And you my scholar.

     (*Laughs slowly*) Of course, you may trip a horse
At Castlerea,

    a sly way out.

      The horse
Is a silly quadruped.

      Goodnight. Goodnight.
(*Silence. Plover call. Far off, a cat. A snore*)

BULLER (*coming in*) Mart, move over on the pack.

MARTY (*sleepily*) You didn't say your prayers.

BULLER (*a bit drunk*) I was thinking.

      Money, Mart.
A golden shower.

MARTY Ah, go asleep.

BULLER A shower of gold.

MARTY That big behind of yours
Is pushed into my bailiwick.

BULLER (*heavily*) We'll trip a horse
   At Castlerea.

MARTY (*little squeal of terror*) Would you make
   Me gallows meat?

BULLER A hundred to one.

MARTY (*shrilly*) Don't speak of it. I'll leave
   Your company.

     That Scholar, there's no luck in him.

BULLER (*hiccup*) A gentle fellow. A noble wit. When Buller hits
   The purple I'll remember him.

      (*Louder*) Scholar.

MARTY Let him sleep.

BULLER Gave me the tip, out of the horse's mouth.
   (*Fading*) Out of the horse's mouth.

COMMENTATOR The horse's mouth,
   And forty-four teeth has the horse;
   Eat, horse,
   And you'll get grass of course.

   But what of the horse
   That rides the jock, the horse that goes
   Roaring upstairs
   To gobble up a rose?

The races of Castlerea. (*The sounds of a race course. A merry folkdance in the background. Suddenly, a piccolo melody*)

BULLER (*excitedly*)   He's here, the gentle soak.

                                            Hey, Scholar, hey.

COUNTRY VOICE   Mister, be quiet. Let him play.

BULLER   Scholar.

VOICES (*angrily*) Hush.

BULLER   Be damned to that. Here's Clancy calling on
        A friend.

 (*Piccolo stops*)

        Scholar.

SCHOLAR (*hiccup*) The bully pedlar. On the rounds
        Of roguery.

                Sit down, drink water, pull

        A face. I see you have a rope.

BULLER (*low. Aback*) A rope.

SCHOLAR   Under your coat, around your waist.

BULLER   My bellyband. I suffer from
        The wind.

 (*Piccolo*)

          . Lord, you see all, do you
        See courage in me? I've lost it by the way.
        And all my money on.

                (*Whisper*) They stationed a guard
        At every fence.

 (*Piccolo*)

                You never thought of that.
        I'm broke.

SCHOLAR   Good – have a drink. We'll butter up
        Your whistle. Give this journeyman a jar –

 (*Piccolo*)

GIRL (*breathlessly*) Are you the piper's friend?

BULLER   Aye, you could call me that –
        Last week.

GIRL   Who is he? Who is he? Will I sit upon
        Your knee and hold your glass –

                        Oh, the large
        Potations he puts down. He has us all
        Dancing mad and worse. We're all in love

With him. Look at his lov–el–y
Little ladycollar.
COMMENTATOR (*accompanied by piccolo*)
                The pied fellow
                Of Hamelin, one foot red and one foot yellow,
                Piped away rats.
                I pipe to bats.

                He was ratsbane,
                Untroubled by his gift, a fairy man:
                I, Christian colour,
                Know Christian dolour.

   (*Piccolo ends. Sounds of dancing stop*)

A LOUD VOICE The great earl's coming up the course.
EXCITED VOICES   Out, out, let me out.
GIRL   Gentle fellow, will you come with me?
SCHOLAR (*hiccup*) Do you think I should?
GIRL   We'll see the earl.
SCHOLAR   I'm blind.
GIRL   Blind?
SCHOLAR   To earls. And to – earls' daughters, dear,
             Most definitely blind.

   (*Piccolo peep*)

                Why am I here
                If that be true?

   (*A great distant cheer*)

GIRL (*excitedly*)   I'm off, I'm off. I couldn't miss
                The sight.
BULLER   A guard on every fence.
                            Why are you here?
SCHOLAR   Don't know – a silken thread – (*hiccup*)
                            As yours is gold.
             Indeed, how did I come?
                    No memory –
             And that is odd. That's very odd.
BULLER   You took
             A good dunt from the Jock that night.
                         Come on,
             We'll take a look. I'd like to see
             Riches roll by.

SCHOLAR   I'll sit and say
              A little prayer – Indeed, how did I come?
BULLER (*a little distant*) The world is here, velvet and silk. They say
              The great pavilion cost a mint. It's roped
              And tassled, silver plate inside, with maids,
              And footmen at all entrances. Along
              The rope are bullies, Leitrim's cudgellers.

(*Distant cheer*)

              He's coming up the course. Bullies keep back
              The crowd. My, there's a press.
                                He's coaching four
              Dark bays himself.
                      A noted whip.
                                The girl on
              The box as well.
                      Now there's an ivory piece
              That won't sell cheap. Dear Lord, I wish I were
              A millionaire.

(*Continuous cheering*)

              Buller, close your eyes
              On Fortune. So.
                      I bartered all
              I had with Mart. I begged and borrowed more,
              And staked it, Scholar,
                          Taking the hint;
              Trip him, says you, the bloody colt.
                              Are you
              Going out?
SCHOLAR   Out?
BULLER   You're on your feet.
SCHOLAR (*surprised*) Why, so I am.
                      That's odd. That's very odd.
GIRL (*breathlessly*)   Gentle fellow, come
              And see the lady. Royalty is on
              The ditch today, the world is gaping, Sir.
SCHOLAR   Whoops, I go the other way.
GIRL   No, no. If you miss this
              You'll sorrow for a year –
SCHOLAR   The other way. (*Hiccup*) A year
              Is nothing to eternity.
                    Whoops, I'm –

	Falling –
GIRL	Oh –
SCHOLAR	Grounded, eh.
GIRL	Give me your hand –
SCHOLAR	*Nil mortalibus ardui est*, which means
	Stand up yourself.
GIRL	Lord, so drunk. I thought
	You'd be my squire today.
SCHOLAR	'Bye, my friends. I'm for
	The West.

                    I'll buy a currach and a still,
And, surfeited, die of one or t'other at
The earliest date.

BULLER (*low*) Far gone.

  (*Piccolo peep*)

SCHOLAR   This is my left croob, this
My elegant righthand shoe;
Please God, they never kiss
And throw me out of – true.

  (*Merry phrase of piccolo. A crowd, merry*)

VOICES (*merry*) The merry piper.
SCHOLAR   Friends, a little room.
Here's a leg – in scholar-prate –
That wlll not toe the line.
My nethers are out of date.

  (*Piccolo*)

VOICES   Room, room for the merry piper.
SCHOLAR   So merry that I laugh
On both sides of my face.
Steady, legs, for once
You carry the state of Grace.

  (*Pip of piccolo. A loud fanfare follows. Horses and a carriage heard*)

      Good Lord, where have I come?
MERRY VOICE Leitrim's passing, Sir.
Push out here if you'd see.
SCHOLAR   No, no, the other way for me.
MERRY VOICE Sir, it's a sight.

                Lads, lift him. Here
You are, Sir, here's a place. The best.

SCHOLAR (*hiccup*) It seems I, willynilly,
Must look down on a lord.

(*A laugh*)

Hoist me up a peg,
Then he must make a leg.

(*Peep of piccolo. Laughter*)

AN ANXIOUS VOICE   Scholar, he saw, he heard.
SCHOLAR (*hiccup*) Pish, of no account.
Nothing under that old front.
WARNING VOICES (*hushed*)   Scholar, scholar.
Let him down, lads. Quick. The cudgel-men
Are out –
SCHOLAR   Am I down then? Very well. Christian size
Is best. (*Hiccup*)
WORRIED VOICE   You'll have to run for it.
SCHOLAR   I do not run
From any enemy.
I merely walk away
With dignity.

(*Pip of piccolo*)

WORRIED VOICE   Lads, gather round him here. Those
Big bullies will break him into bits.
SCHOLAR   I never dodge,
Or hide or flee.
I merely walk away
With dignity.
VOICES RAISED   Keep off, keep off.
A BULLYING ROAR   I want that fellow there.
VOICES   Keep off, keep off.
SCHOLAR (*hiccup*) Am I a cause
For altercation?
A ROARING VOICE ABOVE HUBBUB   Take him, lads. By God,
We'll get him.
VOICES   Gather round, gather round.

(*Blows, shouts, etc.*)

SCHOLAR (*hiccup*) Dear friends, allow
A man to kill his own – like this, like this,
And bury one – like that. Just kick a shin –
This way, a kneecap, that, or black an eye

And butt a nose –
Oh –
The – light – has gone.

(*Silence. A jangle of music*)

SCHOLAR (*muffled*) Ah me, ah me.
> A scholar is in pain.
> This student's reverie
> Is pain, and more pain.

> Plato, friend,
> My dear republic lies
> Up on its nether end
> Gaping up at the skies.

> Poets, shape up
> To all the bullyboys, God rot 'em.
> Fight to the last drop.
> Up, Bards, and at 'em.

JOCKEY   He's waking up.
LADY   Bring warm water, Jockey.
JOCKEY   I'll see to him myself.
LADY   Bring the water.
JOCKEY (*angrily*) Water, there's water here
> And in a bucket too. Good brother, take
> The bloody lot, the horse's portion.
SCHOLAR (*choking*) So – blessings flow – apace,
> *O fons Bandusiae –*
JOCKEY (*impatient exclamation*) There he goes.
SCHOLAR   I smell –

A horse.

(*Pip of piccolo*)

> Good brother horse.
> I see I've come
> To Caesar's tent.
JOCKEY (*acidly*) Leitrim's and my master's.
> A prisoner.
> (*Angrily*) Breaching the peace, by hell.
> Warm water, says
> My lady.
SCHOLAR (*quickly*) Lady.
JOCKEY   The other side of you.
SCHOLAR (*quietly*) Forgive me. So much happens on

	My sinister side – I keep an eye on it.
LADY	Remain where you are.
SCHOLAR (*low*)	Lady, I
	Was going the other way. Truly, I
	Was wending West, some vague appointment with
	An ocean –
JOCKEY	Wandering, by God.
LADY	Don't get up.
SCHOLAR	Must –
	Be on my way –
LADY	Steady him, Jockey.
SCHOLAR	Just man falls – seven times.
LADY	Arrange
	The pillow, get me water, towels, soap.
JOCKEY (*surly*)	No business for you. A serving maid's
	Or mine –
LADY (*imperious*)	Jockey.
JOCKEY	All right. I'll do it. Then out
	He goes –
	This arm is broken, collarbone,
	By God, as well –
	A mess. Now, what the hell
	To do? I'm riding this next match, I can't
	Be everywhere.
LADY	Get water first. I am afraid his head –
	(*Low*) It could be broken.
	Can you open your eyes?
	He's out, quite out.
JOCKEY	I'll get the water.
MEPHISTOPHILIS (*jovial chuckle becoming louder*)	In the arms of –
	Morpheus, is it? Or some royal love?
	Queen Dido cradled some great Trojan thus,
	Aeneas was his name –
	And so you came
	To Castlerea?
SCHOLAR	You brought me –
MEPHISTOPHILIS	A face, a lady's face, not I.
	You followed it.
	I did, indeed, arrange
	Some other items of procedure –
	That
	Riot certainly.
	(*Chuckle*) To bring the man

Unto the lass, and supervise – a bit –
A little –
    (*Ominous*) Breaking an arm, a collarbone,
A wrist as well, and you have ricked a knee;
So, friend, no nonsense. You're incapable
And cannot trip that horse –
                Which is, indeed,
A lucky thing because the guardian on
One fence is drunk, asleep too –
              but you know
All that.

(*Peep of piccolo*)

You brought the bottle.
           Now, know this,
The outcome will be this. You risk four lives,
The Frenchman's first – for Leitrim will shoot him down;
Two pedlars afterwards and then your twin –
And after all that the lady remain unwed.

SCHOLAR   You make a case, I – take a chance –

MEPHISTOPHILIS   On murder? Mortal sin –

(*Piccolo*)

SCHOLAR (*mock*)   Tutor me on mortal sin. I trip
A horse, a lady weds, and she is saved
From you, that's all.
        The rest is God's. I need
Not see beyond my nose. I can abide
Inside my human limitations.
          That
Is what I do.
      I hid a rope inside a fence,
I'll pull it –
      Then drift westward, any place
Where souls are ill. I'm certain now, quite sure
My power comes to me untouched by you.
So if God wills –

MEPHISTOPHILIS   Hah.

SCHOLAR (*loud firm*)   So if God wills and gives me back my first
Vocation, I'll take oils and orders, serve
Inside the Church –

MEPHISTOPHILIS   Hah, Hah-hah.

(*Loud rumbling laughter. Silence*)

LADY (*coming forward*) No fracture that I see.
            Your eyes are open.
SCHOLAR (*drowsy*)   Yes, wide open now.
            (*Yawns*) Also my mouth, it seems.

                                          How do I leave
            This gaol?
LADY (*cold*) I fear – you don't.

    (*Piccolo*)

                        You're father's prisoner
            For one thing, Sir.
SCHOLAR   And broken limbs, you say.
            Still – Onward, Christian soldier.

    (*Piccolo mocks*)

                                          Rise and walk.
            There. Up. Take over, legs. Oh.
                                  A wrist, he said,
            And I have ricked a knee.
                              Lady, you're in
            My debt for some – small wounds. I pass it up
            For you are beautiful.
LADY (*cold*) You're what they say,
            A drunken boy, and most impertinent,
            Abandoned –
                        now, indeed, a muddy wretch.

    (*Piccolo*)

            Yet something more, I think.
                              How have you sunk
            So low? Your eyes, too, are too bold for one
            So young –
SCHOLAR   Lady, I must leave.
LADY   Indeed? How will you leave?

    (*Piccolo*)

                              The guards
            Are on the rope.
                        Why do you wish to leave?
            Is some poor wanton waiting?
                                  Stay and wash.
            I'll find you something to put on.
                                  Stay here.

I'll see you past the guards.
                              I don't know why
I do this thing. You'll sink much lower yet.
Poor jockey – which reminds me, Sir –
                                        One night –
When I was seventeen – we could have met.
Now, where?

(*Piccolo*)

SCHOLAR   Ovid. Catullus, in Petronius,
          Written down by love's left hand.

(*Slight pause*)

                                        Lady, I
          Must go.
LADY (*deep breath*)   Abominable.
                              I will get a coat
          Since I have promised.

(*Pause. Sounds of a racecourse intrude. Horses' hooves. Cheering*)

SCHOLAR   Friend –
GUARD   Hey, you –
SCHOLAR   Open the rope, friend.
GUARD   Aren't you the man –
SCHOLAR   The rope, friend. You're here
          To keep men out, not in –
GUARD   Why, that's fact, but you –
SCHOLAR (*sternly*) Open.
GUARD (*submissively*) All right, all right. But in a minute I
          Will see the catch.
                              Here, out you go.

(*Piccolo*)

          By Christ, he must have dazzled me. By Christ –
COMMENTATOR   The steps we take,
              The forward and the back,
              Are ours indeed –
              But who laid out the track?

              Angel and demon are
              Great powers, it seems –
              Or wishful images laid bare
              In our conflicting dreams.

The last fence. Stiff brushwood, a broad dyke full of water. At one side, propped up, is the sleeping guard.

(*Drunken snores*)

Some yards away the hazelwoods begin, miles of rocks and hazel. Our drunken scholar slips out to the fence and feels for the rope.

(*Far off, the starting bell*)

That's the starting bell. The sounds of the course are muted here. Our scholar searches for the rope.

SCHOLAR   Gone.
MEPHISTOPHILIS (*jovially*)   I took the liberty
                                        My ladies dropped
         Hints in high places.
DISTANT CHEER   The first fence, well over all.
SCHOLAR   Gone.

(*Large laughter of* Mephistophilis)

MEPHISTOPHILIS   The Devil, Sir, looks to his own.
         I see the bully pedlar in the woods,
         His head down on his knees.
DISTANT CHEER   The second fence, well over all.
MEPHISTOPHILIS (*jovial*)   Let us sit down and talk about dead things.
         You don't give over easily.
                                        A plan
         Is forming in your mind.
                                 (*Vast, ironic*) Poor boy, you're living in
         A sort of poem. And really I see
         Some tendency to suicide.
                                        That way
         Or the other, boy, you'll come to me.
DISTANT CHEER   Fourth fence, fourth fence, well over all.
MEPHISTOPHILIS   Women is the poet's fiction, Sir.
         The poet's diction too.
                                        This wish of yours
         Towards suicide now, you say believe in God –
         Yet furnish the contradiction if you die.
         It's suicide to throw yourself against
         This galloping horse.
DISTANT CHEER   The fifth, well over all.
MEPHISTOPHILIS   And the others who will die.
         It's murder, fellow, murder that masquerades

172   *The Hags of Clough*

In decent motives – why, you strut along
                  Shedding blood in lovely odes – as if
                  The whole thing were a song.
DISTANT CHEER   The sixth, well over all.
MEPHISTOPHILIS   So you're determined. So be it.
DISTANT CHEER   The seventh, well over.
MEPHISTOPHILIS   So as murderer and suicide
                  You'll come to me.
DISTANT CHEER   The eighth, well over all.
MEPHISTOPHILIS (*loud, threatening*)   As murderer and suicide –
SCHOLAR   Be quiet, you distract me. What I do
                  Is all for love –
DISTANT CHEER   The ninth, well over.
SCHOLAR   For foolish woman who –
MEPHISTOPHILIS   Will never know your sacrifice, who would
                  Prefer to lie with you.
DISTANT CHEER   The tenth, well over.
SCHOLAR   You bar the way. I am
                  Not lost enough to take her from your hands.
DISTANT CHEER   The eleventh fence, Oh, over, over.
                  And all together still.

  (*Distant hooves*)

SCHOLAR   Well, here's the end. A man will die
                  At any rate.
                              And better die for love
                  Than lesser things –
SUDDEN TUMULTUOUS ROAR Jockey's away, away.
                  A winner –
MEPHISTOPHILIS   In just one hour
                  On this small patch of grass, two men will fight
                  A duel.
                          One will die. The first. You'll hear
                  And – weep for it, a murderer. I like
                  You, Scholar – in my way of course. I like
                  To see a boy enjoy a lady – all
                  This cold Platonic thing is devil's work –

  (*Hooves very near. Continuous cheering. Jockey's voice*)

SCHOLAR (*low*) Out of my way. (*Louder*) Out of my way.
MEPHISTOPHILIS (*jovial*) Well, well. A devil must give way
                  Occasionally.

  (*His huge laughter for a moment. Jockey's shout. Thunder of hooves. Horse, etc.*)

The Hags of Clough   173

SCHOLAR   Up, fellow.
                    Mind out, mind out.

(*A crash. A low moan. The distant echoing laughter of* Mephistophilis. *A horse goes by urged by a French voice*)

COMMENTATOR   Lord, forgive this boy
                His pity, pity;
                Lord, forgive this boy
                His book of poetry.

SCHOLAR (*low wonder*) Buller.
BULLER (*urgent whisper*) Hush, stay down, stay down.

(*Pause*)

                A duel with pistols. Leitrim's fighting mad.

(*Two distant shots*)

                O loving God, the Frog is down.
                                    Now, look,
                I'll leave you here. I carried you and crawled
                This far.
                        Tonight myself and Marty will
                Collect you –
                        (*Deep breath*) Scholar, a hundred to one. You brought
                It off for me.
                            We'll bring you to Elphin
                In easy stages, hidden in the cart,
                But no one knows about you, not a one –
                If Jockey holds his tongue.
COMMENTATOR   Penitence
                Is setting all the sins
                In time and relevance
                Against their origins.

                Condemn, condemn,
                But take up life you must,
                And trying all again
                Take God on trust.

Six months later, the Bishop's palace in Elphin.

BISHOP   Palace. A raindown thatch. I have
           A drop upon my nose since I came here.
           Send that scamp up to me.
HOUSEKEEPER   Your nephew is

No scamp – the only doctor in these parts.

(*Piccolo merry*)

        Come in, and cure old Temper here. My feet
        Are worn with answering bells.
SCHOLAR   Dear Uncle.
BISHOP (*imitating*)   Dear Uncle. Aren't you afraid
        To face me?

(*Piccolo*)

        No? Guess why I sent for you?
SCHOLAR   Stomach aches.
BISHOP   I have a doctor. Do I need a quack?
        (*Roar*) And put away that flute.

(*Piccolo*)

        (*Mild*) No, pipe away.
        It seems in character.
                     I'm worried, half
        Out of my mind.
                (*Roar*) I'm cursed with gossips in
        This diocese.
              (*Lower*) You heal the sick, they say,
        And by no rational means.
SCHOLAR   Say 'obvious',
        Not rational, and I'll concede the point.
BISHOP   Aye, aye, schoolmaster me. Go on.
                   (*Roar*) What are
        You doing with that pencil?

(*Piccolo*)

SCHOLAR   Dear Uncle, you
        Are dying of your diet – so to speak.
        This sheet, keep to it.
BISHOP   Wait.
SCHOLAR   Fats – are furies, Sir.
BISHOP (*roar*) Are you telling me
        To mind my business?

(*Piccolo*)

        (*Lower, milder*) Tell me how you cure –
        And ease my mind. (*Roar*) Not that I want it eased,
        I want an argument to down a fool.

(*Mild*) I know you're good, well, reasonably so.
You'd never league with Hoof and Horns –

                                   I know

The question is impertinent, I do
Not put it of myself.

                       You're troubled too,
You walk the floor all night, and that could be
One way to God – or Satan –

                     (*Roar*) How do I know
If you won't talk to me? You are my blood
And I'm your confessor, and yet since you
Came home half-mauled, you prowl the hills and talk
To Tom and Jack, but never to your uncle.
(*Normal*) And those bosthoons, those mountain-men up there
Make witch doctors. I cannot silence some
Bad priest but they'll make use of him.

                          You dropped
A pious hat in Louvain, but some oils
Remain, you see; they'll make a halo from them –

SCHOLAR (*quietly*) No.
BISHOP (*pause*) No. Well, go on. It's your turn now.
SCHOLAR (*quietly*) You can rest easy, Sir. Whatever I do
          Has no help from the Devil –

                      Not that I
          Work miracles.
BISHOP   I know, but how –
SCHOLAR   My presence calms. I seem
          To understand – and share; that's all – except
          I give out – out of superfluity in myself –
          Something they need, some joy, some sanity.
          I shift the furniture a bit, that's all.
BISHOP   And Satan –
SCHOLAR (*sigh*) Does not intrude –
BISHOP   You are assured?
SCHOLAR   I know – his presence, Sir. And his
          Proceedings.
BISHOP (*low*) You do?
SCHOLAR (*sigh*) Or thought I did. Yet he can prophesy.
          Has Marty been around –
BISHOP   Marty?
SCHOLAR   The pedlar, Mart. He's on my mind all day –
          The little man –
BISHOP   Who brought you home, why he, why him?

SCHOLAR (*pause. Low*) It's a long story.

BISHOP (*low*)   Shall I put on
        The stole?

SCHOLAR (*brooding*) I was warned, Uncle, by Satan himself,
        That Mart, and others, would die did I persist
        On a – certain course.
                    One man died, and died
        Exactly as foretold.
               I took the risk –
        A woman was in it, one – I seemed to love –
        And at that time all that I did opposed
        All Satan asked of me.
                Now – I walk the floor
        At night.
           And wonder.
               (*Quickly*) My intervention did
        No good but ill. Four innocents will die
        If he has prophesied correctly.
                  One –
        Already dead –
                The girl in the hands
        Of beastliness

BISHOP (*firm*) You held a course
        In opposition to old Hoof and Horns?

SCHOLAR   It was not – difficult. I believe in God –

BISHOP   The woman was offered you?

SCHOLAR   She was the bait.
        Her father is – obsessed –

BISHOP   Explain that word –

SCHOLAR   Obsessed – sinfully – with her –

BISHOP   Incestuously – be plain, be plain,
        I deal with sinners –

SCHOLAR   Yes –

BISHOP   And she, the woman –

SCHOLAR   A girl, and innocent –
               (*Low, wrung*) I cannot go to her.
        He bars the way. He showed how I could heal
        The father –

BISHOP (*sharply*) Could you have healed
        Without him?

SCHOLAR   I had no wish to try. At that time, Sir,
        I – doubted the sources of my gift –

BISHOP (*roar*) Those old bald men

In Louvain –

SCHOLAR (*low, wrung*) Even if I could gain admittance there,
And that's impossible – that old earl is
So hedged around –

BISHOP (*sharply*) Wait. Hold there.

                              I am
A soul-saver too, the only one
Anointed in this family.

                          It seems
To me, to put it plainly now, you take
More on your shoulders than a layman can.
Kneel down, and pray a while. And then we'll talk
Under the holy seal.

                    I am relieved
Things are no worse

SCHOLAR This lady, Sir –

BISHOP We'll speak of her.

                     So she's the real hurt
Inside you, eh? We'll speak of her.

                     (*Loudly*) And so
You foiled him, foiled old Hoof and Horns himself,
And now he's got you doubting that you won.
We'll start with that.

                  Give me my stole. It's there
On that pre-dieu.

                 Four men, you said. One dead
Already. When?

SCHOLAR Six months ago. Midsummer Day –

BISHOP Exactly as he prophesied?
Well, that's six months ago. And no one of
The others since?

               Give me the stole. I'll feel
More comfortable with it on.

                 That, too,
Is on your conscience, eh? You think he tricked
You to it?

        Well, well.

          Kneel down

             A weight of care
For one so young.

        A woman too. I hoped
One day I might ordain you –

             now, oh, well,

A woman has her place.
                              The other three
Are still alive, you say. The Master of Lies,
He could be lying, feigning.

(*Knock at the door*)

                    Who is there?
HOUSEKEEPER Who else but me? Who'd face your tongue?
BISHOP (*roar*) Be off out of that
HOUSEKEEPER I've news, most awful news.
BISHOP   Be off – what news?
HOUSEKEEPER Be off, he says, what news.
                              The worst
Could happen in a Christian land. What worse
Than murder?
BISHOP (*irately*) The Lord look down on me.
                              (*A roar*) Go on, go on.
Who's killed, and why, and where, and when?
Another drunken squabble, or some boor
Boycotted, this poor diocese –
HOUSEKEEPER Ah, hould your whistle.
                              None
But little Mart the pedlar –
BISHOP (*pause*) Who?
HOUSEKEEPER The pious little man
Who calls with holy candles, found out there
Near Turlough chapel, dead, and all his goods
Strewn wild.
BISHOP (*calmly*) Number two.
HOUSEKEEPER What's that?
BISHOP   Never mind. Send Father Paton word
I want to see him.
                    (*Roar*) Off with you now.

(*Pause*)

                    Lord rest his soul. Kneel down, my son.
COMMENTATOR   Ease the heart.
                    No man is built
                    To play God's part.

                    Now we can start
                    Whatever God has willed.
                    Now we can start.

The Hags of Clough   179

Some days later our student is on his way to medical school in Paris. He stops at the post inn in Athlone.

(*Noises of an inn*)

FOLKSINGER (*forward a minute*)
> The harvest over, to her door
> Went I, poor stocac; I went to woo;
> But her mother said no, here's a lad without treasure,
> And the colleen he marries will never wear a shoe.

INNKEEPER Dublin-bound, eh? You've missed the coach.

SCHOLAR I'll stay the night.

INNKEEPER I'll call the girl. Dilly, Dilly.
> (*Ringing of table bell*)
>   Devil take it, there's
> A hectoring fellow here – coming Sir,
> Four whiskies, one with butter in it.

SCHOLAR (*exclamation*) Butter?

INNKEEPER (*snarl*) Butter, ever hear the like?

SCHOLAR A pedlar ordered it, a broad red man?

INNKEEPER You're wrong first time. A Dublin merchant, Sir.
> A carriage and pair, and coming from some funeral
> Beyond Elphin.

BULLER (*middle distance*) Landlord, landlord.

(*Table bell*)

INNKEEPER I'm melting the butter, Sir.

BULLER (*drunk*) Did I say to melt it?

INNKEEPER Eh, but you complained last drink.

BULLER Last time was last time. Am I right?

INNKEEPER The customer is always right.
>   If you could put up
> With moneybags, he's going your way, Sir.

SCHOLAR I'll take a room.

BULLER (*roar*) Landlord.

INNKEEPER I'm on the way, Sir, on the way.

FOLKSINGER (*middle distance*)
> My love says to me, you're a light airy fellow
> Who follows the fiddle till morning is blue,
> But what could I find in the bed but a bottle
> If I did elope, says my bold Colleen Rua.

INNKEEPER Now for the room, sir. Dilly, Dilly.
>   You
> Are like some one I've seen –

                              Aye, begod,
            That fellow –
                              Dilly.
DILLY   Here I am, Sir.
INNKEEPER   A tough shaver, like you as two peas,
            Some roadwalker, treading softly on
            The heels of Mister Moneybags within –
DILLY   In jockey-leathers, Sir. I saw him too
            This minute.
                              He was watching you.
INNKEEPER   Lord, the times. If highwaymen can peep
            In public –
                      Take this gentleman upstairs
            To Number Four.
                              I have a rule in case
            Of fire –
                      Lights out, Sir, when you go to bed.
DILLY   This way, Sir. Follow me. It's all
            Made up and water in the pail. In here

    (*Creak of door*)

            I'll draw the blind.

    (*Hooves on cobble. Snort of horses*)

                      Lord, it's a shame, that Dublinman,
            His horses standing there all afternoon.
            Sir, make sure you douse the light.
                                          What time
            Will you be called?
SCHOLAR   To catch the mail.
DILLY   Yes, Sir. Goodnight now.
SCHOLAR   Goodnight. And thanks.

    (*Closing door. Water sounds as scholar washes. Horses below. A knock at
    door*)

SCHOLAR (*muffled*)   Who's there?
JOCKEY (*muffled*) Open.

    (*Creak of door*)

            The velvet boy.
SCHOLAR   Brother.
JOCKEY   Brother, a debtor too.
                      How's this –

The Hags of Clough   181

For gala day?

(*Sound of a blow. A fall*)

Second time I knocked you down.
Are skulls no tougher than the bookstuff in them?

(*Heavy breathing*)

A nice jacket, friend, and sure to fit
A twin. I'll take it off. Your hose, I see
Our mother's needlework
                              Her iron too
On this white shirt.
                         Our baby linen blew
Above the blackcurrant bushes – is she old,
Bowed down –
                   I'll take the shirt. My own is so
Ornate, Lord Leitrim's shirt. I stand in it
And sweat of fifty thousand tenants.
                                           So
Your eyes are open.
                         Here, take that –

(*Sound of a kick*)

                         A kick
From brother horse.
                         I'll tie you while I shave.

(*Faintly, the* Folksinger)

SCHOLAR (*low*) Brother.
JOCKEY (*savagely*)   Not so much brother.
                              Surely there is
A razor in your duffle.
                         Good.
SCHOLAR   You can untie me. I'll not lift a hand.
JOCKEY (*harsh laugh*) A rash promise. Can't you guess,
A bookman, and so wise, what this poor horse
Is going to do?
                   It came to me out there,
An inspiration. I was waiting on
Your chum the pedlar, Buller, bag of guts –
Those horses stiffening in the draughts below.
SCHOLAR   Brother –
JOCKEY (*savagely*)   Brother me again, and I'll –

The Hags of Clough

                              Just do
          What I am going to do.
                                   Six months I racked
          My brains, and never found revenge like this.
          Six months, a scarecrow fellow, nailed above
          My stableyard.
                              In irons on the pigeon-loft.
          A weather-gauge to Leitrim's temper,
                                                  Whipped
          On black days.
                              Do you see my back?
                                                  A net
          Of lashes.
                         My turn now.
                              The little man
          Died soft –
SCHOLAR (*low, horror*) Marty, you killed Mart?
JOCKEY   Who else?
           And flushed the bogeyman below. They were
           Such friends, I knew he'd come to bury him.
SCHOLAR (*low*) And now, it's Buller? You'll kill Buller –
JOCKEY   Me?
           Not me, friend, YOU; a student who
           Consorted with him once, conspired with him
           To throw a horse and make a fortune.
                                             Now,
           Two rogues fall out, d'you see –
                                        O Christ, it's sweet
           Revenge –
SCHOLAR   It's madness. It was I, and I
           Alone who threw that horse. You know the cause
           And reason –
JOCKEY (*ironically*) I believe I do – a fine
           Big jackpot. Gold. A pedlar in fine clothes,
           A scholar –
SCHOLAR   Fool –
JOCKEY (*dangerously*) Easy, friend, I'm delicate –
           And raw –
SCHOLAR (*quietly*) And mad.
JOCKEY (*low*) Mad?
SCHOLAR   I threw that horse. You know
           The reason why.
JOCKEY   The reason why?

The Hags of Clough   183

SCHOLAR   You came
             To me and begged –
JOCKEY   I did, and you refused,
             Then used me to make money. Trip the colt
             You said. That's what you said.
                                         I've thought
             And thought of it.
SCHOLAR (*firmly*) Somebody else has done
             Your thinking, brother –
JOCKEY (*viciously*)   Who'd think for me
             Up there above the stableyard? A flock
             Of pigeons, eh, or the big clock that chimed
             All night?
SCHOLAR (*monotonous*) Some one has thought for you,
             Somebody prompted –
JOCKEY (*loudly*)   No.
SCHOLAR (*monotonous*) Named me, indicated
             A poor scholar aching to be rich –
JOCKEY (*loudly*)   A drunk,
             A lousy drunk, a greedy pedlar, I
             Have thought it out –
SCHOLAR (*monotonous*) Voices, you heard voices –
JOCKEY (*loudly*)   Why not, why not, up there
             At night –
SCHOLAR (*monotonous*) Accusing me, your twin, who never loved
             A coin –
JOCKEY   Wait – you're at your tricks. Take that –
             And that – and that –

(*Sound of kicks? A low groan*)

             Now, mesmerise me, do.

(*Deep breath*)

             Mad. Mad, you said. Just mad enough, says I,
             To play cards as they come.
                                 O Christ, who was
             So innocent as I, so natural
             A beast? I met each day as if it were
             The first created.
                         Now I've blood, a man's,
             Upon my head.
                         The little fellow beat
             Against my hands. A bird. He died like that.

The Hags of Clough

SCHOLAR (*weak*) Brother –

JOCKEY   I'm ready now. How do you like
          The student?

SCHOLAR (*weak*) You'll pose as me?

JOCKEY   He catches on.
                    (*Complacently*) That is my plan.
          An inspiration, eh?

SCHOLAR (*stronger*) Yes, an inspiration.

JOCKEY   I'll down and cadge
          A lift from Bullyboy below. I'll pass
          For his old friend. He's drunk enough to see
          No difference.
                            Outside the town, a mile
          Or two outside, we quarrel, see. He meets
          His end.
                    A fellow in black velvets, his
          Old friend, a scholar, low and drunken, see,
          Will be the man who killed him.
                                Now, mark this,
          Here comes the daisy, I return, I leave
          Your duds, put on my own. And disappear.
          You're nabbed. You did the deed. A gallows for you.
          Well-earned, says I.
                        You brought me down.
                                    Christ, is
          This all your money?

    (*Jingle of coins*)

          Drinking, drivelling while I
          Died on that loft, squandering. You've spent
          Your share –

SCHOLAR (*strongly*) My share was broken ribs, a leg
          And sundry bruises, plus the greatest pain
          Of all – that I had failed, that I was fooled.
          Sit down, we'll talk –

JOCKEY   Sit down, says Jack Tricks. We'll talk, say he.

SCHOLAR   Those voices that you hear –

    (*Faintly, the Hag music*)

JOCKEY   Leave it, friend. I'm off.
                            Dangerous,
          That's what you are. Possessed, my lady said,
          Most dissolute, a power for evil. I

The Hags of Clough   185

Was a fool.
> She climbed the cote last night, she brought
The key, threw off my ankle irons, set
Me free.
> (*Loudly*) Why should those voices lie to me?
You tripped the colt.

(*Hag music more forward*)

> Possessed, she said, possessed.
Abandoned.
> > That's what she said.
> > > I'll go down now
And slit the moneybag.

(*Creak of door. The horses outside are heard. Noises of the tavern become close*)

INNKEEPER I thought you went to bed.
JOCKEY   I changed my mind. I'd like to cadge a lift
> From Moneybags –
INNKEEPER He's just away. He's crying for some corpse
> Called Marty.
BULLER (*forward*) I was the dirty work.
> But he was pious.
DRINKERS (*in chorus*) Poor fellow.
BULLER   Prayers, prayers, he'd patter them
> With any pope.
DRINKERS   Poor fellow.
BULLER   My conscience, that's what Marty was.
> The blindman's dog. And after every bout
> He'd lead me to the first confession box.
DRINKERS   Poor fellow.
BULLER   And sit outside. And if I missed a sin,
> By God, he'd prompt me.
DRINKERS (*automatically*) Poor fellow.

(*One of them gives a hysterical giggle*)

BULLER   Who laughed at me? Who laughed at Buller's grief?
DRINKER   It was a hiccup, Mister, and I beg
> Your pardon for it.
BULLER   Take buttered whiskey for
> The hiccup,
> > Buttering the pony's hay,
That's what the Scholar called it.

                              No one here
                Has known the Scholar, eh? The Devil's own,
                A lovely fallen angel. There was a lad
                Who'd slipped through many arches on his way
                From God.
                              Ah, where's the Scholar now?
                                              The Latin-man,
                The velvet fellow? He'd a piccolo
                Would talk to you.
                              Ah, where's he now, the son
                Of learning?
JOCKEY   No nearer God, I fear.
BULLER   Scholar, by hell, by hell. Now let me turn
                My sober side – it's you –
JOCKEY   Cadging a lift
                From Mister Affluence to Dublin town.
BULLER (*boastfully*) Scholar, I own that place. I'll name
                Streets after you –
JOCKEY   Tripper Alley, eh? Or Nobbler's Lane.
BULLER (*laugh*) We'll drink on that. We've seen
                Great gallopers go by.
JOCKEY   And some that fell.
BULLER   And some that fell.
                              But say that low –
                In Latin, eh?
                              Boys, here's the elegant himself.
DRINKERS (*murmur*) How are you, Sir?
JOCKEY   In a hurry to be off. That road is long.
BULLER   To think I have a friend will shorten it,
                A drink, one drink, the very last –
INNKEEPER   There's one before you, Sir –
JOCKEY   Skip me.
INNKEEPER   And time I closed.
BULLER   The last, then. Let me finish it. By God –
                You melted the butter, did I say –
INNKEEPER   I can't unmelt it now.
                              Down it, Sir,
                And churn it on the way.
BULLER   That's good, that's a good one.
                              Scholar, I
                Know houses on the road, if we can knock
                A landlord up.
JOCKEY   I know a place, it's open all the time,

The Hags of Clough   187

	No one refused admittance –
BULLER	The very place.
	Send round my carriage, you –
	<div align="right">An arm, help</div>
	An old friend, Scholar –
JOCKEY	Ho, with great pleasure, chum.

(*Sounds of carriage and horse, etc.*)

BULLER	I matched a pair of greys
	At great expense.
	<div align="right">Oh Lord, is it dark, so dark?</div>
	Has Buller boozed the light away?
	<div align="right">So dark.</div>
	Poor Marty down below. A murderer
	At large.
	<div align="right">But I'll catch up with him.</div>
JOCKEY	Indeed
	You will. Here, up with you, up, up.

(*Faintly, the Hag music*)

BULLER (*very drunk*) Sometime we'll meet.
JOCKEY   Nothing surer. Sit. You there, drive on.
BULLER   Where's this place you mentioned?
JOCKEY   On the road. We can't miss it, chum.

(*Carriage begins to move off*)

FOLKSINGER (*fading*)
So pay the last respects, and let God judge me,
For He who made me knows what is my due,
And knows the scarecrow fellow love has made me,
A thrall forever to the Colleen Rua.

INNKEEPER Out, lads. Have ye no homes?
          I'm putting out the lamp.
DILLY   Master –
INNKEEPER Eh, what is it? Lads, ye must leave now.
          What is it, Dill?
DILLY   The candle's lighting in
          That young man's room –
INNKEEPER He's gone, go blow it out –
DILLY (*shy*) Sir, someone's there –
INNKEEPER Eh?
DILLY   A mother-naked fellow on
          The floor. I was ashamed –

INNKEEPER Some devilment. Hey you, Jack, Jim –
           Support me here, come on.

   (*Noise of footsteps on stairs. Creaking door*)

INNKEEPER Now, heaven cheer me up. He's gagged,
           And tied, half-dead, look, kicked halfway to death –
           (*Shout*) Dilly, get brandy –
                                    Who did this, Sir?
DILLY (*excitedly*) The lad in leathers, look, he robbed, and left
           His own duds – look –
INNKEEPER Wake up the Watch.
MEN   Aye.
INNKEEPER Get some conveyance on the Dublin Road.
           Christ, he'll rob Moneybags as well.
           The watch, quick. And Jim, the posthorses,
           Here's a kettle, here's a boiling. Who
           Would keep an Inn?
                              A little drink, Sir, here.
           Oh, you've a sore complaint against me.
SCHOLAR   Never mind.
           Get on the road –
INNKEEPER I'll lend you duds of mine.
SCHOLAR   These leathers will suffice.
INNKEEPER They stink to high heaven.
SCHOLAR   So do we all. Get on the road, good man.
INNKEEPER That first. I'll see to you when I
           Come back.

   (*Hallooing and hurry recede. Hooves heard*)

MEPHISTOPHILIS (*chuckle coming slowly forward*) A Jock. A leather Jock.
           Why, you could be
           The man himself.
                           Where to now, Sir? To school,
           To count the bones and number the intestines,
           Or will you masquerade –
                                   A Jock above
           The stableyard a while?
                                  Much safer, Sir,
           To lodge there with a house of pigeons –
                                                  My
           Dear ladies seek you –
                                 NOSE you, seek a boy
           In student's dress –

The Hags of Clough   189

Who overheard one night
And tripped a horse. For all their care
He tripped a horse.
                         That was most noble, Sir,
But very hard on four poor souls, you must
Admit.
                   Quite useless too. The situation is
Unaltered, sir; old skull-cap more flyblown
If anything, the lady pale and drawn –
Lovelorn perhaps –
                         But angry, Sir. She looked
For you all day, and pours the vials out
At dark; no sleep for her, not much –
                                          She goes
Out more, of course, the young crowd round, she's gay
By daylight, simpers above the silver, sails
A sauceboat –
                      Then night falls. My ladies move
Securely in. A stallion roars upstairs.
And there's an accurate summary, now whereto,
Whereto, young gentleman, to school to count
The bones and number the intestines?
                                          I
Leave you to quandary, ahum – to be
Or not to be. No cornuto, Sir,
Wears more horns than Dilemma –
                   By the way
My ladies trailed you here tonight.
                              They watched
You leave, of course.
                         Most fortunate change of clothes.
Goodbye, goodbye, the way is clear. I took
The liberty, so to speak. (*Vast chuckle, echoing*)

(*Leitrim's castle. Our student under lock and key.*)

COMMENTATOR   Decision, it seems,
                      Is thrust upon us from on high;
                      Things happen in our dreams.
                      We catch up by and by;

                      And find waiting for us
                      Dilemmas, conflicts never willed
                      In any act of consciousness,
                      Raging and unfulfilled.

(Bolts, bars, clanging)

GAMEKEEPER   He'll see you now.

>   *(Whisper)* You buried it, the gold,
> The Frenchman's bribe. It brought you back – look here,
> I'll halve it with you, Jock, and some fine night
> I'll steal you off that stack – I know the way –

(Piccolo peep)

> You'll go back there and freeze. Be Jay, at dawn
> You'll be white frost.
>   Jockey –

SCHOLAR   Friend, lead on.
GAMEKEEPER   Look.

(Echoing footsteps)

> *(Surly)* All right, come on. You'll catch it now
> From Guts-and-Gaiters.

(Knock. A half-heard 'Come in')

> My Lord.

LEITRIM *(pause)* Ahum. Our crooked Jockey, home again, to roost –
> To roost, so to speak.

(Underlings' appreciation)

>   What brought you, Sir?
> Your bribe, your buried gold?
SCHOLAR   That's fairy stuff,
> My Lord, another lie you lean on, Sir –
> *(Ironically)* Most noble Sir.
LEITRIM *(high)* Insolent.

(Peep of piccolo)

> A liar, too.

(Piccolo)

> Who plays
> That instrument? Who mocks me here? Who pries?
GAMEKEEPER   By hell, I did hear something too.
> A penny whistle.
LEITRIM   Out and search for it.
GAMEKEEPER   But Jockey –
LEITRIM   I'm Jockey's Lord.

The Hags of Clough

(Peep of piccolo)

> Out. Pick up the whistle player. Out.

(Bang of door)

> You, Rider, I miss something. Is it horse?
> Ahum, some difference.
> > Insolence in your eye.
> And you were never insolent.
> > > *(High)* What brought you back?

(Piccolo)

SCHOLAR   To beard a lord, and listen.
LEITRIM   Listen –
SCHOLAR   To hear lord lie to lord within
          And suppurate –
LEITRIM *(high)* Stop –

(Mockery of piccolo in background)

SCHOLAR   And puff the lordly thing
          Beyond the pale –
LEITRIM   Stop.
SCHOLAR   A vanity.
LEITRIM   Stop, stop.
SCHOLAR   No human unit, just a silly piece
          Of heraldry –
LEITRIM   Stop.
SCHOLAR   A lion spilled
          Out of an inkstand, formal as a seal.
LEITRIM *(squeak)* Jockey.
SCHOLAR   A squeak of paper thunder. You
          Have dribbled out of some clerk's quill –
LEITRIM   Stop.
SCHOLAR   Pipsqueak of majesty. No husband and
          No father.
LEITRIM *(as housebells ring madly)* Stop, stop.

(Doors banging. Hurry of steps)

GAMEKEEPER   My Lord, by hell, did Jockey –
LEITRIM *(quivering)* Tomorrow, Jockey, I will deal with you.
          A whip –
SCHOLAR   Use it on this grotesquerie you call
          Yourself.
GAMEKEEPER *(roughly)* By hell, Jockey.

The Hags of Clough

SCHOLAR   Or come out openly,
               Whip suitor number eight, that's all you've left
               Now jockeys are not trusted –
LEITRIM   Stop him, stop his mouth.
GAMEKEEPER (*roughly*) By God, I will.
                            Oh, Cripes, let go. Oh Jockey.
SCHOLAR (*grimly*) Lie down, dog. This is master's work.
LEITRIM (*choking*) Jockey, I'll have you flayed, I'll pin your pelt
               On the vermin pole.
SCHOLAR   What will you do with suitor number eight?
LEITRIM   Stop.
SCHOLAR   You will not win another match.
               Your secret's out. I'll blazon it. I'll toll
               The bell.
                    I'll leave you now.
                            And you, my dog,
               Show me this pigeon-tower. I'll climb up
               And chain myself – and throw you down the key.
               Security.
                    (*Ironically*) Of locks and irons, yet pop goes
               The Leitrim weasel.
                       My Lord, last night, there died
               A man, you'll hear of him, you drove him to
               His death.
                    Your vanity. Your sin.
                            All night
               From this bird-stack I'll overlook you, sir.
               Your conscience I.
                    I'm ready, dog. Come on.

(*Footsteps, keys, etc. A colt whinnies in the distance*)

GAMEKEEPER (*gulp*) Jockey, if I said anything.
               Jockey, if I –
                    (*High, uncertain*) What's got into you?
               I've shivers down my back.
                       I won't go up.
               Throw down the key.
                      I'll wait, I'll wait (*Fading*)
COMMENTATOR   Humbled in the mercury I touch
               Sad Zero;
               Midwinter is too much
               For such a sunny fellow.

               January, two-faced –

The Hags of Clough

Sees the sun-dialled rose;
If Gods have such short shifts.
I have my winter clothes.

(*The stable clock is chiming sweetly the midnight hour*)

LADY   Up those ladders, rotting steps, a moon
That seems to ride a broomstick –

                              cobwebs too,
Spiders in my hair.

                  And rats.

(*Stallion neighs brutally*)

                  And that
Brute neighing.

            Jockey, I am a fool – to be
A fool twice. I bring the key again.

                    Now take
The irons off.

          We'll leave at once before
I change my mind.

              You upset father; I
Am angry, upset too. He's like a mad
Man pacing in the gallery, his hair
On end, and talking to himself, the lights
Halfblown, the shadows following him, the house
Atiptoe –

          Jockey, why, why – you must have said
Most horrible things –

                Don't sulk with me. Take off
Those irons.

(*Stallion neighs brutally.* Lady *gasps*)

There, that brute again. That brute.
   I've reached a kind of end tonight.

                      I want
To weep.

        (*Low, intense*) Jockey, what happened here
Midsummer Night –

            Remember it –

                Your twin
Was here, you said, and calmed that colt –

                  me too –
Some spacious gaze, I lived in it for days.

And then at Castlerea was this bold boy,
A disappointment –

                Ovid, said he, Petronius,
As if I were a mop. And gone when I
Returned.

        (*Low, brooding*) And yet a – haunting boy.

                              Those eyes,

You know –

        (*Small cry*) How could a boy be trivial
And have such eyes? They opened as I washed
His face, remember –

                I could see, did see
Something that – enhanced me to myself –
Midsummer Night again.

                    Well, well, he's dead.
On Hagshill, Jockey, devilishly mauled.
The Hue and Cry was out for him.

                      They say
He killed that other near Athlone. So you
Were right.

           Confederates.

              To have
A gaze like that and trip a colt.

                   If I
Were small I'd weep a little, not for him
Especially – for all the world, I think,
For me who cannot sleep –

(*Brutal neigh of stallion. Lady gasps*)

                And, Jockey, for
Old times when you could comfort me.

                    Take off
Those irons, take them off. Don't sulk with me.
I'm at the very end tonight, a sad
Small fool, a ninny –

(*Brutal neighing of stallion*)

           (*Low gasp*) That brute is always in
My nightmares now.

           (*Pause*) You've taken my hands, I see
And there's – surprising comfort in it.

                        I
Am small again, perhaps; an urchin you

Protected, wouldn't spoil.

                (*Odd tone*) Oh – my handkerchief –
The breast-pocket, here.

                White hands – not badly kept;
White hands.

     (*Pause. Lady's deep breath*) I knew you all the time, of course.

(*Peep of piccolo*)

    Of course I did.

             (*Angrily*) Will you deny it, Sir?
In jockey-leathers now. And borrowed – fumes,
The fumes of horse, and all the mudland smells
Of gipsy or knockabout.

               You've slept wild since
We met, I think.

          I'll take my handkerchief –
My hands, too, if you please.

              What brings you here –
And masquerading –

            First, did you trip the colt?

SCHOLAR (*calmly*) I tripped the colt.

LADY (*hard*)   For money, and to spite us for
      That beating?

SCHOLAR   For neither, Lady.

LADY   Well then, well then –

             tell, Sir, tell –
      Or did you have a reason?

SCHOLAR   One – that seemed sufficient then.

LADY   Continue, Sir.

SCHOLAR   A lady's well-being.

LADY   Continue, Sir. Who is
      This lady?

(*Piccolo peep*)

         Who is this – lady, Sir? Some twitch,
    Some low thatch, some public piece –

SCHOLAR   Lady, yourself.

LADY (*pause*)   I think I must sit down. Can that
      Small pallet hold the two of us?

              Thank you.
      You may proceed.

(*Piccolo background faintly during this scene*)

                                              The Hags of Clough

You may proceed, I said.
(*Angrily*) Sir, you may proceed.
                              First let me say,
I shall not believe a word.
                    You are, you know,
A student run to seed.
                         A low comedian
With some spoiled gifts.
                         (*Hurrying*) A drunkard too,
A mountebank, a wencher. People say
You are an atheist thrown out of school.
What credit can you have with me?
                              Speak, Sir.

SCHOLAR In fairness – to yourself, you may
Add more;
              Some not in character, but you
Should know it –

LADY Such as?

SCHOLAR Some conference with – the Prince of Darkness. He
Led me here one night indeed.

LADY (*low*) Midsummer Night it was?

SCHOLAR Midsummer Night.

LADY (*low*) Now I should be afraid. Why amn't I
Afraid?
              You calmed a colt and I, perhaps,
Feel grateful.
              (*Quickly*) That body on Hagshill –
                    Jockey's, is it?

SCHOLAR Jockey's, yes.

LADY (*low*) You didn't –

SCHOLAR I didn't kill him, at least not with my hands.
I tripped the colt. It followed.

LADY Poor Jockey, why, why, oh why?

SCHOLAR He wore my clothes.

LADY (*gasp*) Mistaken for you, then.
You are in danger?

SCHOLAR No.

(*Brutal neighing of stallion*)

LADY (*low, quickly*) You hear that brute. You calmed him once,
Midsummer Night. I walked him to his box
Complacently.

SCHOLAR (*quietly*) Next time he neighs, you'll hardly notice him.

LADY   The other, his elder brother, tripped – you say –
             For my well-being –
                            How did I require it?
SCHOLAR   You'll answer that yourself.
LADY   I?
SCHOLAR   The answer's hidden in
             Recurring nightmare.
                            A stallion roars
             Upstairs.
                     And yet no stallion either, so
             You turn your face away, you do not look,
             Examine –
                     But you know. Describe him now.
LADY (*low, pause*) A stallion, that's all.
                            (*Little cry*) A nightmare stallion,
             Almost human, sly, an open mouth,
             Most horrible.
SCHOLAR (*low, monotonous*) Horrible, why? No horse
             Is horrible. You loved the stableyard
             At night, you went the rounds, you drowsed
             In hayracks while the great brutes ate, you loved
             The velvet snort, a puckering nose, you had
             No terror of the teeth.
LADY (*low*) Yes, yes, most comforting.
SCHOLAR (*low, monotonous*) This nightmare monster, then,
             Is more than horse.
                            A man perhaps. You must
             Examine him. He could resemble one
             You know –

  (*Piccolo, sharp*)

LADY (*low, with difficulty*)   No, ah no.

  (*Piccolo, protesting*)

             I said no and no.
SCHOLAR (*low*) Some one you know: close kin, perhaps,
LADY (*high*) No, oh no.
SCHOLAR (*low*) Even your nearest kin, it could well be –
LADY   The miserable chore –
                            To help this poor soul out
             Into unwanted marriage, never asked
             If my affections were engaged. I was
             The chore, the hero's task, or were you, Sir,
             A sort of Pandar?

Why did you take it on?
There is a mythical pattern in such things.
Did you remember it? Being a scholar, you
Must know it surely?
                              Answer, Sir, confess
You know, how the poor girl, a victim still,
Is married off – to any fool who saves her.
You're very silent.
                              And you hold my hands.
This pallet, too, is very small – for two.
And it is after midnight.

(*Colt nickers softly*)

                              And there's my colt –
As mild as mother's milk.
                              (*A sigh*) And I am healed,
It seems.
              So give me back my hands.
                                        Poor father, you
Must heal him also.

(*Colt nickers softly*)

                              Yes, there's my colt
As mild as mother's milk.
                              And there's the moon
Witchlike no more, a happy sailor in
The quiet heavens. I'll sleep tonight. What shall
I dream of, Student?

(*Quirk of piccolo*)

SCHOLAR   Food.
LADY (*with horror*) Food, of food?
SCHOLAR   Beef and mutton, breadcrumbed ham,
              A bird.
LADY   Horrible.
SCHOLAR   And in the morning, mock
              Your father most abominably –
LADY (*quickly*) My father?

(*Squawk of piccolo*)

SCHOLAR   Say things like this.
              Deride and scoff, rally and quizz, ignore –
              So help to cure him.

The Hags of Clough   199

LADY   My father's tempers are
            Notorious, Sir.

   (*Piccolo*)

SCHOLAR   I shall be there before
            The whip.
LADY (*outraged*)   Whip?
SCHOLAR   The whip. When things boil up
            Run out. You'll find me on the lawn,
            The colt and I.

   (*Colt nickers softly*)

LADY (*low*) How softly he speaks now.
SCHOLAR   And yet tomorrow rage – like this.

   (*Colt neighs savagely*)

LADY (*low*) You – almost frighten me
            With knowledge, Sir.
SCHOLAR (*quietly*) Ah no. All flesh is one. We move
            In great simplicities. The colt and I
            Are one somewhere. Believe that. And have no fear.
LADY   I see my hands – have crept back into yours.
            Afraid, poor things.
                              Yet Jockey died, I think,
            Because of you.
                          That other fellow too.
            And my – sweet Frenchman.
                                    Such a lovely boy
            And almost in my heart.
                                  Three men have died,
            Yet these are – student's hands.
                                          So very white.
            A luteplayer's fingers too. Tell me, tell me
            Were you aware, did you know all before
            You threw our colt?
                              You needn't, mustn't answer, Sir.
            I am ashamed.
                        Three men, there could be more
            For all you know.
SCHOLAR   A fourth. A life of penitence –
LADY (*loudly*) I do not care for penitential palms.
            If you have done it, wear your mittens red.
            The halfway heart, the halfway lover is
            Anathema, you must agree.

(*Faintly, the hag music*)

> (*Uncertain*) You must agree.
> I have my value too.

(*Piccolo soars*)

> You look, O Student, you
> Have such a gaze, so cold, so difficult
> For this poor girl to placate.
>   Your eyes
> Are hurting, Student.

(*Pause. Piccolo soars and fades again into background*)

> (*Low*)   Student, did I
> Offend?

SCHOLAR (*low*) Not you.
>   Something used you, for
> A moment I was lost.

LADY (*low*) I was bold, was bad, evil too.

SCHOLAR   Not you, not you. A night
> Of watch and vigil from now on.

LADY (*low*) And now I fear myself.
> There was such pleasure in it.

SCHOLAR (*suddenly, loudly*) Can you pray?

LADY   Can I pray, says he? My hands in his.
> I feel so many hands in yours, I drag
> A jostling horde, bad wives, the lecherous
> Night-wanton, mops in inns, and country molls
> You taught the hedgeschool way, a gross parade.
> Can I, unlearned lady, in all honesty
> Squeeze past this host of trulls?
>   And yet he asks
> If I can pray.
>   My hands, Sir, if you please.

(*Pause. Clock chimes half hour*)

> (*Small voice*) I pray – quite well, of course. Indeed,
> I'm praying now.
>   What do you fear tonight?
> I ask: what do you fear? And if I can
> Give any aid?
>   (*Low*) There in the moon you're skull
> And crossbones.
>   I distract you too

And chatter.

SCHOLAR (*some lightness*) You help – occasionally.

                                                  Now,

I'll see you to your rooms.

LADY (*haughty*) Indeed?

                                  And yet

An arm could be welcome. Well, come then,
Come then.

                        You first, then if I fall,

My Ladyship will be on top.

(*Noises of descent*)

                                This is

Most derelict.

                      Poor Jockey gyved above

His horses, and I couldn't help.

                              They tell

Me, Sir, some other oddities of yours.
You heal and go away.

                        Tomorrow, then,

When you have cured my father, shall you leave
As usual?

                 Here's a night, a marvellous night

Of moon.

                You'll go away, I'm sure.

                              And I

Shall marry as befits my station, some
Great gentleman of blood.

                        And listen to

Odd tales about a straying student –

                           Who

Makes every tavern home.

                    That lamp above

Is mine.

            Who drinks and all the rest, who wastes

Himself in frolic, suborning the poor stuff
That breeds us maidservants.

                        Do you deny it, Sir?

What will you do tomorrow?

SCHOLAR I go to school again.

LADY (*aback*) Oh, why so?

SCHOLAR To be respectable, a doctor who
Can name the bones. To Paris, Ma'am.

          The Hags of Clough

LADY   Indeed,
           The bones are named in **Paris**,
                           Pretty ones
           With bows and garters, **Sir**.
                      This door, it squeaks,
           All should be oiled for secret assignations;
           I must remember that.
                   To **Paris** then
           Tomorrow. I shall follow your career
           With interest.
                To name the bones.
                       Perhaps
           You'll help at my accouchment, Sir. I'll do
           Everything to forward you.
                  I moved
           My rooms some time ago to this lone wing.
           Be careful here. This step has trapped me too.
           Well, well.
                  This window has a view, treetops,
           Lakewater.
                Here I moon sometimes.
                     Six months
           Since Midsummer. Six months. Six hills of time
           So slow to sink.
                I sit and see the swans.
           A girl could waste, could die.
                   Indeed, Sir, I
           Could well be in my monument for all
           The pains you took.
                  (*Low, harsh*) Could you have come before?
SCHOLAR   No.
LADY (*soft sigh*) I take your word for it. A lie,
           A pleasant lie, but still – I'll take your word.
           Well, here we are, and Betty too, my maid
           A long time, sir; knows all my sins.
BETTY (*hurrying forward*) My Lady, my Lady –
LADY (*low*) Student, trouble, I see it come –
BETTY (*at hand*) Your father, Ma'am, and such a fear
           And tantrum. He's inside. He told me leave
           The room.
LADY (*stiffly, covering*) My father isn't well –
BETTY   I know.
           I hid myself. He fingered everything,

	Your gowns, wraps, shawls, your very shoes – and hose –
	Ma'am, he's not safe. He's walking wild –
LADY (*stiff*)	I'll see
	To father, Betty.
BETTY	Jockey, be careful, don't go in.
LADY (*low*)	Student, I
	Will see to Father.
	Betty, leave us, please.
	Wait here.
	Oh, I am ashamed, but then – he's sick,
	You say.
	Will he be violent?
SCHOLAR (*quietly*)	No.
LADY	No?
SCHOLAR	A tired old man, prompted, prodded on.
	We'll find him sleeping in your chair.
LADY (*low*)	You know? You're sure of that?
	Then I
	Can let you in with me.
	I wouldn't have
	You see – another kind of scene.
	Wait, Sir, let me
	Be first.

(*Creak of opening door*)

	Asleep.
	Poor tired old man.
	How did
	You know?
SCHOLAR	It had to come tonight,
	A nominal gesture, little heart in it;
	A tired old man. Unwilling, too, for all
	The prodding.
LADY (*low*)	Student –
SCHOLAR	Lady, the boil has burst. He'll sleep
	Tonight, and never know what happened here.
	I'll take him now.
LADY	No, let him sleep.
SCHOLAR	He'll sleep – and walk, sleep-walk. You go ahead,
	And show the way.

(*Piccolo*)

Up, sweet Sir, the air

The Hags of Clough

　　　　　Is masculine elsewhere. The Bear's hung up
　　　　　His nightshift to the north. We need the cold
　　　　　White sheets –
LADY (*low*) He rises, he obeys.

　　(*Piccolo*)

SCHOLAR　Lead the way, and softly. He
　　　　　Will follow you.
　　　　　　　　　　He has a certain dry,
　　　　　Too-adequate elegance. He'll make a man again
　　　　　Tomorrow.

　　(*Piccolo merry in background*)

　　　　　Marry some titled trot.
　　　　　　　　　　　Or get
　　　　　A maid in trouble.
　　　　　　　　　　　This the door.
　　　　　　　　　　　　　　　I'll see
　　　　　To him.
　　　　　　　　　Tired, a tired old man.
LADY (*sigh*) You'll see to him. I'll stay
　　　　　A while.
SCHOLAR　No, you must sleep tonight – and dream
　　　　　Of mutton, beef and ham –

　　(*Piccolo merry in background*)

　　　　　　Tankards of beer –
LADY (*aback*)　Oh.
SCHOLAR　Foaming porter. Pewter measures. Coarse
　　　　　And yellow cheese.
LADY　　　It should be nightmare night,
　　　　　And now it's merry.
SCHOLAR　Sleep on it.
　　　　　Tomorrow we will throw the tombstones round.
LADY　　　You're walking back with me.
SCHOLAR　Why, so I am.
　　　　　That's not good scholarship, yet here I am
　　　　　Without my book.

　　(*Clocks chime*)

LADY　　　And at my door – an hour
　　　　　Past midnight, Sir.
　　　　　　　　　　And gods and clocks know men

Are never pious after midnight.
SCHOLAR   I go.
LADY   It's etiquette to kiss a lady's hand
          On leaving.
                    There, dear Student, on your forehead, one,
          Just one, in thanks, and trust.
                              Goodnight, goodnight.
MEPHISTOPHILIS (*vast, low chuckle*) Moved, and to extravagance.
                                                        I wish
          Sometimes for flesh, to feel, to know what love
          Can do, to die. And that is whimsical
          In any scene-shifter who pulls a chain,
          Stands in the great Flies, and knowing all
          The script, lets up the curtain.
                              Steady, Sir.
          You move into my properties.
                              Some rent
          Is due.
          No?
              Then state a case.
                    (*Mock rhetoric*) You must acknowledge that
          You use my diagnosis, that I brought
          You here – at great expense – of spirit, hid
          You from my ladies –
                              Hauled you here, against
          Your will, displayed this sordid earl –
                                        All right
          Is on my side –
                    Acknowledged up in heaven, Sir,
          If I may be irrelevant.
                              The cure is mine.
          No?
              Is that fair – to a poor Devil?
                                        Well,
          I'll slip a notch. Admit I'm part of it.
          You're here. I brought you here.
                              And that's
          Beyond all argument.
SCHOLAR (*sigh*) I can't deny it.
MEPHISTOPHILIS But if my finger's in
          The pie, I'm in, if not as master, then
          As partner, portion of the thing; admit
          I'm in, then I'm the cure –

                              No? Well, well, I
            Can argue it.
SCHOLAR   I cure without you. I
            Dropped some weak scruples lately. I am here,
            You led the way —
                         That is admitted, still
            The cure is mine, all mine, and I will make it.
MEPHISTOPHILIS (*loudly*) To profit, to profit by it, win a girl —
SCHOLAR (*low, weary*) I know the law, acknowledge it, and I
            Relinquish any profit there may be —
MEPHISTOPHILIS The girl, ho?
SCHOLAR   Aye, my fee. You offered it —
            And there's that axiom in law forbids
            What Satan offers. I refused. And do —
            Most certainly.
                         But if my service is
            Unselfish, if I do not profit, I
            May use some knowledge you passed on, yet be
            Inside the law.
MEPHISTOPHILIS A Daniel. (*Loud, echoing chuckle*)
            And come to Judgement.
                                How you'll pay
            In misery, in loneliness, become
            Distorted as your patients, honey of life
            Quite savourless.
                         My Hags shall have you yet,
            A plague.
                    Well, well. I fail again.
                                My work
            A nothing.
                      Still we've made it plain you may
            Not cure and profit.
                           So the girl is out
            Of bounds, young fellow, except — ahum —
                                          We've been
            All over that, all over that, all over that —

        (*Fading into vast chuckle. Piccolo faintly heard*)

COMMENTATOR   The dead
              Are half alive; the living half
              Below the sod.
              And nobody has too much life.

              Carry the sad

The Hags of Clough   207

Oaf off the scene. What troubled his life
Will harry him dead;
And the Mute will marry his wife.

LADY (*very lively*) Breakfast, I
    Am ravenous –
BUTLER Chocolate, hot –
LADY Pap, child's pap.
BUTLER (*aback*) Yes, my Lady.
LADY The cold table, all of it. I will
    Begin with ham.
                No lady pieces, please.
    A butcher's round.
                Don't stare at me.
BUTLER Yes – I mean no, my Lady. I am glad
    To see you in such appetite.
LADY A beautiful morning, what
    A ravenously lovely morning, I
    Could chew it bit by heavenly bit.
LEITRIM It lacks
    Some token for a loving parent.
LADY Do I see beef? Oh, mix the rounds for me.
    And mutton, marvellous –
                Exactly what
    I need –
         Did you say something, Father?
                    Never mind,
    It doesn't matter.
LEITRIM (*high, with echo*) Doesn't matter.
LADY Is that a pheasant there?
BUTLER M'Lady, it is.
LADY Bring me that bird.
           No – wait; our muttons first;
    With beer, beer. Now what a timely thought –
    But, dear, who thought of it?
                A draught so rough, the drink
    Of wrangling students, tobacco men puffed up
    With argument.
        (*Laughs*) Oh, that young profligate.
LEITRIM A profligate? Did you say profligate?
LADY Blockhead, not in a jug.
             Beer needs
    A pewter tankard –
        Now how do I know that? Oh most

The Hags of Clough

Extraordinary young man.

LEITRIM (*high with echo*) Young man?

LADY Did you say something, Father – it
Doesn't matter –

LEITRIM (*high*) Matter, not matter? You have not seen
Your father yet, nor kissed him.

LADY A childish habit. Unsanitary too.
Also my mouth is – full, my teeth at work.
Why tug me from such pleasure?

LEITRIM (*high*) Do you mock me?

LADY (*mouthful*) I merely do
The table honour –
Now let me eat good food,
And taste it.
Beer, more beer.

BUTLER Yes, Lady.

LADY Up to the top.
Spare the froth and spoil the mild
And bitter.
Father, you should drink beer. It could
Become a peer.

LEITRIM Beer!

LADY Peer. Distinctly I said peer.
You make no sense
This morning, Father. None at all.

LEITRIM (*high*) No sense?

LADY And now your mouth
Is gaping –
and really, Father, such an open mouth
Does not become you.
You must see a dentist, too.

LEITRIM (*high*) See a dentist?

LADY Certainly, most – absolutely.
Now,
That bird, bring me that bird.
I think I must
Take to the gun again, one way to catch
A husband too.
The woods are full of them –
Not husbands, other game –
Though actually
I could eat one or other.

(*Piccolo query in background*)

The Hags of Clough

But savour both
So differently.
                    Did I say that? Oh, most
Abominable young man.

LEITRIM (*high*) Young man again.

LADY Do I see partridge there?

BUTLER Yes, yes, m'Lady.

LADY Heap up my plate. No ladybits,
No lad-di-daws. I am a buxom wench
Who must be bedded soon –
                    Wedded, I mean
(*Laughs heartily*) Beastly young man.

LEITRIM (*high*) Young man again.

LADY And yet, why not? All fall, and must.
That's not to be ill-used.
                    And *Placens Uxor* –

(*Piccolo quirk*)

A sweet wife. Oh dear, oh dear, Bodega Latin –
Omnis Amor magnus –
                    Dear Student, no,
No more –

LEITRIM (*high*) Student?

LADY (*very quickly, with laughter*) *Sed aperto in conjuge* –
Oh – major –
                    Oh dear I am a learned minx, it seems;
And yet like any honest woman I
Will send my mare to market –
                    Not on head
Alone does woman live.
                    (*Laughing*) Dear Father, is
It mannerly to stare? Your eyes are out
On popsticks, such a silly gaze –

LEITRIM (*high*) Silly gaze.

LADY And so bad-mannered. But then you never show
Good manners –

LEITRIM (*high*) Good manners.

LADY (*briskly chewing*) None. Delicious bird.
I feel I'm really marriageable now.
(*Very fast. In a gush*) *Ut materia appetit formam* – No, no,
Sweet, Sweet,
Sic mulier virum –
                    Whatever it means, it sounds

Too learned at meals –
                              (*Laughs*) Impossible young man.
LEITRIM (*high*) Young man again. Who is
         This soul?
LADY (*chewing rapidly*) Father, come down to earth,
         Walk pleasantly among men, as man and not
         As monument –
                              Oh, dreadful, dreadful youth.
LEITRIM (*beside himself*) Youth?
LADY (*chewing*) To put such in my mouth.
                              I mean the words –
         And not the birds –
                              But now I think – HOW TRUE.
         How true, that's what I think.
                              Indeed, I note
         The public statuary, eloquent platitude.
         So much for earls, poor creatures born to die
         Of all the bronze poured over them,
                              They must
         Strike attitudes it seems, seem spacious, yet
         Are only hollow men.
                              God save the poor –
         Ennobled.
LEITRIM (*high*) The poor – ENNOBLED.
LADY (*chewing*) Dreadful, dreadful youth –
LEITRIM (*high*) Are you possessed?
LADY (*chewing*) Of course, most certainly.
         Beef and mutton, ham and tongue –
         Indeed, by tongue – (*Laughs*)
                              The silly punster makes
         Me laugh –
                              When have I laughed like this?
         Oh, flippant, arrant, errant, punning rogue,
         Oh, naughty young man.
LEITRIM (*high*) Young man, but who, but who –
LADY (*chewing. Laughter*) An arrogant student, Sir, that I
         Must punish soon by – marrying –
LEITRIM   Marrying.
LADY   Revenge, I'll have it. And great joy
          In all the rest.
                              Come soon, come soon.
                                        I'm like
          To have a seizure – before father.

The Hags of Clough   211

LEITRIM	Some young man has proposed to you?
LADY	Why, no. I'll bring the war to him.

        I'll sue him from a height –

                            And then descend

        Into my womanhood –

LEITRIM (*high*) You – you – you –

LADY (*briskly*) Don't stutter, Father. You have all the signs
        Of mental indigestion –

                    I can mince
        As well as most, and tinkle with my feet,
        Daughter of Zion I'll be, show stockings too,
        Gold fringes, blue the shadows on my lids,
        Totter on heels, affect my pace – *Hoc est*
        Dicere, posce, posce, trado –

                    Again,
        He intervenes, but I will have him.

LEITRIM (*high*) Not so, not ever –

LADY (*briskly*) Poor Father, you
        Are more congested than is good for you.
        You'll show me a horsewhip next, I think – but then
        You showed it to my mother –

LEITRIM (*high*) I –

LADY   Really, I
        Am fullgrown today, and not to be
        Put off with whips –

                HORSE-MATCHES either, Sir.

LEITRIM (*uncertain*) Horse-matches.

LADY   A pitiful story. A shoddy, ugly, sad
        And sorrowful affair.

                 Yet good has come,
        And where I would have married any, I
        Have found the only one –

(*Quirk of piccolo*)

                (*Very quickly*) A low comedian?
        A wencher, pothouse fellow, derelict – (*Stops. Angrily*)
        Really, that is too much, Student, at
        This time. I'll not be prompted any more.
        Now, Father, take him as you may, today
        I leave your clutches.

LEITRIM (*high*) Clutches?

LADY (*positively*) Clutches!

LEITRIM (*high*) My love, my care?

LADY   A masquerade.
LEITRIM (*high*) Stop.
LADY   For rank and horrible
              Indecency –
LEITRIM (*high*) Stop.
LADY   For gross obsession, flouting all
              That is most holy –
LEITRIM (*high*) Stop.
LADY   A stupid sin. You made
              Two furies out of us.
LEITRIM (*high, with echo*) Stop, stop.
LADY   My sleep gone mad, your daughter's sleep.
LEITRIM (*high, with echo*) I do not hear a word.
LADY   And now you look
              As you look in my nightmare –
LEITRIM (*high, with echo*) Your nightmare, I
              Do not hear a word.
LADY (*low*) Mouth open, yellow teeth.
LEITRIM (*scream*) I do not hear a word.
LADY (*high, fright*) And I could run –
LEITRIM (*high*) You'll run, you'll run. My horsewhip, bring
              It here, my whip –
BUTLER (*low*) The window's open, Miss. Run out.
LADY (*fading*) Yes, yes.

   (*Brutal neigh of stallion*)

LEITRIM (*high*) The stallion, stop her.

   (*Lady screams. Stallion neighing*)

              Hold him. Hang on to the reins.
              I'm coming. Hold him, hang on to the reins.
              Don't let him go.

   (*Fading as his senses fail*) Don't-let-him-go.

COMMENTATOR   Discover the pin.
              Uncover the sin,
              All in its soiled and shoddy
              Gorgon-headed body.

              It burns bare-faced;
              But watch it waste.
              This that was shocking once
              Has lost all relevance.

The Hags of Clough   213

LEITRIM (*weakly*) My daughter?
SCHOLAR   Safe.
LEITRIM (*weakly*) Thank, God, thank God.
SCHOLAR   Your daughter was
           Never in danger.
                          You confused her with
           Somebody else – perhaps.
                          The colt I walked
           Outside was mild, amenable –
                          Yet you
           Thought otherwise.
                          A double delusion, Lord
           Of Leitrim.

  (*Piccolo background*)

           Why?
                  Some other scene, the same,
           Inside your head?
                          An old old sore, perhaps.
           A wife – who mocked, who was about to leave
           Your Lordship?
LEITRIM (*low*) Who are you who question me?
SCHOLAR   All men.
LEITRIM (*low, weak*) Your eyes.
                          Release me from
           That terrible gaze.
SCHOLAR   I would not if I could. All men
           Are staring –
                      Not in anger, Sir.
                                  In pity,
           In sorrow for a fellow-creature lost
           In some old lie.
                          Why do you think you killed
           Your lady, Lord of Leitrim?
LEITRIM (*weakly grand*) Should Leitrim answer you? I am
           Decorum here, the king's own image, I
           Establish the formal thing that must exist
           Above the ebb and flow…

  (*Mockery of piccolo*)

SCHOLAR   And yet your lady was
           About to leave –
LEITRIM (*strongly*) A Cyprian, a Cyprian.

Some pensioner, with half an arm, in debt
To his own servants, lodgings on the lake,
A rootless fellow with one horse –
                              I threw
Her pious Ladyship out through the glass.
The stallion trampled her, and I looked on,
(*Exalted*) Looked on, looked on, and laughed, laughed.

(*Piccolo soars*)

              (*Low*) You have such eyes, such terrible eyes.
SCHOLAR   They see that scene another way.
LEITRIM (*low*) How could that be? I am a lord.
              I punish or let be. I do not melt
              In pitiful qualms –
SCHOLAR   Poor soul, she could have loved –
LEITRIM (*strongly, in anger*) She mocked me, here.
              I knelt down before her, on my knees, a lord
              Down on his knees.
SCHOLAR   You took your whip, she ran –
LEITRIM (*high*) Ran, ran. The window there.
              The stallion on the lawn, he'd broken out,
              And she was running towards him.
SCHOLAR (*low*) Poor soul.
LEITRIM (*accepting 'poor soul' unconsciously*) Poor soul.
              A beast who answers none but me, who kills
              If hampered –
SCHOLAR   You ran out then. Poor soul.
LEITRIM (*with difficulty*) I ran, calling her. Two men
              Hung on the bearing rein.
                       They let him go,
              The brute, they let him go, they let him go,
              Mistook my words –
                    He was a colt who came
              Hangdog to my call, you see –
SCHOLAR (*low, monotonous*) You said, 'DON'T LET HIM GO', don't let
                                        him go,
              But since he always answered you, the men –
LEITRIM (*loud*) Thought I said 'LET HIM GO'.
SCHOLAR (*low*) And she, poor soul, under the hooves –
              And nothing you could do –
LEITRIM (*groan*) Nothing. Unmanageable then.
SCHOLAR   'Don't let him go', you said.
                        Why, those were words
              You used again this morning –

LEITRIM   My daughter, you
            Were there – and saved –
SCHOLAR   You would have saved
            The other lady as –
                              You would have saved
            Your daughter.
                        You ran out, you called, you said
            The words 'Don't let him go'.
                              The very words
            You used before – to that poor soul, confirmed
            This morning.
                        There was no crime here.
                                          She was
            Unfaithful to your bed, you did not kill,
            But tried to save.
                        No pride demands of you
            To lie.
                  Some ladies need small rooms – and you
            Are something castellated, Sir. You need
            No lie.
                  No lies of any kind. You are
            A man and not a pride.
LEITRIM (*low*) Your eyes are milder now.
            Who are you, Sir – who masquerade
            As my old Jockey?
SCHOLAR   Jockey's twin.
LEITRIM   He's dead. He threw a colt of mine.
SCHOLAR   It was I. You know the reason, Sir.
            Those horse-matches, your daughter's suitors
            Who lost to you.
                        A sin, a crime this time,
            A real and no imaginary thing.
LEITRIM (*low, sad*)   I do confess it. Devil-wrung
            So long.
                  She was so like one I had lost.
            Did I confuse them too? You look so wise,
            A judge, a judge. Last night I dreamed of you,
            You led me away, was it from – her?
SCHOLAR   Her very room.
LEITRIM (*wrung*) Dear God, did I –
SCHOLAR   No.
LEITRIM   Thank God, thank God.
                  (*He breaks down in sobs*) Can I ever face her after this?

SCHOLAR   She's here, she's coming in the door –
LADY (*softly*) Father.
LEITRIM (*shaken*) My daughter, my dear daughter.
LADY (*airily, tender*) My Student has arranged you, my young man.
            Here's washing water, Sir. A change of clothes;
            Father, when he is all down from Olympus,
            You two will breakfast,
                              Talk of me,
                                        Divide
            Me into dowries, portions,
                              Student, away, away and wash.
            I've laid out clothes, I've rummaged wardrobes, found
            Some elegant things you'll wear.
                              Off now, away.
            (*Pause*) Why, you have fallen asleep, dear Father.
                                        Well, well.

COMMENTATOR (*merrily read*)
            Lust, lovelorn,
            You cannot stint her.
            Men and women born
            To make work for the printer.

            Sleep, Earl
            Of Nothing. Harms
            Are little if some girl
            Have you for a knight-at-arms.

LEITRIM (*yawning*) Yes, I can eat. The cold table, all
            Of it.
BUTLER   Yes, m'Lord.
LEITRIM   Where is this fellow, I can't wait.
            Begin with ham.
LADY   Father.
LEITRIM   A butcher's round. A beautiful morning, what
            A ravenously lovely day. Do I see beef?
            Mix up the rounds for me.
BUTLER   Yes, m'Lord, certainly, m'Lord.
LADY   What keeps him?
LEITRIM (*munching*) Beer, that's well. You fool,
            A pewter tankard.
                              Did you say something, love?
            It doesn't matter.
LADY (*annoyed*) The bell, please pull it, PULL
            All the bells. I'll jangle him or be

A mute forever.
                              You, upstairs, and call
          My lord.
FOOTMAN (*uncertainly*) My Lord?
LADY (*angrily*) My lord, not yours.
BUTLER (*whisper*) The boy like Jockey, fool.
LADY (*softly, dreamily*) I do not even know his name.
                              No matter, we'll
          Invent one as we go.
                              Something quite
          Pedestrian that I can arm at dusk
          Along the Bois.
LEITRIM (*chewing*)   Up to the top, fill up.
          Who'll spare the froth will spoil the mild
          And bitter.
                              Who said the Bois, who mentioned that
          Dear city?
                              Fellow that I knew told me
          A lot. I meant to go. Why not, why not?
          I'm free and fifty-one. Quite spry.
FOOTMAN (*uncertainly*) That boy, I mean your lord –
LADY   Well – well –
FOOTMAN   He's nowhere to be found.
LADY (*angrily*) Well, search, search for him, range,
          Range everywhere. He must be found.
                              Father –
LEITRIM (*munching*) Do I see pheasant, woodcock too?
          Did you say something, love –
                              It doesn't matter.
LADY (*furiously*) Yes, it doesn't matter. You
          Need search no more, you, fellow, call
          Him back –
LEITRIM   Mutton, another round.
LADY   You understand.
FOOTMAN   Yes, m'Lady.
LEITRIM   This ham is crummy –
LADY (*low, tremulous*) It doesn't matter –
LEITRIM (*munching*) Why, it must and should. The pig
          Is noble when he's ham, and with respect –
LADY (*furiously*) Let him go. Let him go.
LEITRIM   Eh, what ails the child? You make
          A lot of noise. Good food should have respect.
LADY (*almost a sob*) He's gone.

218   *The Hags of Clough*

LEITRIM	Who's gone? Oh. Without his breakfast?
	(*Munching*) Foolish fellow.
COMMENTATOR	Paris. City.
	All the bright sky over;
	Abelard lived here,
	Wrangler, scholar, lover.

Sing-song the man,
Heloise to her convent gone:
Sing to the rose
The tune the sow-gelder blows.

Another year, much changed; another earl, much married; another climate, very varied. The Paris of the great.

COUNTESS	The minx is eligible, but –
	I'm in despair.
	One minute it's this lord, another that,
	Now it's a Wit, a paltry priest; the next
	A Doctor of Divinity, and he
	In turn gives way to some Moustachio
	Or landed fellow with a vine down south.
	Please speak to her.
LEITRIM	Ahum.
COUNTESS	Ahum – is not enough. You're weak with her,
	Deny her nothing.
	And now my nephew's coming home
	And we must leave his house.
LEITRIM	Glad to be off, I'm 'fraid.
	Prefer, I think,
	Some fellow speaks my lingo – too.
COUNTESS	Must we go there?
LEITRIM	Ahum.
COUNTESS	So dull, in the barbarous blue. It rains,
	I believe.
LEITRIM	Ahum.
COUNTESS	There you go.
LEITRIM	Affairs need my attention –
COUNTESS	You've agents, bailiffs.
LEITRIM	Aye, but do you see – the dapping –
COUNTESS	Dapping –
LEITRIM	And there's the shooting –
COUNTESS	Shooting –
LEITRIM	Places, precedence, all kinds of rows

	If I'm not there. Keepers like it too.
COUNTESS	Indeed. Well, come along. If we have guests,
	We must be hosts to them.
LEITRIM	What do we have today?
COUNTESS	Music. Some new pianist
	With raving hair.
LEITRIM	Ahum, quite good – with raving – ahum.
	(*Laughs*) With raving –

COUNTESS Sir, your daughter – you forget her – call,
Accompany her, I'll go ahead down stairs.
Not that way, Sir. This corridor –

LEITRIM Damned house, never remember. (*Fading*) Never remember.

COUNTESS (*exasperated*) And speak to her, and strongly, Sir.

FOOTMAN My Lady –

COUNTESS What is it?

FOOTMAN Le Comte – your –

COUNTESS (*loudly*) Raoul –

NEPHEW (*approaching*) Dear Aunt –

COUNTESS Home. I thought it would be next week –

NEPHEW (*merrily*)So did I. But inns are holes, and roads
Are inns with more holes –

Frankly, I tired, I think
To travel is to exaggerate.

And so
You've married again, and look so well.

COUNTESS Ahum. Your house, you'll wish us to vacate –

NEPHEW Never. Honeymoon, dear Aunt. I'll bunk
Down anywhere, cockloft or attic – it
Is yours –

An earl from barbarous parts, that is
Most wonderful, most suitably – bizarre.

COUNTESS Dear Raoul, what really hurried you home?

NEPHEW (*aback*) Eh?

COUNTESS Come. An aunt is made
For confidences.

(Nephew *laughs*)

Some new woman, eh?
What is she like?

NEPHEW (*laugh*) I don't know.

COUNTESS Don't know?

NEPHEW Never met her, but you will – tell me all
About her –

COUNTESS   I will tell you –
NEPHEW (*merry*) And perhaps receive me, make us known
            To one another –
                        Your stepdaughter, dear Aunt –
            I heard, and hurried home. A tempest, I
            Was told, Artemis, Diana with a bow,
            Uranian Aphrodite, beautiful
            Barbarian who rides great horses like –
            Who was she? – Hippodameia, the dame
            Who galloped chariots, the very moon
            Of woman –
COUNTESS   Such rubbish. Who's been talking?
NEPHEW   Ma'am,
            The buzz of beauty, it goes round –
COUNTESS   A very ordinary girl –
NEPHEW   But –
COUNTESS   Some looks, and much
            Bad temper –
NEPHEW   But –
COUNTESS   You'll meet her. If you fall, well, well,
            She's rich –
NEPHEW   Don't disenchant me, Ma'am –
COUNTESS   And very variable. Who told
            You all this silliness –
NEPHEW   Why, now I come
            To think of it – nobody definitely –
            Words here and there, in Naples, Rome, or some
            Post-stop, Geneva, Florence, really –
            Gulled, was I?
COUNTESS   Dear boy, I'll get your luggage up –
            The baggage will wait – inspection.
                                    Take this room
            For the time being.
NEPHEW   Is the room adjoining occupied –
            I have a friend –
COUNTESS   Male or female?
NEPHEW (*laugh*) Madame, half a Leech, a young
            And ravishing doctor, half-made. We've laughed our way
            Across the Alps and down. A notable.
            A journey, I must say, diversified
            With some odd happenings, miracles I should say.
            I'll bring him in, with your permission, Aunt.
COUNTESS   My house is yours, dear boy. Or is

It vice versa?

(*They laugh pleasantly*)

So nice to have you home.

COMMENTATOR   Home is where
                The heart is, that's what they say;
                But where is home
                If the heart has gone astray?

LEITRIM   You cannot leave alone.

LADY   Neither can
        I wait for you, dear Father.

LEITRIM   Perhaps you'll give
        Some reason I will understand.

(*Piano heard in background*)

LADY   Oh, say
        I'm tired of pianos, soirées, routs, gallants,
        Of people, anything.
                          Look on my desk,
        That calendar, you'll see a date I marked;
        Red-letter night – and morning. I go home
        To hold some kind of anniversary –
        (*Low, harsh*) My last hope.
                          (*Cry*) Pride, I've none no more.
                                              He could –

        Recur, if that's a word to use, like his
        Anniversary – and mine, be drawn
        There too, the yard, the tower, the window where
        We – talked, my room; I kissed his forehead, that's
        A little thing to be sure, but – (*Weeps, low*)

LEITRIM   Ahum.
        I fear I'm in the dark. Some young man –

LADY   He was in Paris, did a term, and left.
        I found he did. I made my escorts bring
        Me round the wineshops –
                          Shameful, yes, but I
        Have shame no more.
                          (*Picking up*) You know him, Sir.
        He healed us both – you, forever, me –
        I never was so sick, it seems. I know
        I'm going mad –
                          (*Loud*) With pride, frustration, shame –
        (*Low*) It's love, that's all.

The Hags of Clough

LEITRIM   I'll order the carriage then.

LADY   Thank you, Sir.

LEITRIM   You should have told me this.

LADY   I was ashamed –
Determined too – it seemed such moonshine, such
A lot of silly nonsense.

LEITRIM   Do you mean
To travel all night –
                    Well, you've an hour or two.
I'll get you company, some one to sit
In front with the driver –

LADY (*tired*)   Thank you, Father.
                        We've packed.

LEITRIM   Child.

LADY   Better now. I'm sorry I
Am such a fool.
                    (*Fading*) Hysterical, a very ass
And numbskull.

COMMENTATOR   Such in one room; and in another near, as in old come-
dies and high romance, a certain straying Student.

NEPHEW   More wine?

SCHOLAR   The plague of honest guts.

NEPHEW   Well, more for my dishonest indigestion.
What a let-down.
                    I am an old campaigner, I,
Accustomed to my victories, and yet
Defeated on my doorstep, so to say –

(*Piccolo*)

I hurry home, for what? To see her leave,
Depart, pick up her skirts and run.
                                I'm low,
I'm lost. And find no sympathy.
                            But then
You are no wencher.
                    Wine?

SCHOLAR   I've done.

NEPHEW   Why won't you stay?

SCHOLAR   If I start now I'll catch
The packet, walking easily.

NEPHEW   Why walk? There's transport here.
This lady – ah, I am a fool, you'll eat
My lure, this jack-o'-lanthorn piece who's danced

Me down the Alps.
                              Well, so be it; you are
A friend, I yield my place.
SCHOLAR   Too easily.
She's warts, I'm sure, hot armpits, black teeth,
She snuffles, limps –
                              I'd better walk.

(*Merry laughter*)

NEPHEW   It's very odd. She got into my head
And hurried me home. And yet I never saw
The lady – true.
                              And where I heard of her
I have forgotten. Odd.
                              And now I'm out
Of love. I have no wish to see her. Odd,
It's oddly, curiously odd.
                              There's rain,
You cannot walk in that.
                              Sit down again.
SCHOLAR   I really must go.
NEPHEW   But why, down in the toe
Of Sicily, when I found you, there was none
Of this mad bustle –
                              drowsing like a vine,
Dear Doctor, till I woke you up. and now –
Your footsoles itch, why, why this sudden most
Provoking haste?
                              A woman? I'll lay odds
Some She is calling.
                              (*Sighs*) Well, old fellow, come
Accept the transport. What the gods provide,
Accept. There's rain. A winter gale – or two
In one.
              Come.
SCHOLAR   It seems I must –
NEPHEW   But such reluctance, why, why?
SCHOLAR   I've learned to look
Two ways at once.
                              And then I'm going home –
To some unhappy thing.
NEPHEW (*softly*) Tell me. A woman, eh? I'm wise
On that vast subject – aye, my friend, I've had

My breast on that particular thorn –

(*Piccolo*)

SCHOLAR   I see some holes, indeed, some – rosy wounds.
                  She will be married now, some coat of arms
                  Like you –
NEPHEW (*merry*)   And in the doctor's bag there is
                  A pair of horns?
                                    (*Another tone*) I'm off the mark – regrets,
                  Dear fellow.
                              Why do you go if pain's
                  The end of the journey? Don't deny it, you
                  Are suffering.
SCHOLAR   Dear friend, *remedium*
                  Amoris – there is none they say, no cure
                  For love. That is not altogether true –
                  I hope –
NEPHEW   You hope. What will you do?
SCHOLAR   Not much. I'll visit an old place,
                  Look down from a pigeon-loft, hear horses move
                  Below.
NEPHEW   No more?
SCHOLAR   Hear news of her along the road,
                  How she is married, where, what life she leads –
NEPHEW (*quickly*)   You'll look at her –
SCHOLAR (*low*)   Perhaps, myself unseen –
NEPHEW   And turn the thorn
                  Inside your breast?
SCHOLAR   There could be some
                  Finality in that. Great pain may cure
                  A lesser pain.
                              If she be happy too,
                  And settled –
NEPHEW (*quickly*)   Did she care for you?
SCHOLAR   All fall for Doctor Miracle a while.
                  He leaves, and very comfortably, friend,
                  They live without him.

(*Pip of piccolo*)

                              I expect to find
                  Some arrogant young matron, lady of
                  A great house whom none will cross, she will
                  Be Domina, very Roman, ruling all,

Receiving the great, responsible, she'll see
Her husband goes to church, her boroughs send
Sound men to Parliament –
NEPHEW (*sigh*) May God preserve
This gentleman from such.

              Let us go down
Before the carriage leaves you to this rain.
(*Laughs*) May God preserve this gentleman from such
A paragon.
         Come along.
SCHOLAR   I'll trudge, I think.
NEPHEW   Never. I'll pull a rapier
And keep the door. If you will walk,
Stay here the night –
                Yes, stay. Why must you catch
This packet anyway?
SCHOLAR   A sort of anniversary.
NEPHEW   Then you'll ride in style –
Or stay –
        Friend, listen to the rain.
Hear it. I doubt a carriage can get through
On such a night.
        Well?
SCHOLAR   Have it your way, but –

   (*Piccolo*)

               If she have warts –
NEPHEW   Frolicsome elbows, friend,
Is all you have to fear. Let's down at once.
I heard wheels roll, I think. The cobble sends
Up echoes to an old inhabitant.
             Do you like
My house?

(*Piano music played by a virtuoso begins to be heard. It comes forward as they go downstairs*)

        Piano player. Great gal, my aunt,
All for the light fantastic. Once she blew
A fortune on some fiddler –
           say she liked
Strings on her bow.
        This fellow's good.
I hope she's sensible, will throw no more

        The Hags of Clough

Money down the strain.

(*Piano ceases. Applause*)

COUNTESS   Ah, there you are. Come in, come in.
NEPHEW   First, dear Aunt, would it be possible
           To give this obstinate fellow leg-room in
           That vehicle outside –
COUNTESS   Too late, I fear –
NEPHEW   Gone?
COUNTESS   I said goodbye in here. I could not face
           The portico, the rain –
NEPHEW (*quickly*)   I'll see –
COUNTESS (*fondly*)   Impulsive boy, but spoiled,
               Quite spoiled.
                        What a pity, Sir, had we
               But known –
                           Indeed, the favour would be on
               Your side – a suitable escort –
NEPHEW (*loudly, from background*)   Halloo, halloo.
               Here, come along. Still here, not left –
COUNTESS   How nice –
               And lucky – for you both. Well, au revoir,
               And bon voyage, Sir –
NEPHEW (*middle distance*)   All arranged. Quick, now –
               (*Whisper*) This barbarous lord –
COUNTESS (*fondly*)   Dear nephew, his wife is present –
NEPHEW   Stands in the downpour, hatless I think, and at
           The horses' heads –
                        A groom, so charmed was he
           To have an escort for his Miss –
SCHOLAR   Madame, I am obliged –
COUNTESS (*fading as night noises of storm and horses grow*)   Au 'voir,
           Au 'voir.
NEPHEW   This rain – is rain. In quick.
                           Mademoiselle,
           Your most devoted servant – If I could
           See you in this dark. Please make yourselves
           Acquainted. I can guarantee my friend
           Is – notable.

(*Door bangs*)

           There, with a blessing, go. Au 'voir.

(*Carriage rolls away*)

The Hags of Clough   227

LEITRIM Ahum.

NEPHEW Apologies, Sir. This downpour plays
     The devil with my manners –
            Really,
     There was no need to hurry them away.
     I could have made them known to one another.
     Well, well.
         It's very odd. Indeed, I see
     I must learn etiquette again –
             But what
     The devil possessed me?

LEITRIM (*fading*) Ahum, ahum.

NEPHEW (*fading*) You speak – excellent French I see.

(*Thunder. Roll of carriage wheels*)

COMMENTATOR On such a night as this –
       Dear Dido and her willow wand –
       Even on such a night as this
       Can love get out of hand.

BETTY Dear God, this is a night
    For rosaries.
        Your rug has slipped. Please, Sir,
    Just pass this end around my lady –

LADY No.
    I'm babied like a cradle.
          You have caught
    Some rain, I think, Sir. Take this scarf, and dry
    Yourself.
       The scarf, where is it, Bet? It is
    So dark –

BETTY Lord, it's a night –

LADY There, Sir. Your hands are very wet –

(*Thunder peal*)

BETTY (*quaver*) That shook the heavens down.

LADY And you, I think, good Sir.
         Are you afraid
    Of lightning, of a silly peal?
         Hold out your hands,
    I'll dry them. (*Busy*) Handmaid's work.
          Well, well, it's odd,
    We all have fears of some kind, yes.
         There was

A time when I was terrified to sleep.
Somebody – took my hands –
                              Hey presto, there
Was Sleep, a gentle minister, that now
I court – and – woo –
                    But his were special hands,
Most delicate, yet strong, and very calm –

(*Gasp. A loud gasp*)

BETTY (*concerned*) My Lady, what is it?
LADY (*pause, remotely*) What is – what, Betty?
BETTY   You got some start, a shock?
LADY   An old memory, I think. Our hands
            Continue to remember –
                              Odd –
                         Even after we
            Have quite forgotten.
                         Shall we sleep or talk?
            I think this gentleman is dumb. And so
            I'll vote for sleep.
                         (*Yawns obviously*) Sir, do my poor legs
            Discomfort you?
                         Betty, change places. You
            Sit here beside me, Sir.
BETTY (*loud whisper*) Poor man, I think
            He must be deaf as well.
                         (*Loudly*) Sit over, Sir,
            Beside Her Ladyship.
                         That's better now.
LADY   Now tuck the rugs about us. There. That is
            Much better, yes.
                         The night has changed I think.
            I feel a moon. The thunder's gone. Now we
            Can sleep.
                         Betty, go asleep.
BETTY   Yes, Ma'am.

(*A faint, distant peal*)

            Still thunder on the left
            Out there.
LADY   A little light now.
            We poor humans, we poor women, need
            A little light – inside and out.

                                  But go
Asleep, poor Bet.
                    Me too. (*Yawns*)
                                   Your shoulder, Sir,
Is very knobbly. (*Yawns*) Pity you are dumb
And we could talk.
                        And be polite.
                                   Yet centuries
Of conversation, I'm afraid, have left
Me savage.

(*Betty snores*)

        Sleep, poor Bet.
                     Heigho, the rain
Has passed, quite gone.
                              Your coat is wet, cravat
As well.
            It's no great matter. I have slept
On worse.
              They say the hand is everything.
Our stars and signs are in it.
                                  Here's a hand
Has done great damage, yet a healing hand
I think.
            Preserve me, Cosmas, Damian,
It is a wencher's too.
                          Poor me, to have
It tilt my nape, to grope about my poll,
The other stealing round my back.
                       (*Harsh, low*) No, Sir. I'll not be kissed, not yet
Till morning and daylight, or never, Sir.
Why did you leave?
                      Don't tell me, it
Would all be lies, all lies.
              (*Sobs low and suddenly with abandon*) Aye, nestle me –
Like some poor stray –
                      I said I'd not be kissed.
(*Wildly*) Why did you leave, why did you leave? I've died
A thousand deaths. I've beaten every dive
In Paris, catfooted each low place, disguised
Myself, ashamed, ashamed –
                         Why, why?
                                    You seemed

To love me too, till I abased myself
And wooed you like a whore.

                         Why did you leave?

SCHOLAR (*low*) We'll come to that.

LADY (*roughly*) First, am I loved?

SCHOLAR (*agonised*) You're loved, indeed.

LADY (*roughly*) How much, how much?

SCHOLAR So much I doubt if I
        Can ever leave again.

LADY (*high*) Leave?

SCHOLAR (*low*) It's hunger and thirst, this love; accidia
        That sees no God, no good, that never sleeps.
        I am entirely haunted –

LADY (*sigh*) You feel me then, I mean the loss
        Of me?

              A loss like pain. There's nothing left
        At all. The days are emptied out before
        They come – (*Stronger*) Student –
              Tell it to me, tell
        It, I will have you wracked – like this poor fool –
        Poor ninny –
            It was illness, wasn't it,
        No minute but you died?

SCHOLAR (*very low*) Yes.

LADY You whisper very low, and still I think
        It's such a fanfare all the world can hear.
        So much is satisfactory, indeed –
        It's illness any silly girl may cure –
        So simply, Sir.
             Now, conjugate that verb
        'To leave'. 'To leave'.
              I hear no joybells ring,
        But perhaps I'll cope with it.
              (*Calmly*) Now that I'm here
        Upon your heart, I'm adequate, I think.
        The moon is out, our moon. The clouds have gone.
        One thing – where were you travelling tonight?

SCHOLAR You know, you know.

LADY I must be told.

SCHOLAR (*murmur*) A stableyard, a tower with pigeons, one –

LADY (*murmur*) High window over treetops.
              Now, Sir, to this
        Ridiculous verb.

	(*Louder*) You must admit it is
	Absurd, inconsequent, unnatural.
SCHOLAR	No, most logical.
LADY	That word is ominous, a cap-and-gown
	That smells of candles, snuff, a blear-eyed word;
	I'm not afraid of it, and yet –
	(*Loudly*) Go on,
	Continue, Sir –
SCHOLAR (*low tenderness*)	Dear – heart.
LADY (*loud*)	Our tender time will come, not now,
	Not yet –
	There is this terrible verb 'to leave';
	It must be cleared away.
	Then off with it.
	You've stamped on larger things, put hell in place,
	Sent demons packing, cracked the choking shell
	Of nightmare, healed the crazy and the ill,
	And let loose innocence again –
SCHOLAR	Ah, hold;
	I have some gifts. They come from God. I am
	A creature too, no more. All healing is
	From God.
	But when your father ailed, I used
	Knowledge not mine –
LADY (*low*)	Midsummer Night, you walked
	With – Satan, you said. He showed you then
	The way –
	(*Loudly*) Showed me – to you, made me
	The bait and lure, used me for hook and line –
	(*Desolately*) I see.
	You cured but cannot profit. If
	You do, your soul goes down below. I know
	The axiom. (*Sudden burst of weeping*)
SCHOLAR (*low, agony*)	My love, my love.
LADY (*low*)	We'll stop the carriage here. Tap on
	The shutter, Sir.
	The shutter, Sir, knock knock.
SCHOLAR (*low*)	Not yet.
LADY	Your soul is precious, Sir.
	Your powers, great as they are, will die at source.
	Knock at the shutter then.
SCHOLAR (*low*)	Not yet. Not yet.
LADY	Knock, Sir. Your soul is valuable. You are

A prize, it seems –
     A battle-piece between
The poles of good and ill.
        So knock and save your soul. I see
You're greatly valued – you receive those vast
Attentions –
    Good soul, knock; Sir, you must knock.
Here's all eternity depending on
A pair of knuckles. Stop the carriage, Sir.
Time is a coffin passing by. And I'm
Poor flesh to be such bait.
     (*Muffled*) My mouth is on
Your mouth, yet you must save yourself.
         I'm bait,
That's all. A piece of pretty bait. Lift up
Your eyes – Oh, not to me. Look overhead –
And say what you see.

SCHOLAR (*low*) You, nothing else.

LADY   I must not blot
   The heavens out –
     (*Loudly*) Please knock. Have done with this.

(*Pause. The noise of the carriage wheels forward a moment. Chirrup of driver*)

   You cannot knock?
      (*Some triumph*) You cannot – is that so?
   You cannot knock.
     I'll do it for you then.
   See – how I rap. All love – and yet –
      (*Loud cry*) I knock,
KNOCK, KNOCK.

(*Carriage stops*)

   It stops.
    (*Low*) And yet I think we hang
   Above the pit – you do not leave.

(*French voice of coachman*)

       Am I
   Then worth so much?
     (*Loud, raucous*) Am I worth all?
   Drive on, drive on.

(*Carriage sounds take up*)

A hearse it may be, but
Our lives, our lives. And if we're lost, we've loved.
That's all.
You cradle me again. It seems
Enough. It's large enough.
This instant is
Eternity, I think. Let love make laws
For you and me.
(*Cry*) I can't live otherwise,
And if God empties all the upstairs rooms
We'll furnish out the cellar, camp abroad,
Inhabit one another –
Here's our love,
Its dignity is its necessity.
We can't deny it, so we'll accommodate
The marvel as we may.
Student, make room
For me, invent a world that will hold
Us two and if it's temporary, well,
The fleeting thing is sweetest – that's what they say –
(*Cry*) Oh, my darling, say it must and can
Be so, it must and can –

SCHOLAR (*tenderly*) It must and can, it can and must
Be so.
(*Loudly*) It must and can be so.

LADY (*low, warmly*) Yes.
Kiss me now. Two new-born creatures,
Brief as the mayfly too –
My love, my love.

(Mephistophilis *heard far off and approaching with a vast chuckle*)

MEPHISTOPHILIS So the head's
Inserted in the pretty rope. I could
Be sorry.
Break the piccolo. Come –
The healer's instrument, or deal with me
As I direct.
(*Loud*) Break, break the staff.
Come, break
The healer's instrument –

(Mephistophilis *overwhelms the microphone. A sudden silence. Loud breathing.* Buller *coughs*)

The Hags of Clough

BULLER (*half drunk*) You're sweating like
    The hangman's bread-and-butter.
                    All right, you dreamed
    Some hustler done you in –
MARTY (*weakly*) Beyond Elphin, near Turlough chapel, choked –
BULLER   Here's buttered whiskey, cure for all,
    For nightmare too –
MARTY (*weakly*) My windpipe aches.
                  Oh, take that mess away.
BULLER   Mess. It has redemption value. I
    Will slip a pint to Peter as I pass
    The horned and holy gate.
             Lord, look at Scholar, Mart.
    Now there's a soul in torment –
               Save us, he
    Will break the little piccolo.
               Scholar, hey.
    Devil-dodging, haunted, eh?
MARTY   You won't see angels on
    A diet of whiskey drops.
BULLER   Scholar. Hah, good. Some sanity
    Looks out at me –
            Stop wringing that sweet thing –
    You'll break it, man.
SCHOLAR (*distressed*) Wouldn't break for me.
    It wouldn't break.
         (*Low, calmer*) Where am I – oh, the red
    Pedlar –
        Mart here too, the little man –
               O God
    O God –
MARTY (*weakly*) I'm here, but shook. I had a fearful dream.
SCHOLAR (*heavily*) I think I know your dream –
MARTY   How would you know it, man?
SCHOLAR (*low*) Yes, how – should I know? That's relevant,
    Oh God, how relevant it is –
              How do
    I know –
MARTY   Beyond Elphin, a chapel near,
    Some gallow's joker wrung my neck –
BULLER (*hiccup*) Nobody, Mart,
    Will stretch that little stem of yours. I'll see
    To it, we're buddies, tender chums.

The Hags of Clough

(Sound of a passing coach)

　　　　　　Another vehicle pass by. The great
　　　　　　Move in.
　　　　　　　　　　A lady is eighteen tonight.
　　　　　　The county celebrates.
　　　　　　　　　　　　　Cellarmen, pantryboys,
　　　　　　Were up and down all day. Oh, wine will pour,
　　　　　　And ladies jig from hand to hand.
　　　　　　　　　　　　　　　　Eighteen
　　　　　　Tonight that lady, proud, unlovely bitch,
　　　　　　An arrogant galloper –

MARTY *(testily)*　Go easy now.
　　　　　　What's she to us that you should mention her?

BULLER　　Scholar, have a nip of this. A servant maid
　　　　　　In black and white donated it –

MARTY　　You'll get us locked out of the castle, I
　　　　　　Can see it come –

(Sounds of a carriage passing by)

BULLER　　Another carriage on the way.
　　　　　　A lady is eighteen. Her ribs are made of gold.
　　　　　　Proud, contumelious –
　　　　　　　　　　　　Who rides all down –
　　　　　　　　　　　　　　　　Who killed
　　　　　　A fox within the portals of the church
　　　　　　And sprinkled the parson with the reeking brush;
　　　　　　Aye, when he protested she, the chit,
　　　　　　Baptised the minister –

MARTY *(out of patience)*　Your tongue, your tongue,
　　　　　　We are in Leitrim's campus here –

BULLER　　Ungovernable. They say she jumped
　　　　　　A funeral procession, swam the flood
　　　　　　Of Shannon, laughing in the saddle while
　　　　　　Some sprig who dared the spate with her was drowned.

MARTY　　I give you up –

BULLER　　Who burned a family out
　　　　　　For taking salmon in the moon. A trull
　　　　　　In her spare time, the Jockey's Moll, they say
　　　　　　She trailed that tabby from her cradle days –

MARTY *(whisper)*　O Lord, O God –

BULLER *(hiccup)*　Her mouth is red,
　　　　　　Yet I've seen bigger paps on babes.

(Sound of passing carriage)

              Another load
   Of lords goes by. The moon is up.
             The laces show.
                O Lord, to have
   A tall brick house, a stately lady in
   The four-poster –
MARTY (*wild*) He's off, he's off.
BULLER A city merchant with
   A carriage, greys to match; a playhouse piece
   Upon the box on Sunday, driving out
   To take the air in Sandymount, a most
   Respectable tall hat –
         (*Urgent, low*) Scholar, let you and me
   Discuss a horse. A hundred to one. We'll share
   And share alike –
        (*Low*) O Lord, he's a haunted lad
   Tonight –
MARTY What's he to us?
   That fellow troubles heaven, I think. Let him
   Go on his way.
BULLER (*hiccup*) He's a mad carcass, but
   A comfortable body too –
          Who'd trip
   That colt but he? Who'd have the pluck? Who'd dare
   A daunting earl like Leitrim's lord?
              I'll sit
   With him.

(Another carriage passes)

   Great lords roll by.
         Scholar, here's you and me,
   Our toes in turf-ash, poor men's toes, while not
   A mile from here there's jubilation –
              For
   A lass with little tender teats.
          (*Hiccup*) By hell,
   You have a piercing stare.
SCHOLAR (*quietly*) That fellow on
   The wheel, that Ixion, he took a cloud
   For Juno, tricked, bewitched –
         The heavens laughed
   At him.

Now tell me when you saw this child
You speak of –
                        First, this gossip of her person, where
Does it come from, the kitchens or the roads?

BULLER   God's truth, it's everywhere.
                                    Ask Mart for more

MARTY (*testily*) Mart holds his tongue about the better folk.
Let you hold yours.

BULLER (*hiccup*) Mart's hat is off
To every thruppenny bit.
                        (*Belligerently drunk*) Those eyes of yours
Look into me like lamps.
                        Let Buller be.
What's she to us that we should mention her?
We stand and see her pass.
                        Poor people hug
The ditch, pedlars give way, that's right, we doff
Our hats and catch the splash.
                        Here, have a drop
Of this. Be merry. A servant maid in black
And white donated it.
                        A gabby girl.
                                    We stood
Behind a bush and watched a lady pass
The trodden woodride, linked to a lordly lad.

(*Hiccup. Another carriage rolls past*)

A piece of ivory now.
                        The fop beside her
Floating all his pennants, yet that doll
Was absent, far away.
                        The toast tonight.
The wine will pour for her – a waste of wine,
The shadows eat her up.

(*Soft piccolo background*)

                        A slow decline,
That's what they say. Poor virgins are
Most prone to it.
                        The Fall will see a funeral.
What's that to us?
                        (*Loudly*) I've only the one song
To sing tonight – the odds, the odds. Stand in

With me, Lord Latin, under a golden shower.
(*Pause. Change of tone*) You're putting on your shoes. Are you
away?

SCHOLAR (*as if to himself*) No man asleep is damned, but waking – when
His wits are all alive – that's something else.

BULLER   Are you away?
Let's meet at Castlerea,
Scholar, Scholar –

SCHOLAR (*a little distant*) I'm for Elphin, my friend.
If I
Am right, I'm on the dodge, the future on
My heels –
Yours too, and Mart's. So, down upon
Your knees and pray for us, for you and me
And little Mart.

BULLER (*hiccup*) God help you, but you have it bad.

SCHOLAR (*heavily*)   I'll do my part. I'll run, get far away
Before the clock strikes twelve –
(*Low, strained*) My head aches more and more.
The night is huddled, watching us. I feel
A gaze I know, that terrifies me –
(*Quick babble*) *Quos inquit arcere, si volunt viatores,*
Clara voce Deum appellare –

(*Clock begins to chime twelve*)

No one is damned while sleeping, but awake,
His wits alive –
But I succumbed in sleep,
I'm not reliable – I could be tricked
Again –

(*Clock ceases chiming*)

That chime was twelve.
(*Incredulously*) Twelve struck.

BULLER   Twelve struck, old weights-and-chains, the croaker on
The wall.
And on the stroke the Jockey leads
A yearling in, a priceless colt, a gift
From lordly father to his lady daughter.

SCHOLAR (*happy relief*) Twelve, and I'm not there.
Why then, I've had
Only another nightmare, built a house
Of thunder out of nothing –

The Hags of Clough   239

> Made Juno from a cloud,
> Dared heaven, and was sweetly lost.
> > > > > > Asleep
> It seems I swell.
> > > > *(Back on earth)* So that's the end of it,
> Thank God. A warning fable, one to mull
> And analyse.
> > > > > Buller, goodnight.

BULLER Away? Ah, come to Castlerea. You have
    A sort of crippled halo –

SCHOLAR Friend, goodnight.

(Sound of door opening and shutting again)

BULLER *(grumbling)* I'll trip that colt myself, that's all, that's all.
    Move over, Mart.

MARTY *(waking crossly)* I cannot get a wink. What time is it?

BULLER *(yawn)* Struck twelve.

MARTY Only eleven then. *(Yawns)* That clock is out of chime
    For years, and you should know it, calling here.
    That fellow gone?

BULLER   The devil go along with him.
    (Fading) Oh, leave your wizenpipe alone. No one
    Will snatch it, Mart. No one, while Buller's by.

(Piccolo in background)

COMMENTATOR A moon-blown night,
    Some staggering rogue in sight.
    He plays the piccolo,
    A wandering fellow.

SCHOLAR This road, and the devil take all roadmenders,
    Is puddle alley.

(The distant roll of a carriage)

> > > A carriage on the way,
> This one will miss the toast.
> > > > Don't think of her –
> Well, think of her, the kitchens know it all –
> A coarse and rumpled baggage, kitchen talk,
> They know it all downstairs –
> > > > > *(Low)* And yet, and yet.
> Where now, whereto?

                    Avoid the towns, the crowd
That gathers –
                    God, O God, this gift abuses me –
And yet a reason in a wayward life,
The sole, the whole.

(*Carriage coming near at a smart trot*)

                              I have a dizzy head.
Don't think of her. Does sleep expose a man
Or burn the rubbish up –

(*Carriage forward*)

                              I have – a dizzy head.
That dream shows tendencies to suicide
As well.
              A warning fable.
                              My head, my head.

(*Horses and carriage noises overwhelm the microphone.* Coachman*'s voice
lifted in fright. Silence, except for snorting horses*)

WOMAN'S VOICE What happened, John –
COACHMAN This bloody fellow stumbled right
              Before the horses –
WOMAN'S VOICE I'll see to him. A lamp, John.
                                        His pulse
Seems normal –
                    Smells of the bottle, I'm afraid.
Well dressed, quite good-looking – he is, indeed,
Quite good-looking.
                         There is a wound, his head –
We cannot leave him here –
COACHMAN If he's hurt it was no fault of mine.
WOMAN'S VOICE We'll take him with us, John. Here, lift
              Him up –

(*Fading*)

              Hurry, hurry. We must be there by twelve.
COMMENTATOR This story bites its tail,
                    Comes round, comes round. You dreamed
                    It all before, but now
                    You're visible, washed, brushed and combed –

(*Big clock is booming twelve o'clock*)

WOMAN'S VOICE   In time, just in time.
                              Indeed, and positively, Sir –
              A rare gallant now I have patched you up.

(The toast is given distantly, as in previous scene)

              There's Ladyship. A dreadful hoyden, Sir.
              A whip-and-spur young dame, most merciless
              On your poor sex.
                              Thinned down I see, indeed
              Quite shadowy. What a marvellous colt,
              The darling, the darling –

(Sudden savage neighing as in previous ballroom scene. The piccolo soars)

COMMENTATOR   An end at last, if end
              It be. This story can
              Show nothing one can trust –
              Ending where it began.

The End

The Hags of Clough